ON THE
SWING
SHIFT

TONY COPE

ON THE

SWING
SHIFT

Building Liberty Ships in Savannah

NAVAL INSTITUTE PRESS
Annapolis, Maryland

This book has been brought to publication with the generous assistance of Edward S. and Joyce I. Miller and Marguerite and Gerry Lenfest.

Naval Institute Press
291 Wood Road
Annapolis, MD 21402

Library of Congress Cataloging-in-Publication Data

Cope, Tony.
 On the swing shift : building liberty ships in Savannah / Tony Cope.
   p. cm.
 Includes bibliographical references and index.
   ISBN 978-1-59114-123-5 (acid-free paper) 1. Liberty ships—Georgia—Savannah—History. 2. Shipbuilding—Georgia—Savannah—History. 3. World War, 1939–1945—Naval operations, American. 4. Merchant marine—United States—History. I. Title.
 VM391.C67 2009
 338.4'76238245—dc22

                            2009027763

14 13 12 11 10 09   9 8 7 6 5 4 3 2
First printing

For Ellen . . . more than all of the raindrops

Contents

Photographs

ACKNOWLEDGMENTS

On the Swing Shift would probably not exist had it not been for Evelyn Finnegan. A number of years ago when I was working on another project in Savannah, I asked a friend, Archie Whitfield at the *Savannah Morning News*, to include a request in his City Beat column for photographs of Savannah during World War II. Finnegan called and told me of a series of photos that she had of her mother, Nonnie Skinner, christening a Liberty ship at the Southeastern Shipbuilding Corporation during the war. I knew that there had been several shipyards operating then, but Finnegan's photos reminded me that few people my age—and almost none of lesser years—remembered anything about that part of Savannah's participation in the war effort. Finnegan's call gave me the idea for this project.

Many others in Savannah helped to make this book possible. Scott Smith at the Coastal Heritage Society gave me invaluable tips for sources and made available the resources of his organization. The Georgia Historical Society was also a great source for both information and photographs. Capt. Clifford Thomas, who sailed on many of the Savannah-built Libertys and who was the first person I interviewed, not only shared his own experiences, but also pointed me to other Savannah seamen who had sailed on the Savannah ships. I particularly appreciate Thomas breaking his rule, in my case, of not suffering fools gladly.

The many shipyard workers, Merchant Marine seaman, U.S. Navy Armed Guard sailors, and launch sponsors and their families whom I interviewed were, with few exceptions, excited to share their experiences, which was much appreciated. I am only sorry that many are not still with us to see their experiences related here.

Marine historian Bill Hultgren, who has probably the largest collection of Liberty ship photos in existence, was very generous in sharing many of those photos with me and in encouraging me through the years. Thanks are also extended to Sue Cole, a friend and former secretary at the Oatland Island Education Center, who spent many lunch and afterwork hours typing up letters to sources and research notes for this, at the time, longhand specialist.

I particularly want to thank Elizabeth Bauman, my editor at the Naval Institute Press, who from the original submission of this work has been both excited and encouraging about its prospects. Thanks also to Ed Lamb, who copyedited the manuscript and made this a better book while also being a calming influence on this at-times agitated author.

A big thanks also to my daughter, Georgia Hopkins, whose computer skills saved my literary life on many occasions.

Perhaps the biggest thanks go to my wife, Ellen, who, throughout this process while having to listen to all of my complaints, dealt with all of my aggravations with various problems and was still able to provide the encouragement, the compassion, and the love that really made this book possible.

Finally, completing this book has been a long process on both sides of the Atlantic Ocean, and there are many more people who deserve my thanks for their advice, assistance in various ways, and encouragement. To all of them, I offer my grateful appreciation.

Chapter One

The "Jim"

On a raw February afternoon in 1733, five pettiguas—large canoe-type boats—accompanied by a 70-ton sloop brought thirty-seven-year-old James Edward Oglethorpe and 114 English settlers to the foot of a high bluff on the Savannah River, a place the local Creeks called Yamacraw and which the settlers would soon rename Savannah. The bedraggled group of colonists was greeted by the firing in the air of small arms by Captain Francis Scott and a contingent of the Carolina Regulars left on the bluff by Oglethorpe when he had scouted the area several days earlier.

Hours later, this tired, cold, and already somewhat disillusioned band of settlers had to interrupt their unloading of stores from the sloop for another ceremony when the *mico*—chief of the resident Creek tribe— arrived with his retinue. Oglethorpe had met the *mico*, Tomachichi, earlier and established a warm friendship that would last until the aging chief's death several years later. But this was the first sight the rest of the group had had of the local Native Americans, and some of the settlers must have had one eye on the Indians and the other on the steps carved into the bluff leading back down the river. More than one must have longed to be anywhere else in the world when the medicine man detached himself from the crowd of brown faces and approached Oglethorpe, dancing, in "antick postures" and waving feathered fans over and around the English leader "whilst the king and others followed, making a very uncouth hollowing." This fifteen-minute ceremony was followed by the *mico* and the men of the tribe all shaking hands with English leader "in a regular manner" and the presentation of a bison skin.[1]

A little more than two hundred years later at a point just a mile or so downriver from the site of that historic encounter, another much larger and noisier celebration was to take place as the Southeastern Shipbuilding Corporation launched its first Liberty ship, the SS *James Oglethorpe*.

A heavy mist enveloped the shipyard in the early morning of November 20, 1942. But as the time for the launching approached, it began to dissipate as if driven away by the ebullient mood of the thousands of local citizens, workers, and dignitaries invited to witness the spectacle of this new type of cargo ship being added to America's victory fleet.

The *Oglethorpe* was ready. She had spent 183 days on the shipyard's No. 2 ways, rising from her keel plates, as hundreds of welders, burners, shipfitters, and laborers swarmed over her. The keel plates had been laid on May 22, 1942, the anniversary of another milestone in Savannah's long list of contributions to America's maritime history. At 9:00 AM on that date in 1819 the SS *Savannah* left a cheering crowd on the city's waterfront, traveled downriver past the site where the *Oglethorpe* now waited, and began the historic first steam-assisted voyage across the Atlantic.

But this was the *Oglethorpe*'s day. Pennants were flying on her deck and superstructure. Her bow was draped in red, white, and blue bunting. Every seat on the flag-bedecked platform built for the occasion on the slab just under the ship's bow was filled by a high-ranking dignitary. At ground level in front of the platform, the band from the nearby U.S. Army Anti-Aircraft Artillery Training Center at Camp Stewart played martial airs to inspire the huge crowd waiting for perhaps the biggest moment in any ship's life.

As the band played and the crowd waited, the ship sat, tall and erect in its ways, held fast by a single plate on either side of her bow. She was flanked on one side by the nearly launch-ready SS *George Handley*, and on the other by the still-bowless SS *James Jackson*. Work on both of those ships had been suspended for the *Oglethorpe*'s launch ceremony, but both would join the *Oglethorpe* at the outfitting dock for their final preparations for sea.

Henry M. Dunn, a member of Southeastern's Board of Directors and the company's local attorney, stepped to the microphone, asked the crowd for quiet, and introduced the Army band. With an almost immediate clashing of cymbals and rolling of drums, the first bars of the "Star Spangled Banner" echoed throughout the shipyard. As the band played, a wind off the river caused the flags and bunting to billow, adding to the fervor of the moment and producing goose bumps among many of those standing at attention. In the invocation that followed, the Right Rev. Msgr. James J. Grady, chancellor of the Catholic Diocese of Savannah–Atlanta, wished the ship godspeed and asked for a safe return after her many voyages.

Before introducing Congressman Hugh Peterson, Dunn praised the workers who had played a part in building the ship: "In celebrating the launching of Georgia's First Liberty Ship, the lion's share of the credit goes to the men and women of the yard. These fine results could not have been attained but for them."[2] Peterson also congratulated all involved, and U.S. District Court Judge Archibald B. Lovett then spoke of the forces seeking to tear down the liberties established by Oglethorpe in founding the colony of Georgia.

As reported in the *Savannah Evening Press*, Lovett said,

Today is much the same as the day when General Oglethorpe set sail from
Graves, England on the good ship *Anna*. Forces are endeavoring to tear
down what the United States has been building for over 200 years. The
job that General Oglethorpe did, he did well and permanently; his well
made plans to defend the ideals which were the governing influence of
his undertaking here were right and worthy to be maintained and are so
woven into the fabric of American life that if need be we will give all that
we have, even our lives, before we surrender them, for without them life
is not worth living.

He went on to tell the audience that "we come today to launch the ship
bearing the name of a great Englishman. As he labored to establish us here,
we now labor jointly with other Englishmen and others to preserve not only
what has been established but also that which has been maintained successfully
here and in that jewel isle set in the sea for more than two centuries—the right
of men to be free, to set up governments to serve them rather than to become
themselves servants of the State."[3]

Adm. Howard L. Vickery, vice chairman of the U.S. Maritime Commission,
speaking to the shipyard workers who were watching the proceedings from the
tops of cranes, scaffolding, and buildings, said, "Victory depends upon what
power we will be able to present overseas. That power depends on ships we
have to carry supplies. I know that you men will not be content until you have
delivered the ships."[4]

The admiral appeared to forget for the moment what Henry Dunn had
stressed: that men *and* women had worked on the new ship. Anna C. Hunter,
a longtime writer for Savannah newspapers, found this situation sufficiently
unique to mention it in her article on the launching. "The presence of a number
of women in workmen's togs occasioned interest today, the groups of workmen
in shipyard's helmets being interspersed with overalled feminine workers."[5]

Admiral Vickery's remarks had to be cut short, and William H. Smith,
president of Southeastern, was unable to deliver his speech at all because the
final steps for launching depended on the tide being at its highest point. The
prevailing winds had pushed the tide and, hence, the launch up a bit. Time and
tide wait for no dignitaries, especially in the Savannah River.

M. C. Nettles was ready, however, waiting for the speeches to end so he
could get on with his very important part of the ceremony. "I was a burner and
had the burning crew on the No. 2 ways," Nettles recalled in one of the dozens
of interviews with former Southeastern workers conducted for this book. "I ran
the whole ways and the slab. Burnt the first ship loose when it was launched."

Photo 1. Launching the first ship, the SS *James Oglethorpe*, at the Southeastern Ship-building Corporation, November 20, 1942. The SS *George Handley* is visible to the left. *Photo courtesy of the Georgia Historical Society*

Nettles and another burner were positioned on either side of the *Oglethorpe*'s bow underneath the platform full of dignitaries. On the command of the shipwright foreman, the burners used their acetylene torches to cut through the sole-plates still holding the *Oglethorpe* in place. As the torches, each keeping pace with the other, cut through the last segments of the plates, Lucy Heard George, the wife of Georgia's senior senator, smashed a bottle of Brut Cuvée 1857 against the ship's bow, and the *Oglethorpe* began her first and shortest journey.

Newspaper reporter Sarah Wilkerson described the moment: "Down the whale's way and the gull's way and the right of way for victory yesterday morning went Georgia's first World War II Liberty ship when Southeastern Shipbuilding Corporation's 10,500 ton 'James Oglethorpe' slid smoothly down the ways to ride the muddy waters of the Savannah River."[6]

At the moment the *Oglethorpe* began to move, a celebratory clatter of riveting broke out over the shipyard, and a roar went up from the thousands of guests and hundreds of workers, almost drowning out the U.S. Army Band as it played "Song of the Victory Fleet" (see Appendix A). Had they heard the din of this cheering crowd and the military band, the Indians who first met the English settlers back in 1733 would probably have disappeared into the surrounding forests forever.

Not quite everything had gone according to plan during the launch ceremony. Leon W. Judy, a nineteen-year-old machinist at the yard, remembered one particular hitch that many seamen would have considered a bad omen: "When the champagne tied to the rope was released to be broken on the bow of the ship, it missed and had to be repeated."

As she slid stern-first into the river, the *Oglethorpe* was taken in tow by three Atlantic Towing Company tugs—the *Robert W. Groves*, the *Cynthia No. 2*, and the *William F. McCauley*—to keep her from running aground on Fig Island, which sits across the river from the shipyard. Maneuvered to the wet, or fitting-out, dock, the *Oglethorpe's* flags and bunting were taken down and stored for the next Liberty ship's launching, and the work was begun to complete her construction.

With the ceremony over, the crowd began to disperse. Some citizens went on to a luncheon at the DeSoto Hotel or other gatherings in honor of the day. Most went back to their jobs or homes. Shipyard workers returned to the task of getting the *Handley* and the *Jackson* ready for their launching ceremonies. For both guests and workers alike, it had been morning that filled them with a sense of accomplishment, a sense of doing something to begin to hit back at enemies who had struck cowardly blows.

November 20, 1942, was a morning that none would forget, and the *Oglethorpe* was a ship they would not forget. She was not the first ship launched in Savannah during World War II; that honor went to the USS *Symbol*, a 220-foot Navy minesweeper launched July 2, 1942, by the Savannah Machine and Foundry Company. Nor was the Southeastern-built *Oglethorpe* the first vessel constructed in Savannah to bear that proud name. On Independence Day, 1918, another large, cheering crowd watched as the Terry Shipbuilding Company launched the SS *Oglethorpe*, a 287-foot ship capable of carrying 3,600 tons of cargo to the troops fighting in World War I (see Appendix B). This latest *Oglethorpe*, however, was important to a shipyard that had experienced very troubled beginnings and to Savannah as the first of many ships to be launched from a yard that would eventually employ more than 46,000 workers and make a tremendous contribution to the city's economy.

At the wet dock, the *Oglethorpe* faced another eighty-six days of construction before she could be turned over to the U.S. Maritime Commission and her operator, the South Atlantic Steamship Company. William N. Tiencken of Isle of Hope on Savannah's south side, a fifty-two-year-old veteran merchant mariner who had already survived a torpedoing earlier in the war, was signed on as chief engineer on December 14, 1942. On that date he secured a pass, went aboard the ship for the first time, and was introduced to various shipyard officials by the assistant superintendent for South Atlantic. Within a couple of days Tiencken was joined by H. S. Gaffey, who signed on as the

Photo 2. The engine room of the *Oglethorpe* during fitting out. The ship's chief engineer, William N. Tiencken, is shown on the far right. *Photo from Jimmy Hodges*

Oglethorpe's first assistant engineer, and by ship's master Capt. Albert W. Long of Fort Lauderdale, Florida.

Tiencken's log gives some insight into the problems faced by a brand new shipyard building its first ship. On December 17, he reported that "work generally appears to be of a satisfactory nature, but is progressing slowly and in my opinion way behind schedule." On the 21st, Tiencken noted, "Today was unusually cold and windy—work noticeably slowed down." On the 26th, he wrote that "delivery date has been set ahead by Mr. Reitmeyer of the Maritime Commission to January 18th—my opinion is ten days or more beyond that date."

By January 16 the chief engineer's frustration had become obvious: "There are now more men doing less work on the ships than I ever saw in any yard. As an engineer and an employee of the operators this is no concern of mine, but as a citizen, and I hope a useful one, of a country at war, it looks like mighty poor business, and I for one will want to see men doing at least a half a day's work for a day's pay before I take kindly to an idea being advanced to draft wives and daughters for defense work."

The yard continued to throw men at the problems. In an entry on January 18, Tiencken, "Men are so packed in passageways and compartments wrote [that

Photo 3. Tiencken and his wife, Mary, before his sailing on the *Oglethorpe*. Tiencken was reported missing at sea after the ship was sunk. *Photo from Jimmy Hodges*

it is] almost impossible to move about ship." On the 23rd he wrote, "Shipyard men so thick in engine room it is almost impossible to force a passage through them—and certainly impossible for more than a few to work through the crowd." Four days after the deferred delivery date comes the entry, "There is practically no single item entirely complete on the ship yet."

Most of the problems were finally solved, and after successful dock and sea trials, the *Oglethorpe* was delivered to the Maritime Commission on February 13, 1943, some fifty-five days after the contract delivery date. Captain Long, Chief Engineer Tiencken, and forty-two other merchant marine crewmen—twenty from Savannah—signed shipping articles on February 22. The *Oglethorpe*'s cargo of steel, cotton, and foodstuffs was loaded in Savannah, and on February 25 the ship moved away from the dock and sailed down the Savannah River, past the city and past Fort Jackson.

Eight thousand shipyard workers dropped their tools and lined the docks to wave and cheer as the *Oglethorpe*, which the crew had begun referring to as the "Jim," passed by about noon. This salute was returned by waving seamen who had paused for a moment from their duties of coiling mooring hawsers, fastening strongbacks on the hatch covers, clearing the detritus left by the longshoremen from the ship's decks, and generally preparing her for sea. The *Oglethorpe* sailed past Fort Pulaski, past the little house of Florence Martus— "The Waving Girl"—on Elba Island, through Tybee Roads, and out into the Atlantic Ocean, where the ship was put on a northern heading that would take her to New York.

Chapter Two

New York, New York

O n the *Oglethorpe*, besides the merchant crew, were Lt. (jg) James E. Bayne, twenty-five members of the U.S. Navy Armed Guard, and a reporter and a photographer from the *New York Sunday News*.

Just a couple of hours out of Savannah, First Officer Otto Lechner met the reporter Sloan Taylor on the boat deck and warned, "You will sleep in your clothes and with the lights on in your room. You will keep your Mae West and your 'zoot suit' [survival suit] where you can get into them on a second's notice."

"We are going to traverse a critical area, sir?" Taylor asked.

"Damn critical, mister," Lechner replied."[1]

He wasn't exaggerating. During the past year more than one hundred merchant ships had been sunk along the coast from Maine to Georgia, an area designated the Eastern Sea Frontier by the U.S. War Department. During March 1942 the Port of Savannah was virtually shut down because of the U-boat menace. This was the period known to the U-boat crews as the "Second Happy Time"—the period during which German submarines were able to operate almost completely unhindered by an American military system unprepared for this type of warfare.

By the beginning of 1943 U.S. defenses along the East Coast had improved to such an extent that most of the U-boats had been moved to the North Atlantic and merchant ships were traveling without escorts. The *Oglethorpe*, however, was about to enter an area off Cape Hatteras, North Carolina, known as "Torpedo Junction," an area that would have special meaning to her merchant crew members. Just a year or so earlier the *City of Atlanta*, owned by the Ocean Steamship Company of Savannah, was sunk by U-123 in the vicinity of Diamond Shoals, North Carolina, with the loss of forty-three of forty-six crew members. Many of the *City of Atlanta*'s crewmen had been from Savannah and were friends of those in the *Oglethorpe*.

Lechner took the two newspapermen below to the officer's mess and showed them how to get into their emergency gear. The life jacket, or Mae West, went on first, then the zoot suit. "The zoot suit, not to be confused with the bizarre raiment worn by many young hoodlums," Taylor wrote in his article, "is a rubber garment covering the entire body except the face. The ends of the sleeves are gloves, the ends of the legs are boots, and a tight helmet covers the head. The whole thing is one piece. In a zoot suit you feel and look like a turtle peeping out of its shell. The official name of the zoot suit is the Goodall Overboard Suit, Type R."[2]

Taylor and photographer Joe Costa were riding the *Oglethorpe* to chronicle the trip from Savannah to New York and give their readers an idea of the routine aboard a merchant ship in time of war. Soon after leaving Savannah the reporter and photographer were invited to the captain's quarters where Captain Long told them that officially they were entered on the crew list as wipers, but told them, "Don't let that fool you. The Jim [the crew's nickname for the ship]—all of it—is yours. Go anywhere you like, take any pictures you want. I am proud of this vessel and proud of my officers and crew."[3]

About mid-afternoon of the first day out of Savannah, Long conducted an abandon-ship drill. While high-pitched bells rang throughout the ship, the merchant crew went to their stations, and according to the New York reporter, "The armed guard, alert young Navy bluejackets, sped to their guns in the bow, stern and barbettes. Lt. (j.g.) James E. Bayne, commander of the armed guards, went to his station on the flying bridge, the officers and seamen were at their stations almost before the echoes of the bells had ceased."[4] Taylor and Costa were assigned to the gripes on No. 1 lifeboat, while the seamen handled the lifeboat falls. The boats were lowered outside the rails and made fast against pudding booms, where they remain as standard procedure while the ship was at sea. Long, surveying the proceedings from the bridge, seemed pleased and signaled that the exercise was over.

At about 11:00 PM that first day, general quarters was sounded for the armed guardsmen. A lookout had sighted blinker signals off the ship's starboard bow. Long ordered the ship's radio officer, Harvey Kweit, not to answer or to acknowledge the message, which was, "Put in at next port."

"The hell with that guy," exclaimed Long. "That blinker is violating wartime regulations." He ordered the engine to full ahead and told his second officer, Joseph L. Duke, to "hold the course."

Three minesweepers with an escort were sighted the next morning, but no messages were exchanged. That afternoon, the Armed Guard crew conducted gun drills with their 3-inch, .50-caliber bow gun. Taylor timed the rate of fire with a stopwatch but was warned not to use the data, as it was military information.

A twenty-four-hour storm struck the ship on the third day out. As Taylor described it,

> The rails shipped seas that swept the decks and the bow cast up spray almost to the truck of the foremast.

"Bad stuff," I suggested to Captain Long.

"Not at all," he replied. "That's spray. If we ship green water there'll be plenty to worry about."

Swirls of vapor covered the sea as far as the eye could reach. I was about to mention it, but Captain Long anticipated the question: "We're in the Gulf Stream," he said. "The water is warmer than the air—that causes vapor. When the air is warmer than the water we have fog."[5]

About noon the Jim entered a confused sea caused by a sweep of seas from one gale running into seas from another. The ship pitched and rolled, and lines were strung from the quarterdeck bulkhead to the aft deckhouse so the crew could continue with their duties without being swept overboard. "The deck was a quagmire of grease from a couple of oil drums that had been squashed in the storm," Taylor wrote. "It was mighty risky business walking that deck in total darkness, despite the lines. The Captain got us out of the rough sea by altering his course."[6]

Later in the afternoon there was another alarm when a small vessel operating with lights was sighted about five miles dead ahead. Again, the Armed Guard went to stations, and the *Oglethorpe*'s speed was reduced to four knots. This was another false alarm, as the unidentified vessel turned out to be just a fishing boat.

On the fourth day out, Sunday, the 28th, three Civil Air Patrol planes and two military aircraft flew over the ship on antisubmarine patrol, and later that afternoon at 4:00 PM, the *Oglethorpe* hove to off the lightship *Ambrose* to take a New York Harbor pilot on board.

The *Oglethorpe* arrived in the Hudson River at 7:00 PM but was unable to dock until the next morning. She had been delayed about twelve hours because of the storm. Anthony "Andy" Von Dolteren, a utility man on the ship, wrote to his wife, Bertie, that "I can see New York from across the river, but can't get there tonight."

Von Dolteren had joined the ship in Savannah especially to get to New York, but not to see the sights. The thirty-eight-year-old Savannahian had several months earlier signed the papers for his underage son, Joseph, to join the Navy. Joseph had written to his parents from Norfolk, Virginia, saying that he was being shipped overseas and would be leaving soon from New York. The elder Von Dolteren would not hear of it; he did not want his son sailing into a war zone. He quit his job at Southeastern, where he had helped to build the *Oglethorpe*, signed on to the ship on February 22, and sailed for New York in an attempt to find Joseph and get him out of the Navy.

The family had written to Joseph, telling him to wait at the corner of Broadway and 42nd Street every day at a certain time. His father would try to meet him there. In his letter to his wife that first evening in port, Andy Von Dolteren wrote, "I am going to try and get in touch with Joe as soon as I can get ashore." He also told her about the newspaper story about his ship: "We had a newspaper reporter on the trip up to New York who went around taking pictures of the ship and everything and the pictures will be in the paper about the last of March so I am going to get the address of the paper and send it to you so you can write and get a couple of copies sent to you."

The reporter, Sloan Taylor, and the photographer, Joe Costa, left the ship the next morning to begin working on their article, which would appear in the March

Photo 4. Anthony "Andy" Von Dolteren, a utility man on the *Oglethorpe,* was reported missing at sea after the ship was sunk. *Photo from Dorothy Wise*

29 edition of the *New York Sunday News.* The crew began a seventy-two-hour leave, and Andy Von Dolteren began the search for his son.

New York on Monday, March 1, 1943, found her waterways jammed with more than one hundred fully loaded ships waiting to be formed into convoys for the dangerous trip across the Atlantic. Most of the seamen were sure that they would be heading for Great Britain, but they also knew that any ship could be diverted by the Navy to any destination. All prayed they would not be going to Russia.

The day was bitterly cold, and there were thick sheets of ice coming down the rivers and banging against the sides of the ships. Snow squalls swept through the city and through the anchorages.

The *Oglethorpe's* crew was lucky. Some crews did not get liberty. If there was no reason for a ship to dock—if it was fully loaded, fully provisioned and bunkered, and did not need repairs—it stayed at its anchorage. The *Oglethorpe* did have a reason to dock. A British naval order had recently been issued stating that no ship was to sail in convoy to Britain without being loaded with extra deck cargo. Deck cargo loaded in New York normally consisted of crated U.S. Army vehicles and aircraft. Some ships also took on bulky cargoes such as landing craft and railroad engines, and such heavy and

Photo 5. Joseph Von Dolteren with his grandmother (left) and his mother, Bertie (right), in front of the family's house in Savannah. His siblings and aunt are on the porch. *Photo from Dorothy Wise*

unstable pieces of equipment were not welcomed by crews who would have to face the storms of the North Atlantic.

The *Oglethorpe* loaded trucks, ambulances, tractors, and planes destined first for Liverpool, then for the Soviet Union, in addition to the cargo loaded below decks in Savannah.

New York Harbor was under very strict security. Ships mounted antisabotage watches, and the docks themselves were heavily patrolled. During World War I there were a number of acts of sabotage in the dock areas. Away from the docks, however, New York was an almost wide-open city, and wartime New York was generous and hospitable to seamen.

Merchant seamen generally had more money than their Navy counterparts, and this was often a source of conflict on the armed merchant vessels. Accordingly, some venues, such as the USOs, were available to Navy seamen but off limits to the *Oglethorpe*'s merchant mariners. Others, such as the Eagle Wing Theater and the Stage Door Canteen, were open to all. There were free tickets to movies, Broadway shows, sporting events, and other outings. There was the Empire State Building; Carnegie Hall, where Bruno Walter conducted the New York Philharmonic Orchestra; and Radio City Music Hall, which featured the big band music of the era. There were a variety of clubs for foreign seamen. The American legion opened its doors, and many local families welcomed seamen into their homes. Then there were the bars and nightclubs, some of which were posh and expensive, while others featured lesser-known or unknown entertainers but required no cover charge and offered relatively cheap drinks.

The experience of a British seaman from a ship that would sail from New York three days before the *Oglethorpe* illustrates the excitement of this period in the city. The man walked past the Paramount Theatre and saw it was advertising a well-known band and "a new discovery." He went in to listen, and after the band had played several numbers, the "new discovery" appeared, only to be greeted with the "piercing shrieks" of some two or three dozen young girls. Frank Sinatra had made his New York debut with the Benny Goodman Orchestra.[7]

Andy Von Dolteren did not have time for the clubs, bars, or shows. In another letter to his wife, he wrote, "I've still got all of my money except what I spent for carfare, hunting Joe. I haven't even went to a show as I have been continually hunting Joe every spare minute I have." It was cold and snowing "to beat the band," he noted.

Three days had passed, and Andy had still not found Joe, a discouraging development he described this way:

> Every night I go to 42nd and Broadway in hopes of seeing Joe but I haven't as yet met him. I have stood on the corner so long at a time that it seemed as if I would freeze not having an overcoat to keep me warm. When I came aboard last night and laid down I had a fever and woke up about 2 or 3 o'clock dry and thirsty and got up to get a drink of water and came to find out that the pump was broke. I was not able to get a drink until I melted down some ice cubes out of the icebox. . . . I don't feel much like going ashore, but I'm going back to 42nd and Broadway in the hopes of seeing my boy.

Lieutenant Bayne, the *Oglethorpe*'s gunnery officer, had also tried to find out something about Joe from Navy colleagues but could not come up with anything. Andy had traveled all over Manhattan and Brooklyn. He had gone to the Catholic church, but they were not able to help. He went back to 42nd and Broadway on Wednesday night at 6:30, but "it got so cold around nine o'clock that I just had to give up and come back aboard the ship," he informed Bertie.

The cold, the snow, the incivility of the people, and the frustration of not finding his son had become too much for the quiet family man from Georgia. Andy was fed up with New York; the city was not a pleasant place to be. "Now the streets were all wet and sloppy and if you don't have galoshes your feet get damp and cold," he wrote. "I sure will be glad when we leave here as I never have and never will like this place. Everybody up here is like those in Norfolk—you ask them a question and they don't know or else they just don't want to tell you."

Another Georgia boy was also less than enchanted with New York. Twenty-one-year-old Thomas C. Napier Jr. from Ringgold, Georgia, an able-bodied seaman on the *Oglethorpe*, found the big city a bit too much to take. "I did not like New York," he told an interviewer after the war. "It was completely different from my life in the country. It seemed like the sidewalks were about 40 feet wide and full of people half going one way, half going the opposite way. Where they were going and why they were walking so fast was a puzzle to me."[8]

Most of the *Oglethorpe*'s crew, however, enjoyed the layover in New York and would leave with stories to tell and memories that would last a lifetime. But this was wartime, and with their seventy-two-hour leave up, it was time for the *Oglethorpe*'s crewmen to get back to work and get their ship ready for the voyage ahead.

Life on board the Jim had been made a bit more cheerful while the ship was docked. A radio had been placed in the merchant crew's mess, and many of the songs popular at that time, such as Connie Haines and Jimmy Dorsey's rendition of "Kiss the Boys Good-Bye," Vaughan Monroe's "When the Lights Go On (All Over the World)," and "Praise the Lord and Pass the Ammunition" would have had special meaning for men preparing to leave home and sail into a war zone. For those leaving wives or sweethearts behind, the Andrews Sisters probably best expressed their feelings with the admonition "Don't Sit Under the Apple Tree (With Anyone Else But Me)." If the title was too subtle, the line "Don't go walking down Lover's Lane with anyone else but me" made their thoughts very clear.

For the crew members from Savannah, hearing Johnny Johnson singing "That Old Black Magic" or Bob Eberle and Helen O'Connell getting together on "Tangerine" would have also been special. The lyrics for both songs were written by Savannahian Johnny Mercer. Mercer's down home lyrics and his soft southern drawl reminded these men of home, making his radio show, *Johnny Mercer and His Music* with the Paul Weston orchestra and a variety of guests, very popular. Certainly, Andy Von Dolteren was happy to have the radio. As he wrote Bertie, "Now we can have music whenever we want to."

By the time the *Oglethorpe*'s decks were loaded, there were more than 160 ships in New York Harbor and at anchor in Halifax, Nova Scotia, that were ready to sail in the next convoys, which were designated SC.122 and HX.229. Because of problems with finding enough escort groups, the British Admiralty decided that it would take only 128 ships in these convoys. When another escort group was put together, this number increased, and HX.229 was spilt into two sections, as HX.229 and HX.229A. There would still be more than twenty ships in the New York area that would have to wait for the next convoy.

There were eight Liberty ships in the three groups, seven of them just out of the yards making their maiden voyages. The *Oglethorpe* was to be part of the forty-ship HX.229.

After all of the cargoes had been loaded, all of the fuel tanks topped off, and all food supplies stored away, space was sought for some of the always-large number of servicemen and few civilians on essential war duty who were waiting to cross to the war zone. They had to be squeezed in wherever some sort of accommodations existed. Two U.S. Navy enlisted men were assigned to the *Oglethorpe* as passengers.

On Sunday, March 7, the masters of the merchant ships and the captains of the escorts for convoys SC.122, HX.229, and HX.229A attended a convoy conference at the office of U.S. Navy Port Director Capt. F. G. Reineke at 17 Battery Place on the Manhattan waterfront. A young British naval officer, Sub-Lieutenant A. D. Powell of the HMS *Chelsea* considered himself lucky to have been given an opportunity to attend.

As Powell later recounted,

> The New York harbor master addressed the company at considerable length. I remember that it took about half an hour to get us down the water and clear of the swept channel. One had the feeling that most of the Masters were impatient to get on with the procedure. I remember wondering whether the harbor master had ever left the safety of New York harbor himself. As far as I can remember, the Commodore of the Convoy, Commodore M. J. D. Mayall, RNR, spoke next and went over the diary routine in detail. Next came the senior officer escort. I remember him saying how important it was for ships to keep well closed up for each ship to maintain the designated speed of the convoy. Stragglers would be a menace and it was quite likely that they would have to be left to fend for themselves as escorts could not be spared.
>
> At the end of the Conference, the commodore asked whether anyone present had never been in a convoy before. I remember there were two American masters who put their hands up. One I think had never done any ocean sailing; his experience was confined to the Great Lakes.[9]

During the convoy conference, the masters were told what positions their ships would take in the convoy. Those who had inside positions would be relieved, but those on the flanks and in the coffin corners—the last ship in either outside column—would not be smiling. Captain Long learned that the *Oglethorpe*'s position would be 94, making it the fourth and last ship in the ninth column. This assignment was not ideal, but it had the slight advantage of being on an inside column. Each captain was also given a sealed envelope containing the straggler's routes that was not to be opened until twelve hours after sailing. The main course the convoy was to take was not given to anyone for security reasons.

The shortage of escort vessels was stressed during the convoy conference. Such a shortage was a given at this stage of the war. Details on the estimated strength of the U-boats were also discussed, and the ships' masters were warned that the Germans were operating farther west than usual. One topic that always came up in these meetings, sometimes acrimoniously, was whether naval gun crews could open fire without waiting for a master's permission. Events later would indicate that this point was decided in the favor of the masters.

The next day, Monday, March 8, with thoughts of liberty set aside if not forgotten, the crew of the *Oglethorpe* checked the tiedowns on the deck cargo, tested equipment, and went through all of the last-minute activities necessary to be ready to sail. The ship was now anchored off shore, and Andy Von Dolteren wrote one more letter to his wife. This one, sent from the ship, had to be examined and passed by a U.S. Customs officer, so Andy could not tell Bertie that he was leaving that day.

He reported that he had gone down a last time on Thursday to try and find Joe, with no success. Unbeknownst to Andy, Joe's ship had sailed for the Mediterranean before the *Oglethorpe* had arrived in New York. Disappointed at not finding his son, and with thoughts of the dangerous voyage ahead, Andy's letter was subdued:

> I never did get to see Joe and don't think I will. We are anchored off shore and I don't go ashore. I just stay aboard and read and think of you and the children. . . . I hope that by you getting my letters helps you to get along without me for the short while though it will seem so much longer than it really is . . . when we are back together again. I will try to make up for being away from you. . . . Think of me always and the time will not be long until, My Sweetheart, the only one that I love, we'll be reunited again, maybe never separated again. When you see that three or four days has elapsed between letters you can be pretty sure that we have gone. . . . So, Darling, be good for the sake of one who loves you very much. Until we meet again, I give you my undying love.

This letter was signed, "Your devoted husband, Andy."

When she read this letter, Bertie had a premonition that she would never see her husband again.

At 11:00 PM on March 8, the *Oglethorpe* weighed anchor and began to move downriver. She steamed past the New York skyline, past the terminals of the famous transatlantic liners, out between Governors Island and Waverly Island,

and through the narrows between the Upper and Lower bays. The forty ships of HX.229 fell in line, continued first south and then southeast along the Ambrose Channel, which had been swept for mines earlier in the day. None had been found.

At the *Ambrose*, harbor pilots were dropped off, and the process of forming the convoy began. The *Oglethorpe* had begun her very dangerous voyage to Liverpool, England.[a]

[a] I acknowledge use of *Convoy: The Battles for SC.122 and HX.229* by Martin Middlebrook (New York: Penguin Books, 1978) for some of the information about the period in New York prior to sailing.

Chapter Three

This Ship Will Do Us Very Well

Amerca's merchant fleet was as unprepared to fight a two-ocean war in December 1941 as was every other U.S. sea service. Some of the nation's merchant ships had been built at the end of World War I, but only a handful were constructed between 1919 and 1935. In addition, there were in 1936 only ten shipyards with forty-six ways capable of constructing ships of 400-plus feet.

Nervously watching the looming crises in Europe and the Far East, the U.S. Congress passed the Merchant Marine Act of 1936, calling for fifty vessels to be built over the next ten years. This number was doubled in 1939, and doubled again in 1940. Still, when Pearl Harbor was bombed, 92 percent of the 1,442 ocean-going ships in America's merchant fleet were at least twenty years old, and most were incapable of attaining a speed of twelve knots. There were also no ocean liners comparable to the British "Queens," which could be converted for carrying troops.

Great Britain, which had been at war for two years by 1941 and was losing merchant ships to the U-boats faster than their yards could build them, could not afford the luxury of a ten-year U.S. shipbuilding plan. The too-few shipyards Britain had were short of workers and materials and were within range of the Luftwaffe. For them, American shipyards, which were out of range of both German and Japanese bombers and still in a peacetime mode, had to be the answer.

In September 1940 a five-member team representing the Admiralty was dispatched to the United States with instructions to spend up to £110 million to buy sixty 10,000-ton tramp vessels per year from U.S. shipyards. There were, however, problems. First, all of the American yards were at capacity with U.S. contracts for naval and merchant ships. Second, and more significantly, the design for the ship the Admiralty wanted was for a type that American workers were not qualified to build.

The British wanted ships with riveted hulls, and while there were a relatively large number of trained riveters in the British yards, that was not the case in the United States. Untrained workers could learn to weld faster and easier than they could learn to rivet, and with steel in short supply, welding used almost 600 tons less in building a 10,000-ton cargo ship. In addition the cost of welding was considerably less. The Admiralty's representatives argued that hulls that were riveted were more reliable, and their crews had more faith in them. In the end, the envoys were forced to give in to the reality of the situation.

In their attempt to find the yards to build their ships, the Admiralty delegation met Henry J. Kaiser. Kaiser had no shipbuilding experience, having started out as the owner of a photography shop before moving into the sand and gravel business and then into construction. A salesman with a tremendous ability to organize, his company had built the Hoover, Bonneville, and Grand Coulee dams and the San Francisco Bay Bridge.

Working with Todd Shipyards, Inc., Kaiser convinced the envoys to enter into two contracts. The first was for thirty ships to be built at the Todd-Bath Iron Shipbuilding Corporation in Portland, Maine, and the second was to build thirty ships at the Todd California Shipbuilding Corporation in Richmond, California. Kaiser's sales pitch must have been very convincing as neither shipyard had been built. The site of the Portland yard was frozen ground over a rock foundation, and that of the Richmond yard was a mudflat. One might have thought that the Admiralty delegates would also have been susceptible to a sales pitch to purchase the Brooklyn Bridge and oil wells in Florida. Both Kaiser and the British, however, knew what they were doing; the first *Ocean*-class cargo ship was delivered in just eleven months. Other shipbuilders would joke about Kaiser referring to the bow and stern of a ship as the "pointy end" and the "round end," but they did not joke about his ability to get things done. The design of the *Ocean*-class ship, with some modifications to suit the American merchant fleet's needs, would be the chosen for the Liberty ship.

The Liberty's official designation was EC2-S-C1—*E* for "emergency," *C* for "cargo," *2* for a class of ships 400–450 feet in length at the waterline, *S* for "steam powered," and *C1* indicating a specific ship type and its modifications. The *E* was the key element in this designation. This was to be a ship that was to be built for the duration of the war, with some saying that if a Liberty completed just one voyage, it would have served its purpose. A report from the U.S. House Appropriations Committee in late January 1941 describes the Liberty ship as "a five year vessel," and observes that "for the demands of normal commerce in foreign trade [the Liberty ship] could not compete in speed, equipment and general serviceability with up-to-date cargo vessels."[1]

The design for the Liberty, selected after a tremendous amount of debate within the Maritime Commission, called for a ship 441 feet 6 inches in length overall, with a beam of 56 feet 10 3/4 inches, a loaded draft of 27 feet 9 1/4 inches, and a deadweight tonnage of 10,850. The ship would have a welded hull, a single mid-ship house, and an oil-fired triple expansion engine that could drive her at eleven knots. In five holds, a Liberty could carry 9,146 ton of cargo, which was the equivalent of 300 railroad freight cars (see Appendix C). When shown a drawing of the proposed ship, President Franklin D. Roosevelt, who loved all things nautical, described it as "a dreadful looking object" and gave it the nickname that would follow it through the war: "I think this ship will do us very well; she'll carry a good load. She isn't much to look at though, is she? A real ugly duckling."[2]

Two hundred "ugly ducklings" were ordered, and the problems then became where, and by whom, they were going to be built.

During 1940 and 1941 the Maritime Commission, realizing that there were not enough shipways to provide for both the naval and merchant tonnage that was going to be required, began constructing seven new shipyards at Tampa, Florida; Pascagoula, Mississippi; Beaumont, Texas; Tacoma, Washington; Long Beach, California; Oakland, California; and San Francisco, California. This number was increased in early 1942, when three more yards, two of which were to be built by Kaiser, were approved. At the same time, a federal contract was awarded to complete a privately funded shipyard in Savannah with six ways.

The yard in Georgia was chartered in September 1941 under the name of Savannah Shipyards, Inc. It was the brainchild of Frank Cohen, a New York businessman who previously had been a promoter of insurance companies. Described by Joe Gerbasi, who came to Savannah with the company, Cohen was "some kind of entrepreneur and master salesman." According to Gerbasi, Cohen chose Savannah as the site of the new yard "on account of the Savannah River. Savannah was far removed from any major metropolitan area, and he could build these ships in secrecy. If you had put that yard on Staten Island or the Battery in New York, it would have been bombed in no time." The fact that riverfront property was available in Savannah and that its cost was relatively low in comparison with that in major metropolitan areas may also have entered into Cohen's thinking.

The site, just two miles downriver from the city, was described by the Savannah Shipyard's newly appointed president, William Crowley, as "ideal." Like many of Crowley's later pronouncements, this was stretching the truth a bit. According to M. C. Nettles, a burner at the yard, "It was a soupy mess. It was riverbank, is all it was. Nothing out there; it was just woods." Twenty-eight thousand sixty-foot pine pilings and 355,000 cubic yards of fill would be required to provide a stable enough foundation for the ways and buildings of the new shipyard.

Gerbasi, the office manager for the company, had other problems. Savannah merchants kept raising the prices for materials needed by the yard. "I went to this one guy . . . and asked, 'Why do you go up every time we buy exactly the same item? You double it, all the time double it,'" Gerbasi recalled. "He told me, 'Well, you see we don't know you people. You come down here from New York, and you are trying to run a construction business. We don't know if we are going to get paid.' By God, we were giving them some sizeable checks each month, but that was their attitude." Savannah's trusting city fathers would have done well to adopt the same attitude of caution toward the newcomers.

Savannah, like the rest of the country, had experienced twelve years of economic depression, and the city was excited about the prospects for the shipyard. An editorial in the *Savannah Morning News* of April 5, 1941, exclaimed, "Of momentous local interest . . . was that a shipbuilding company involving an estimated 40 million dollars and the probability of more than quadrupling that huge amount is now assured for Savannah. It is easy to envision the new industry will be the largest of its kind ever established here, eclipsing by far the ship construction operations during world war days on the same site as that selected for the new plant."[3]

Photo 6. Southeastern Shipbuilding Corporation site in May 1941.
Photo from the Sou'Easter, n.d.

The day before, Crowley had announced that twenty-five ships would be built in the city at a cost of $40 million as part of the order for 212 ships Roosevelt had said would be built for Great Britain. These ships would be 500 feet long and 10,000 tons deadweight. According to Crowley, "If we fulfill our threat in building these ships, the Maritime Commission has assured us they will give us all we can build. We asked for an initial order of 100 ships. We think the Commission has that in mind and that ultimately we will get that many."[4]

In fact, there was no contract, official or unofficial, and none had been promised. Cohen had met with Admiral Vickery, the director of the Maritime Commission's technical division, who had said that while the commission had no objection to the construction of Savannah Shipyards, the commission was in no position to offer any assurance of a contract. With no promise of a contract, but with a lease from the Savannah Ports Authority and confidence that, given the war situation, no shipyard would be idle for long, Cohen began to build his shipyard on the Savannah River and announced that the first keel would be laid on August 1.

On July 18, 1941, just two weeks before the first keel laying for the first of the vessels Crowley had promised would be built, he announced to the press that Savannah Shipyards was the low bidder for a Maritime Commission contract for nine 250-foot, 2,800-ton coastal vessels. The first keel was to be laid in mid-August, and the first vessel was scheduled for completion six months later. Many in Savannah were disappointed, but Crowley stated that by the time the nine coastal vessels were completed, contracts for larger ships would be in place.

Crowley had again jumped the gun. Several days after his announcement, the Maritime Commission rejected the Savannah Shipyards' bid to build the coastal vessels. Savannah's leaders were now not only disappointed, they were nervous.

So was the Maritime Commission. But with ever-increasing certainty that America was going to be involved in the war, the commission could not afford to let a shipyard in whatever state of construction and under dubious leadership sit idle. Cohen had been correct. On October 11, 1941, a real, honest-to-goodness, bona fide, official contract was announced, not by William Crowley, but by the Maritime Commission. Twelve Liberty ships were to be built in Savannah. Cohen was excited, Crowley was excited, and Savannah was excited. But two months later, the Japanese bombed Pearl Harbor, and within three months, all of those hopes were dashed.

The Maritime Commission had never been completely confident in its dealings with Cohen and had attached a number of provisos to the contract with Savannah Shipyards. A thirty-day deadline was established by which time adequate staff was to have been recruited, $750,000 in working capital would be produced, and evidence that the yard would be completed within thirty days would be exhibited. On December 26, 1942, the thirty days expired, and not one of the provisions had been met. With America now at war, the Maritime Commission was desperate to get ships built, and it had lost confidence that Savannah Shipyards could build ships.

Consequently, the twelve-ship contract was cancelled by the commission, and the yard was taken over through the process of condemnation. After a long trial, Savannah Shipyards was awarded $1,378,638.36 in compensation. During that trial Crowley was asked on the witness stand what experience he had that qualified him to be president of a shipyard, and he replied that he did not know why he had been chosen for the post.[5] Perhaps, it was his ability to manufacture contracts out of thin air.

Chapter Four

If You Build It, They Will Come . . .
and Build Ships

With Savannah Shipyards defunct, the Maritime Commission had to move quickly to find a new company to operate the yard in Savannah. After negotiations with ten different managerial teams, the decision was made on February 3, 1942, to allow the newly incorporated Southeastern Shipbuilding Corporation to take over operations at the shipyard. Four days later a contract to build thirty-six Liberty ships was awarded to Southeastern. According to the terms of this contract, the first ship, the *Oglethorpe*, was to be completed and delivered on December 20, 1942.

The members of Southeastern's board of directors and its managerial team had extensive corporate and shipbuilding experience. The man appointed as president, William Smith, was a former executive with Todd Shipyards, Inc. All of this experience was going to be needed to begin to get shipbuilding under way on the Savannah River.

Southeastern inherited a yard that was far from completion and where much of what had been constructed was poorly done and would have to be rebuilt. Of the three hundred workers recruited by Savannah Shipyards, only twenty had shipbuilding skills and experience, and ten of those had left when their original employer's contract was cancelled. The remaining nucleus of ten experienced men was soon augmented with the hiring of skilled workers from other shipyards and other types of industries, as well as a huge number of people who had never seen the inside of a factory, much less the inside of a ship.

To paraphrase the line from a popular movie made many years later: "If you build it [they] will come." And the workers did come—from Sylvania and Statesboro, Brooklet and Beaufort, Claxton and Clyo, and Bluffton and Bloomingdale. Others came from Pooler and Port Wentworth, Guyton and Garden City, and Hinesville and Hardeeville. As Jeff Dukes, who began working at the yard as a seventeen-year-old said, "The place was like a magnet. It just drew people."

Farmers left their fields in the hands of wives and sons, came to Savannah, and took courses at local vocational schools to qualify for jobs at the shipyard. They came from other professions as well. Many had been well-known musicians, such as the leader of a fifteen-piece band that had to disband because twelve of its members had joined the armed services. A fullback for the Chicago Bears, a professional baseball player, the star quarterback for the University of Georgia in the mid-thirties, and a successful heavyweight boxer all changed professions to help with the war effort.

There were former school principals and teachers, one of whom was a tutor for the Rockefeller children, as well as Frederick M. Stetson, whose background had to be among the most interesting. He had attended Harvard University, gone on to a world-famous art school, studied in Switzerland, served in the U.S. Merchant Marine, was a licensed pilot, had been a race car driver, had sold insurance and advertising, and was the author of several books for children.

Some workers came from jobs that had disappeared. As American factories converted from the production of domestic goods to defense work, salespeople for such products as automobiles and major appliances found themselves with nothing to sell. Many who came to work at Southeastern had been considered unemployable before the war. Women, African Americans, southern white migrants, ex-convicts, teenagers, the elderly, and the physically handicapped all found jobs at the shipyard.

For Dewey "Shorty" Beasley, Southeastern was not his first choice for a job. "I tried to volunteer for tail gunner in the Air Force," he said. "That area where the tail gunner was so small that they wanted short people, but I was only four feet seven inches, and they wouldn't take me." Beasley later received a draft notice and went to Fort McPherson in Atlanta for his service physical. As he recalled, "That was the first time I ever rode the train. I passed everything until I came to this captain who was measuring people. He slides that rule down and said that it was the end of the line for me: 'If you fall into a rice paddy we wouldn't be able to rescue you because we couldn't see you. You go back and build those ships. We got to have those Liberty ships.'"

Beasley did build ships and became a welder first class. Because of his stature, he was able to work in the confined space of a ship's inner bottom without the discomfort experienced by taller welders.

Eighty-year-old S. E. Mauney became a drill press operator in Southeastern's sheet metal shop. In fourteen months he missed only four days. When asked by a staffer of the *Sou'Easter*, the shipyard's in-house publication, if he attributed his good health to clean living and not smoking or drinking, Mauney replied, "Heck no, I guess I must have spent $2,000 on cigarettes and liquor, I've had my share of it."

Al Williams was a student at Savannah High School. He and another student who knew one of the executives at the yard were told that they might be put to work burning with a torch, but they would have to pass a test first. "We didn't know anything about burning," Williams said. "So two days before, we went to this garage, and a guy there showed us how to light a torch. We went to take the test, and we were competing with men who had been doing this for years. We kept popping the torch because we didn't have it the right distance away, but we got the job anyway."

Many came to work at Southeastern with other members of their families. The five Cox sisters came from the Okefenokee Swamp area, and all became welders. Five Moores—a father and four sons—were outdone by the Harrises, who were represented by a father, four sons, and a daughter-in-law. The largest family working together at Southeastern, and perhaps at any shipyard in the country, was a group from New York State consisting of thirty-three brothers, sisters, cousins, aunts, nephews, and nieces—the Rileys, Whites, Corrigans, and Dalys.

Many of the people who went to work at Southeastern did have families, and most needed housing. Some were already living in Savannah or in outlying communities, but many, like the extended family from New York, were relocating from great distances and would require some type of residence near the shipyard.

Workers at Southeastern were also competing for housing with compatriots working at the other defense plants in the area, such as the Savannah Machine and Foundry, which would be building minesweepers for the Navy, and the McEvoy Yard, with its contract to construct 5,800-ton concrete oil barges. The Union Bag and Paper Corporation produced as much as 500 tons of cardboard each day to make V-boxes for the Army, shipped tons of machine-dried pulp to Allied nations, and turned out more than 25 million paper bags. The Steel Products Co. manufactured thousands of large trailers for the U.S. Army engineers, while the Southern States Iron and Roofing Co. produced 25,000 bomb casings each month.[1]

Two other Savannah companies were heavily involved in the war effort. The Mexican Petroleum Co. sent 12,000 tons of asphalt to battle zones each month, and the Pierpont Manufacturing Co. produced millions of boxes from its own timber for the Allied armies. By May 1945, there were 38,000 people in Savannah holding defense jobs that which were considered absolutely essential to the war effort. Few communities would be prepared to deal with an influx that sudden and that large, and Savannah was no exception.

In April 1941 concerned city officials, representatives of the Savannah Chamber of Commerce, the Real Estate Board, and the U.S. Works Projects Administration met with Sigurd Mylander, a field adviser of the U.S. Division of Defense Housing Coordination. Mylander suggested that the first step in dealing with the looming housing shortage would be to create a listing of all available houses, apartments, and rooms and to establish a local committee on housing. This committee was set up, with Abram Minis Jr. named as chairman.

The following month Crowley announced the purchase of one hundred acres just behind the Savannah Golf Club on which the shipyard planned to build a neighborhood named Irvin Gardens that contained five hundred homes for workers, a school, a firehouse, a recreation center, and a park. According to Crowley, "Our idea is to build a village that will be not only a model for Savannah, but for the entire country."[2]

The houses were to be designed for both skilled and unskilled workers, and each was to have space for a garden. Houses for unskilled workers would be slightly smaller than those for skilled workers and cost between $3,000 and $3,500, requiring a monthly payment of just a little more than $20. Because of shortages, substitute materials would be used; wood would be used instead of metal for framing, and no metal gutters or downspouts would be attached; those would be added after the war. It was also announced that cut stone or wood would replace bronze for plaques. One has to wonder how many plaques Crowley envisioned.

Crowley's plans for Irvin Gardens went the way of his plans to build Liberty ships when the U.S. government took over the shipyard after Pearl Harbor.

Photo 7. Deptford Place under construction, June 28, 1943. *Photo by Girard, used courtesy of the Savannah Housing Authority*

Another private developer later constructed the 273-unit Pine Gardens subdivision on the same site, with each unit selling for $3,500.

After Southeastern began operations, three government-owned housing projects were built for workers and their families under the auspices of the National Housing Authority. The 150-unit Moses Rogers Grove, named for the captain of the SS *Savannah,* the first steamship to cross the Atlantic, was built on the north side of President Street and adjacent to the shipyard. Tattnall Homes, with 750 apartments that featured hardwood floors, plaster ceilings and walls, coal-fired circulating heaters, gas-powered ranges and hot water heaters, and linoleum floors in the kitchen and bathroom, was constructed south of Liberty Street along Pennsylvania Avenue. The largest of the three projects, with 850 units, was Deptford Place, which was built south of President Street but further east and closer to the Wilmington River. In all three projects, rent for one-, two-, three-, and four-bedroom apartments was $32.00, $35.00, $38.00, and $40.50, respectively.

On September 14, 1942, newspaper reporter Bill Fielder wrote an article for the *Savannah Morning News* that was a good indication of the wartime mood of Savannahians during that first year after America's entry into the war. The article, headlined, "Trees and Grass to Aid Protection of New Project," states,

> If Hitler's or Mussolini's boys ever get as far as Savannah with any idea of bombing the city there are going to be two targets that will give them plenty of trouble. The reason is that enemy planes would have a tough job finding them. . . . An integral part of the plans for both projects (Tattnall Homes and Moses Rogers Grove) is camouflage. . . . This camouflage has already been thoroughly tested by federal agencies and has proven very satisfactory.
>
> So thorough is the job to be done that almost every blade of grass, tree or other natural feature will be incorporated in the final result. Roofs and exposed parts of the buildings will be painted with a special camouflage paint in designs that will blend inconspicuously with the natural surroundings. . . . The buildings of four to six units will be dispersed over a large area. This will reduce the likelihood of extensive damage.[3]

Looking back, the fear of an enemy attack from the air seems a bit far-fetched. But in 1942 that fear was very real. Several months before Fielder's article appeared, a large crowd attending the Civilian Defense School at Savannah's Municipal Auditorium had been warned by U.S. Army Air Forces Col. Robert A. Selway, "Savannah has an airbase, shipyards and industries which the enemy would like to see destroyed. The Axis Powers have two aircraft carriers and other ships which can catapult planes which could reach Savannah." Selway, from the Savannah Army Air Base, urged citizens to prepare and maintain an effective blackout, saying, "We have to use every trick, every deceit we can. The blackout is a deceit. . . . Remember this; if the enemy can't find a target they can't hit it."[4]

About the same time, Robert W. Groves, chairman of the Savannah-Chatham County Defense Council, requested that a group of local architects, engineers, and contractors serve with A. S. Goebel, chairman of the Division of Public Works, on a committee to determine which buildings in the downtown area might be suitable shelters against bomb fragments in the event of an air raid. Citizens were warned that if an attack occurred while they were at home, the safest place to be would be under a table on the second floor if incendiary bombs were falling, or in the basement if high explosives were being dropped. Basements in Savannah were actually the ground floor because below-ground basements were impractical, as the city sits in an area that is not very high above sea level. In either eventuality, the level of protection would not have been great.

The author, who was a small boy living in Savannah at the time, was very careful each night to make sure that the blackout curtains in his bedroom were tightly closed to prevent light from the coal fire from becoming a beacon that German bombers or U-boats could use to aim at and destroy his house on Gaston Street. No one really knew the capabilities of the enemy, but with Edward R. Morrow broadcasting the grim news from Britain and the other stories coming out of Europe and Asia, there was genuine fear of an attack against Savannah.

There is the question, however, of why blackout regulations were so strict in residential areas when the shipyard, operating a full midnight shift, was lit up like a forest of Christmas trees. "It was lit up well enough," said former welding leaderman Red Pitts. "Once in awhile they had a practice blackout, but you'd be notified ahead of time. They'd turn all the electricity off just in case there was such a thing as the Germans coming over this far." Also, during the Christmas season, shipyard workers could look back at a city ablaze with lights. Pitts continued: "I remember at night during the Christmas season looking from where I was working and seeing that big beautiful star on top of the Savannah Bank Building." At fifteen stories high the Savannah Bank Building was the tallest building in the city, and any light that might have escaped from the author's bedroom window would have paled in comparison.[a] By the end of 1943, however, when the shipyard was working three shifts and the Battle of the

---

[a]The real threat was not from U-boats shelling the city. The danger was enemy submarines using the lit-up coastline to silhouette and torpedo merchant vessels sailing up and down the coast.

Photo 8. Neighborhood garden at Tattnall Homes. *Photo by G. C. Hopkins, used courtesy of the Savannah Housing Authority*

Atlantic, while certainly not over, was being won by the Allies, the threat from U-boats to the east coast of the United States had lessened considerably.

Finding space in the camouflaged housing projects was not easy. When Nick Creasy began working at Southeastern, he was living on his father's farm up in the country. As he explained, "I always wanted to stay in Moses Rogers Grove so I could be close to the yard, but I never got an opening. They had a long list of people waiting."

For those who did find an apartment, however, every effort was made to make them feel that they were part of a community. Tattnall Homes and Deptford Place had health care programs, community centers, and both also had children's centers. At the Deptford community center, for instance, residents there could enjoy community sings, family games, a summer recreational program, craft lessons for women, teenage activities, Tuesday night movies, and library services. A Boy Scout troop was formed for older boys living in Tattnall, Moses Rogers Grove, and Pine Gardens. A. D. Sharpe, a boilermaker at the shipyard, served as troop leader.

Each government-owned housing project had a branch post office, barber shop, variety store, and lunch counter. A Western Union sign outside of Mrs.

James Young's apartment in Moses Rogers Grove indicated that she was one of thirty women helping that company overcome a messenger shortage by receiving and delivering messages in their projects. Tattnall Homes had a motion picture program. A committee of shipyard workers living there was organized and collected one dollar from each family to buy the projector and the screen. Movies were shown twice a week, and admission was free. A trip downtown today from the location of those projects would take about five minutes. During the war, the lack of time and money, coupled with gasoline rationing, made a recreational trip downtown almost impossible.

Each of the housing projects built for Southeastern's employees had its own civic club, which would represent the families in community affairs and help take care of the welfare of residents by providing money, food, or clothing when necessary. "Thus," a *Savannah Morning News* reporter noted, "by helping themselves and drawing in the various agencies in Chatham County, the little community of Deptford and others like it not only aid the war effort, but are making a place where their children can have a decent background as far as health, religion, recreation, education, child care, protection, and safety are concerned."[5]

By the middle of 1944 more than 20,400 defense workers and their families in Chatham County were living in accommodations provided through the National Housing Agency's War Housing Program. But with production in area defense plants having peaked and begun to decline, the emergency housing needs of the area were considered to have been met, and the Savannah War Housing Center was closed.

All of the public housing units built in the Savannah area were temporary by design, constructed for the emergency, and to be torn down after the war. Because substitute materials had to be used in construction, the contracts for all of the government-owned housing projects specifically directed that the units were to be razed within two years of peace being declared. Like the Liberty ships built by the workers who lived in them, the projects were built for the duration of the war.

As was also the case with the Liberty ships, the duration came and went, but a need, a use, for them remained. When the war ended and military personnel began returning from overseas and bases around the United States, it was realized that there would still be a critical need for low-rent housing. In September 1945 it was announced that Tattnall Homes, Deptford Place, and Moses Rogers Grove, all previously restricted to shipyard workers, would all be opened up to veterans, with rents remaining the same. All three housing projects were operated by the Savannah Housing Authority for many years after the war.

Deptford Place was demolished in the late 1970s to make way for an industrial park. Tattnall Homes was renamed Savannah Gardens and was still in use until the early twenty-first century when it, too, was razed. The original camouflage colors had been painted over many times, and few of the later residents knew that the apartments they were living in were once considered possible targets for the Luftwaffe. Moses Rogers Grove was the last to go, in the early 2000s, succumbing, too, to the need for space for the rapidly growing city.

Shipyard workers who could not get into one of the projects had to look for rooms or apartments in the city. That, too, was difficult. Almost every issue of Southeastern newsletter, the *Sou'Easter*, carried pleas such as the following for help in finding rooms:

WANTED: Two room apartment or garage apartment for myself and husband who is stationed at Hunter Field.[6]

WANTED: Two meals a day with a private family residing within walking distance of the yard.[7]

When sheet metal apprentice Jeff Dukes' father died, his uncle, Wilton, told his family that he would take care of him in Savannah. As Dukes recalled, "Housing was very tight. We found a room on Gwinnett Street. In those days [the neighborhood] was just beginning to be frayed and tattered. We rented a room with two strangers, but only stayed about a week. Those guys were from up in the country somewhere, and every cotton-picking night they would get their guitars out and sing Ernest Tubbs and Roy Acuff songs. We couldn't sleep." It was easy to understand why Dukes did not want to hear that music at home; that was all he heard all day long at work. "I was never much of a country music fan," Dukes explained. "But I want to tell you, Ernest Tubbs and Roy Acuff were the heroes of that shipyard. I heard people singing Ernest Tubbs and Roy Acuff songs around me constantly. It drove me crazy." The young shipyard worker and his uncle soon left Gwinnett Street and found a room at 111 Jefferson Street.

Describing the new rental, Dukes said,

A lady lived downstairs and rented rooms upstairs. She also fed us a meal or two. I was young and would get hungry about bedtime. I told Uncle Wilton that that lady had a big refrigerator in there with lots of leftovers and I sure would love to have the privilege of going in and raiding that icebox. She was a divorcee and the age of my uncle. He said, "Let me work on that." Well, they ended up marrying, but in the meantime, shortly after their first date, she invited me to use that refrigerator any time I wanted to.

When the long drive from up in the country and the early hours finally got to be too much for Nick Creasy, he found a room in the city. "I was staying downtown around Oglethorpe Avenue," he later explained. "I was getting room and board for five dollars a week, and they fixed me a lunch to take to the shipyard. Five dollars a week!" Not everyone was that fortunate. Large families, particularly, had problems finding housing.

The largest apartments in the government-owned housing projects had only four bedrooms, and some families were just too large. Dukes remembered one:

> There was a family from Doctor Town; you talk about people from Tobacco Road. . . . His name was Wash and his wife's, Henrietta. They eventually had thirteen children. Well, they couldn't find anything to accommodate them. Just across the highway [President's Street] from where Eli Whitney School is today, there was a beautiful field with some large oak trees. Wash somewhere came up with a large tent, like a circus tent—an ugly brown, not colored at all—and he erected it under those trees. Didn't ask anybody, just put it up, and he and Henrietta and those kids lived there while he worked at the yard. Wash and Henrietta had the prettiest place in Chatham County to live . . . in a tent.

Wash could walk to work at Southeastern every day, as could the residents of Moses Rogers Grove and Pine Gardens. For workers who lived farther away, transportation could have been a problem. One of the factors considered by the federal government in making the decision to take over Savannah Shipyards was that there were no plans to transport workers from other parts of Savannah to the yard. W. L. Marshall, who spent three days inspecting the facility for the Maritime Commission, found that "there is no established bus or public transportation facility serving the plant from Savannah or the surrounding area and we were informed that . . . no plan had been worked out with the transportation operators to transport such shipyard workers having no other means of conveyance."[8]

Southeastern, with the advantage of having the mistakes of the first company pointed out, wasted no time in seeing that such transportation was organized. In February 1942 a city ordinance was adopted that granted the Savannah Electric and Power Company (SEPCO) permission to operate a bus line from the Bilbo Canal near the yard into the city, around Wright Square in the downtown area, and back to the yard. However, SEPCO, which was already operating buses to Savannah Machine and Foundry and McEvoy Yard, stated that it did not have the capability to transport between 10,000 and 15,000 workers to the three shipyards every day.

Photo 9. The first shift leaving work. *Photo from the* Sou'Easter, *n.d.*

The Savannah City Council began to study other plans, and Mayor Thomas Gamble announced that work trains and boats had been suggested as the most practical solution to the problem. Potentially, three rail lines could have used to move workers to Southeastern. The Central of Georgia's old Tybee Railway Line, on which trains ran to the resort island until 1933, could be reopened at least as far as the yard. The Atlantic Coastline (ACL) railroad could also operate a service beginning at Bull Street and Victory Drive, with stops at Gwinnett Street and other points, as well as run a train along River Street that would stop at West Broad Street, Bull Street, and East Broad Street. With passenger car availability already stretched by the need to transport service members to bases throughout the country, it was suggested that old boxcars could be fitted with seats or benches for Southeastern's workers.

Passenger boats, too, could be utilized, picking up shipyard workers at the Bull Street docks and moving them up and down the river to all three yards. While these plans were never implemented, they were not farfetched. Other shipyards around the country did use both railcars and boats to move workers to and from their worksites. In Savannah, however, it was decided to use as many buses as could be found. "They had these maritime buses, kind of like City of Savannah buses, but they would only carry people to the shipyard. You'd have to have tokens. I don't think you could buy tokens from the driver. They wouldn't accept any money," said Creasy.

For some Southeastern workers, particularly those coming from outside the city, catching the bus was an adventure. Creasy initially found the system difficult to navigate: "They had shipyard buses all the time. You could catch one anywhere up there [downtown], but I didn't know anything about riding buses. I didn't know where to get off, didn't know the names of the streets. One night I got off at the wrong place and had to walk ten blocks." Jimmy Hodges had to catch a city bus down to Oglethorpe Avenue, then get on the shipyard bus to complete his journey. The proposed ACL train would have passed within yards of his house.

Buses helped to ease the transportation problems to some degree, but most Southeastern employees, like their counterparts around the country, preferred to use their own cars or to catch a ride with a fellow worker. "Most everybody was carpooling. Anybody that had a car that would run would charge you like $3 a week. That was a bargain," said carpenter Harold Miller. As that story indicates, carpool drivers did pretty well. Creasy bought a 1939 Oldsmobile for $200 and recalled, "I was hauling four or five riders so I was making a little money." That money probably helped meet his $10 a month car payments.

Likewise, welder Joseph Williams had a 1939 Mercury Club Coupe and packed it with six fellow workers to make the drive from Clyo each day. He later explained, "It was hard to get gas to get to the job and back until I contacted Major Fawcett down there. He was in charge of all that. I told him I was hauling six men to work and if I can't get enough gas, we wouldn't be into work. 'How much do you need, Joe?' 'Enough to get back and forth and maybe a little bit to spare.' He got me all the gas I wanted."

Getting gasoline was not supposed to be that easy, but the shipyard did encourage carpooling and the Want Ads section of the *Sou'Easter* was always filled with requests for rides or riders, such as the following:

WANTED: A ride to and from Garden City. Mrs._____ first shift.

WANTED: Four or five riders for third shift, vicinity of Henry and Waters. See_____.[9]

Finding a ride or riders was only the first step. Very definite rules had to be followed by carpoolers. Supplementary occupational gasoline was approved for a three-month period, and that fuel was to be used only for going to and from work. Any personal business such as going to a doctor, buying groceries, or traveling out of town for recreation had to be done with the A ration sticker.[b]

---

[b]The rationing of gasoline in the United States went into effect in December 1942, and A, B, C, or T ration stickers had to be displayed on the lower right-hand side of the front windshield. An A sticker allowed the driver three gallons a week, while a B sticker provided a supplemental allowance for essential driving. The C sticker allowed drivers to select one of seventeen activities that would call for an increased supplement, and the T sticker meant that vehicle's driver was allowed unlimited fuel.

Only one round trip to the yard was permitted each day, and riders had to sign an application that the driver then submitted to the shipyard ration board. Drivers were not permitted to drive more than five blocks out of their way to pick up riders, and gasoline was allocated on the basis of fifteen miles per gallon plus two miles per day for traffic conditions. Mileage was based on twenty-six working days per month, which meant that a driver working strictly five days a week could end up with extra gasoline. Drivers and riders were threatened with "special investigators" who were supposed to check on riders signing up with more than one driver and drivers who actually rode with others part of the time. Anyone caught in one of the situations was to be denied gasoline in the future. Shipyard drivers were given the C ration sticker for their windshields, as their cars fell in the special category of transportation of marine workers.

Gasoline was rationed in America not because there was a shortage of gas, but because of the serious shortage of rubber for tires. In an attempt to extend the life of tires, gasoline was rationed and a national speed limit of thirty-five miles per hour was imposed. Workers were constantly reminded that there was a very definite shortage and that the type of tires they would be given, if any, was determined by the type of job they had, the number of riders and the total number of miles traveled each month. Joseph Williams recounted the difficulties both the rubber shortage and the speed limit imposed: "I had myself, George John, Larry, Billy Hollister and a black man named Green, and we packed that old Club Coupe. One of those boys said, 'Why don't you drive a little faster, Joe?' I drove 45 mph on account of the tires. I had to save those tires. Every once in a while, we'd blow one. They were synthetics and hard to get."

Carpool drivers did find it easier to deal with rationing than did the average citizen, however. Ed Carson, who worked in the mold office, had a 1937 Plymouth, and he remembered, "I picked up a car full. I had a priority ticket to buy gas, tires, parts, and all that because of working at the shipyard." If a shipyard worker could not get those items at the rationing office, there were other ways. As gantry operator Robert "Buddy" Smith confessed decades later, "I had a car, and I could get gas. I tell you there was a lot of black market tickets going around at the time. You could get all the black market tickets you wanted. But gas, if you bought it on the black market, was 50 cents a gallon. Normally it was 15 or 16 cents."

Civilian automobile production in the United States was stopped in early 1942, making the shipyard workers who bought those 1937 Plymouths and Oldsmobiles fortunate indeed. Sue Donahue said she and her mother, Lillie Pearl Dickenson, "planned" well. "We had a Ford," Donahue explained. "We bought it in the fall of 1941. We always thought that was a stroke of good luck because we had a new car that carried us through all the war years. We had trouble getting gas, and also people would steal the tires off of cars, so on the farm we had to put up a building to secure the car."

Photo 10. Office worker Virginia Sue Dickerson in the shipyard parking lot. *Photo from Virginia Sue Donahue*

The shortage of automobiles and the rationing of tires and gasoline were not the only problems faced by workers who had to travel some distance to and from Southeastern. Carpooling meant less time at home. Williams noted that "sometimes we'd work twelve to sixteen hours. Very seldom did we work just an eight-hour shift. I gave myself an hour and a half to get there. We had no paved roads . . . every bit a dirt road and not very well taken care of. During those times I'd get an average of four hours at home. I had to eat a little, hurry up and sleep, and charge right back down there."

In an attempt to spend more time at home or for other reasons, many workers paid little attention to posted speed limits. Complaints from residents in the communities near the yard prompted both a special effort on the part of the city police and a warning in the *Sou'Easter* that read, "Many shipyard employees have an idea that a defense worker should be allowed to drive as fast as he pleases. . . . Parents between our yard and town, particularly those living in Pine Gardens, Tattnall Homes and the Gordonston sections are greatly disturbed over the way our workers tear through their neighborhoods at the turn of shifts."[10] The article went on to warn workers that they might face a fine of $100 and the loss of their gas rationing if they were caught speeding.

Not everyone who got caught had to pay the penalty. Jeff Dukes, for one, got stopped but got off. He had just started working at the yard, and he arrived one day only to realize that that he had left his badge at home and would not be able to get through the gate. His uncle told him to take the car and go back and get it. "I took off," Dukes said. "I was nervous, and I was afraid that they were going to fire me. I was new at everything, particularly the ways of motorcycle cops. Right at the Casey Canal, there was a cornfield with real tall corn in it, and there was a cop sitting on a motorcycle behind that corn. He stopped me. Having left my badge, I had also left my wallet [at home]. I reached over in the glove compartment and got out my uncle's license. He wrote the ticket out to Wilton Dukes. . . . The bonds of family almost disintegrated."

Jeff and his uncle were faced with a problem. Jeff had to go to court to pay the ticket written for Wilton, but if the arresting officer was there, somebody was going to catch on to the fact that Jeff was not forty-one years old. At the same time, if Wilton appeared in Jeff's place, the arresting officer would recognize that he was not the person to whom the ticket had been given. "We were in a real catch-22," Jeff said. "I agonized over that because I wanted to be a pilot in the Army Air Corps, and I figured that this would destroy me with a record of deceiving the government, deceiving the law."

As with finding gasoline in spite of rationing, however, there were ways around even this situation. Jeff Dukes continued: "There was this guy, a pipefitter. He was a local loudmouth . . . fast-talking, lawyer type. He said he could handle everything. We went with him up Liberty Street to the police station, and he said, 'Boy, how much money you got?' I told him $20. He took it and told me to sit in the car. When he came out he said that everything was taken care of. That was my first experience with the criminal world." So much for the $100 fine and the loss of a gas ration.

Transportation and housing were problems throughout America during the war, with workers and their families moving to areas where work was available and with servicemen and their families relocating to military bases around the country. Finding housing, transportation to work, and supervision for children were problems in Savannah as well. Many Southeastern workers had to get up very early in the morning, and others returned home early in the morning. Such schedules often precluded any real social life. And while a large number of people were earning more money than they had ever seen, with factories converted to defense work, there was little to buy; with rationing, what was available was severely limited.

Times were tough, but no light escaped from the blacked-out third-floor bedroom window on Gaston Street to guide U-boats up the Savannah River, and the Germans never did bomb Tattnall Homes, Moses Rogers Grove, or Deptford Place. Nick Creasy undoubtedly spoke for many when he said, "That was some exciting time. That was probably the most exciting time of my life—in that shipyard."

Chapter Five

Wendy the Welder at Southeastern

M en were not the only ones leaving farms and other types of employment and moving to Savannah to work at Southeastern. Many women were joining them. While women did work in U.S. defense plants during World War I, the number entering that formerly all-male territory during World War II was much greater. Also, with the existence of national magazines, nationwide radio broadcasts, and movie newsreels, there was far greater publicity for "Rosie the Riveter."

The increase in the number of women working in production jobs was dramatic. At the beginning of 1940, there were thirty-six women in such jobs throughout the country. By 1943 that number had increased to 160,000. At Southeastern, a small number of women were hired early on. Some, in fact, worked on the *Oglethorpe*, but the numbers did not become significant until the first six months of 1943, when the monthly average percentage of women workers at the shipyard reached 9.3 percent. That rose to 13.8 percent in the final six months of 1943. Two thousand women were helping to build ships in Savannah during that period.

While shipyard managers generally welcomed female workers, many male workers did not. To most men, a woman's place was still in the home. Southeastern welder Joseph Williams remembered the reaction when the first women production workers were hired at the yard: "There was big moan and groan that went through the yard. . . . 'It's all over now; they won't get any production, now.'" The government, however, used the symbol of Rosie the Riveter to illustrate the need for women workers in defense plants and to help smooth the way for women into the industrial workplace. The first issue of the *Sou'Easter*—and almost every issue that followed—gave examples of how well women were doing their jobs as well, sometimes observing that female workers were performing better than their male counterparts. Placed under a photograph of five women welders in their overalls and hoods in the inaugural issue of the *Sou'Easter* was the caption "Expert Welders" and the statement that the five were not just average women welders, but "are some of the very few girls at Southeastern who weld shell plates, overhead, vertical and horizontal. Orel Horn says that putting girls in difficult

Photo 11. Welding crew at the shipyard. Nell Miller is third from the right in the front row, and leaderman Al Pittman is at the right end of front row. *Photo by Robert A. Smith*

work has spurred the men to greater efforts. The men work better for they are afraid that the girls will show them up."[1]

In addition to the mini media blitz in the *Sou'Easter*, Southeastern often placed female workers in high-visibility situations. As a reward for high attendance or superior work, a number of women workers were asked to serve as sponsors or maids or matrons of honor for the launching of a ship. Myrtle L. Cowart, a worker in the fabrication shop christened the SS *James H. Couper* as it slid down the ways. Nonnie Skinner, a junior keypunch operator launched the SS *Thomas Wolf*, with Rosemary Walsh, a senior clerk in the International Business Machines office as the maid of honor. Thelma Hodges, who worked at the shipyard for seventeen months, recalled, "I was the first female to burn a soleplate to launch a ship. That was the SS *Crawford Long*. They put my picture in that magazine with the other pictures of the launching."

All of these efforts, plus the fact that women were for the most part excellent workers, helped to smooth their way at Southeastern. Most male workers remembered women on the production line being well treated. "They were fine and did excellent work, especially the welders," said outside machinist Leon Judy.

Walter Simmons, who worked in the cafeteria, thought female workers were treated "pretty decently." Simmons said he "didn't see anything that was abusive at all. . . . There was the normal whistling and giggling going on, but I don't think they were offended by that in those days." Several male workers also remarked on the wolf whistling and agreed that it was natural for the times. For example,

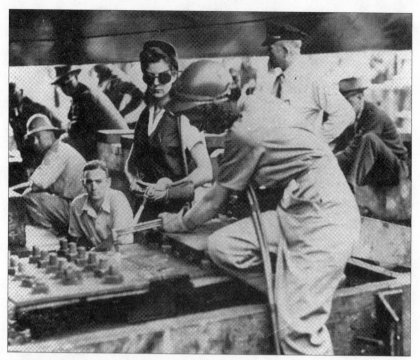

Photo 12. Burners Dorothy Feltes (facing camera) and Grace McGovern cutting the sole plates to launch the SS *Langdon Cheves*, May 22, 1943. *Photo from the Sou'Easter, n.d.*

Jeff Dukes, who started at the yard as a teenager, said, "In the fifteen months I was there, I never saw anything that appeared to offend the women involved. In fact, the shipyard was the first I ever heard women using foul language and telling dirty jokes. . . . The ones I saw were tough enough to be where they were without being downtrodden."

The women who worked at Southeastern, too, remembered the whistling and the kidding. Welder Ruby Clifton recalled, "I was married and had a child and was treated very well, but the guys liked pretty ladies. I don't know if they didn't get a little preferential treatment too, the pretty ones. If you act a certain way, you get treated a certain way. If you flirt you get flirted with."

Jimmy Hodges, a rivet catcher, did not remember any problems. In fact, he thought that the men had a lot of respect for the women. "They worked good," Hodges said. "You didn't see any playing around or nothing." Some may not have seen it, but it was there. As the war continued, the disregard for traditional social conventions increased. Shelley Winters, a struggling young actress at the time, wrote in her autobiography that during World War II, "under the guise of patriotism there seemed to be a general loosening of morals and manners, with everyone living for the day or night and to hell with tomorrow."[2]

What was going on in the community was bound to invade the workplace. The combination of women separated from husbands or boyfriends by the war, the feeling that no one knew what tomorrow would bring, and the growing number of women going to work in defense plants and being thrown together with available men—available in the sense that they were in the proximity— in a situation that most had never experienced before led to a big problem for management at shipyards. Sex in the workplace became a part of wartime living. As the Johnny Mercer song "On the Swing Shift" goes

> Life is fine with my baby on the swing shift
> On the line with my baby on the swing shift
> It's the nuts
> There among the nuts and bolts
> Plus a hundred thousand volts
> Shining from her eyes.[3]

Shipyards created the position of women's counselor ostensibly to help men and women deal with the new experience of working together on the production line, but the counselors were also put in place to keep an eye on employees and minimize the number of liaisons during working hours. Southeastern published a dress code for women, again ostensibly for safety. But as a counselor at an another shipyard said, the clothing rules were based "as much on the principles of concealment and sexless propriety."[4] Another yard reported that its women's counselor, in drafting a dress code for women, had "lowered the boom on allure."[5] That woman and her peers were fighting a loosing battle.

Many women at Southeastern either ignored the dress code or adapted it to accentuate their best features. As one supervisor said in an interview in the *Savannah Morning News*, "You take that number over there," pointing to a statuesque blond in denims, "she would look good in anything."[6]

One might think that in a workplace with some 10,000 other people around that it might have been difficult to find the time or privacy for liaisons. In a shipyard that covered ninety-six acres and had more than sixty-five buildings, not to mention a number of ships in various stages of construction, however, amorous couples had little difficulty finding a secret, or sometimes not-so-secret, spot for their activities. Carpenter Harold Miller recalled, "This guy nudged me and said, 'Come under the ship on No. 1 way.' This ship was a couple of weeks from launching. There was plenty of space under there. You could crawl under there and hide. Here was this guy, a shipfitter, and he was screwing a welder. Well, she was a welder, but she was a whore too. She made a lot of extra money."

Red Pitts, who supervised a crew of forty welders, was aware of such extracurricular activities. "They had women out there that you could have right down in front of this crowd," he said. "I'm not kidding about that! One of my welders, he was a kid seventeen years old. . . . He was welding, and this woman walked up to him and put her hand there. He almost jumped overboard. He couldn't weld anymore until she left. The first thing I knew, I saw a fellow take her off down in the ship. Once in a while, we'd find condoms down in the inner bottom. Those people didn't care."

Some children may have been conceived at the yard, and according to welder Shorty Beasley, "Some women had babies out there, you know. I remember one time, they found a baby and didn't know who the mother was. They just found a newborn baby." While Nick Creasy remembered that "a whole lot of stuff went on out there," Red Pitts put it all in perspective, saying, "They had a whole lot of ladies out there, and they had a few tramps. If you were a tramp, you were treated like a tramp." There must also have been some men who were less than gentlemen at Southeastern.

Most women who worked at Southeastern did their jobs well. While at first most were hired to work in the more traditional roles reserved for women such as receptionist, secretary, clerk, telephone operator, cafeteria worker, and chauffeur (all thirteen executive chauffeurs at the yard were women), women were very quickly also hired and trained to become welders, shipfitters, crane operators, burners, and pipefitters—practically any job that was necessary in building a ship.

Officials at other shipyards around the country believed that the greater patience of women equipped them better for welding than men. Kaiser management also found that women could be trained quickly to do a better job than men on installations of complicated electrical connections that involved fine finger work. Men at Southeastern made these same discoveries. As a burner, M. C. Nettles worked with a number of women on the production line. He recalled, "There was one good thing about a woman. If you tell her to do something, she'd do it. Everything was freehand. A woman is a lot steadier than a man and could make a prettier cut."

Fifteen of the welders Red Pitts supervised were women. According to him,

My best welder was a girl. She came out there to work, too. Some of the boys would mess with her a little bit, but she'd buck the devil out of them if they fooled around too much. There were several of them that were good workers, but she beat anything. I've never seen anybody that could take 3/16 electrode and run a vertical up a 3/16 plate. She had that certain little lick too. A man, he'd go about so far and then he'd start weaving, making it twice as big as it ought to be. Boy, she came out to work.

Photo 13. Sisters Nan Hiott and Bertha Brown stand on the corner of 37th Street and Drayton Street ready to go to work. *Photo from Nan Hiott*

Some jobs at Southeastern required physical strength that most women were not thought to have. Even if a woman could weld as well or better than a man, there was concern that she would have difficulty carrying heavy electrical lead wires. Many women quickly put such concerns to rest. As Ruby Clifton noted, "We had to drag our own welding cable. We didn't have anybody to do that for us."

Some women did have problems, though. Rates of separation and absenteeism were much higher for women at Southeastern than for men, and a few women learned quickly that the dirty, dangerous, noisy work at the shipyard was not for them. Among those who stayed, some found dealing with various problems at work difficult, and many had to take time away from work to keep up with their domestic duties. Married women who worked at the yard would come home exhausted after putting in a full shift only to face a husband and children waiting for dinner to be cooked and laundry that needed to be washed. These were the 1940s, and the man around the house was definitely not the "new man" of the late twentieth century. For unmarried women the cry was "Jingle, Jangle, Jingle—Thank God I am Single."[7] When former female production line workers interviewed for this book were asked if they had participated in any of the company-sponsored activities and entertainment, invariably the answer was, "When would I have had the time?"

There were no child care facilities at Southeastern, and while such facilities were available at some of the housing projects constructed for shipyard workers, those were small and could not meet the demand. The Tattnall Homes children's center had space for thirty-six 2-6-year-olds. That was 36 spaces for 750 families. Mothers who could not get their children into a center often had to leave them with friends or arrange to work the night shift so they could be with their children during the day. Mrs. Herschell Dickey took care of the problem in her own way. She had eleven daughters, so when she started work at Southeastern, the older girls took care of the youngsters.

School was also a problem. The thousands of families that had moved into the Savannah area to work at the three shipyards and the other defense plants brought a huge influx of children that strained the resources of the Savannah-Chatham County Public School System. Double sessions were set up at many schools, but there were no schools in the residential areas built specifically for Southeastern workers. Students had to be bussed to the already overcrowded inner-city schools, creating even more scheduling problems for parents working at Southeastern. The school system purchased land at the corner of Pennsylvania Avenue and Elgin Street and applied for federal funds to help build a school to educate the children of shipyard workers. By the time the Pennsylvania Avenue School opened in 1945, though, employment at the yard was already in decline.

Women in some defense plants did not receive the same pay as men for doing the same job. In shipyards operated by the Maritime Commission, however, equal pay for equal work was the policy. There was not, however, equal opportunity for promotion. While there were several female leadermen at several yards and while a *Sou'Easter* article of July 1, 1943, suggests there may have been a few such women at Southeastern, no records survive that definitely show any women served as crew leaders in the Savannah yard. Even though most men had adjusted to working with women, some had considerable problems working under them.

Tommy Preston was a second-class shipfitter at the yard and an article in the *Sou'Easter* noted, "Tommy is usually selected to act as leaderman whenever the regular leaderman can't be on the job and things run smoothly under her direction. Looks like she's headed for that title in her own right. Good luck, Tommy."[8]

When it became apparent that the war would result in an Allied victory, women were the first to be laid off. Some 12 million servicemen would be returning home to find work, and while there would be an increase in the manufacturing of formerly rationed domestic goods, the jobs created in that sector would not make up for those lost in the closing defense industries. Most women would be going back to domestic life or to lower-paying service and clerical jobs.

According to welder Lula Paine, the day the war ended, all of the women production line workers at Southeastern were laid off. There were some gains, however. Many women were able to save part of their salaries to help buy houses and provide a higher standard of living for their families. Welder Ruby Clifton used her savings to help her husband Pete start what was to become a very successful business on the west side of Savannah-Chatham County.

Women learned during the war that they could hold a "serious" job, that they could work in a world that was formerly "for men only," and that they could do a job as well as any man could. Women also learned that they could make home repairs, drive and maintain a car, and balance a checkbook without the help of a man. As *Newsweek* commented at the time, "Keeping women in the home following this war may prove as difficult as keeping the boys down on the farm after they'd seen Paree."

Things did not change right away, but the seed was planted, and it would germinate and flower decades later. If the benefits from their work during the war were not immediate for women, the benefits to the country were. As one shipyard official put it, "America's wartime achievements in shipbuilding could not have been realized without women workers."[9]

Chapter Six

You Were a Laborer No Matter What Skills You Had

If the appearance of women on the production lines of the nation's shipyards was considered unusual, for African-American workers in southern shipyards it was business as usual. Many were hired, but they were hired to perform the most menial tasks at the lowest pay regardless of their skills, past experience, or potential. At Southeastern the situation inside the gates mirrored the situation on the outside, and Savannah was both geographically and philosophically Southern.

African Americans held the lowest-paying jobs and had to travel to those jobs in the back of the bus. They lived in the worst neighborhoods, often in houses that would have to be improved to be called substandard. For African Americans, Savannah was West Broad Street (now Dr. Martin Luther King Jr. Boulevard) with its shops, banks, theaters, bars, restaurants, and nightclubs. If they walked just a couple of blocks east, however, they were in a very different Savannah, where "Whites Only" signs on doors and windows told them they were not welcome. A few blocks further east, the signs became unnecessary; everyone knew who was and who was not welcome to eat in the restaurants, use the public toilets and drinking fountains, and attend the churches, schools, and movie theaters. This was not just custom, the way things were. It was the law.

Georgia's segregation laws were not supposed to apply within the boundaries of the shipyard east of the city, as they had been superseded by federal statutes. In early 1941, as American industries began to gear up for the country's entry into the war, very few African Americans were being hired, so A. Philip Randolph, president of the Brotherhood of Sleeping Car Porters, threatened to march on Washington, D.C., with 50,000 supporters if the situation was not corrected. Congress dawdled, and a date was set for the protest. On June 25, five days before the march was to take place, President Roosevelt issued Executive Order No. 8802, which prohibited discrimination in defense plants and established the Fair Employment Practices Commission (FEPC) to enforce equitable treatment of federal workers. In compliance with the executive order, the U.S. Maritime Commission inserted the following clause in all of its contracts:

Fair Employment Practice: The contractor agrees that in the performance of the work under this contract, it will not discriminate against any worker because of race, creed, color or national origin.[1]

This clause appeared in the first contract for Liberty ships the Maritime Commission awarded to Southeastern and all subsequent contracts, but it was completely ignored.

When the FEPC tried to act on the first discrimination complaints arising from problems at southern defense plants, executives and managers defended themselves by saying they had to be concerned with policies "consistent with maximum production."[2] Translated, this defense meant that if the government wanted weapons and supplies to win the war, it should not rock the boat.

Accepting this reality and finding it necessary to insist on stiff production quotas, the Maritime Commission acted to ensure that nothing interfered with the construction of ships by forcing the FEPC to agree to consult with it before issuing any fair employment compliance order to a shipyard. The Maritime Commission was thus able to stall or derail the issuance of compliance orders and shield the shipyards under its supervision. Unlike African-American newspapers around the country, which were urging readers to strive for the "Double V" of victory over discrimination at home as well as victory over the Axis powers, the Maritime Commission considered victory over America's enemies abroad to be the number one priority.

While some southern shipyards adopted unique practices in an effort to appear to be in compliance with Executive Order No. 8802 such as training African-American workers in skilled jobs but then assigning those individuals to work on segregated production lines and ways served by separate toilets and, in the case of one yard, separate bomb shelters, Southeastern made no attempt to comply. There was no integration of workers, and Southeastern certainly provided no skills training for African Americans. Rather, Southeastern employed a large number of African Americans as laborers and helpers. The exact number is unknown, however, because while the Maritime Commission kept statistics on a vast number of things in wartime shipyards, it kept none on the number of African Americans employed.

Twenty-four-year-old Sam Williams' problems at the yard began the day he went to ask for a job. "I filled in the application," he recalled. "Had to stand against the wall. You couldn't sit down. Wrote down that I was applying to be a diesel mechanic oiler [the job he had been doing outside of the yard]. I carried the application to the window, and they tore it in two. Told me to get another application and let them fill it out. You were going to be a laborer no matter what skills you had."

Williams would spend two very difficult years at Southeastern fighting for skilled African Americans to be recognized as more than laborers, fighting for higher pay, fighting the treatment that he and other African Americans had to endure, and, perhaps, just fighting for visibility.

Fifty years later some whites who had worked at the yard did not remember that African Americans worked there. "There may have been some there, but I don't remember them," said one. "I guess there may have been some."

Other whites remembered that there were African Americans working at the yard, but as one said, "I don't remember there being any problems at all between . . . the whites and blacks. There were a good many out there. They wasn't welding or burning. I don't know what they did to tell you the truth." Gantry operator Robert Smith's memory was better: "I know that there were no black heavy equipment or crane operators. As far as I know the only blacks that I can remember were doing cleanup work, laborers."

According to welder Nick Creasy, "There was never any confusion about it, you know. If [African Americans] wanted to work out there, they was treated like everyone else. You hear a lot of things . . . that they was treated bad in society. They was treated bad at that time, no doubt about that, but I never did see anything unusual about getting along. If you worked out there, you worked out there." Those "things" never sat well with Sam Williams. His frustration was illustrated by an incident that he remembered very well:

> There was this panel, a part of the ship that they needed, and the white riggers couldn't get it high enough so they could weld it. This piece was too heavy, and they dropped it two or three times. Our engineer was white. He was a wonderful person. He told [the riggers] he had a crew that could put that piece up there. We had to go all the way around the yard to get there, and he had all those white riggers stand there to watch. We did it. We got it up there. We did skilled work others couldn't do, and we was treated like dogs.

Along with not having access to skills training or craft positions, there were no housing projects built near the yard or anywhere else for African-American workers and their families. Also, African Americans were allowed to work in the cafeteria, but they could not eat there. "You had to buy over the counter at the canteens and walk away," explained Williams. Not one ounce of the daily delivery of sixteen tons of ice went into the water coolers marked "Colored Only."

The treatment of African Americans by some of their white fellow workers mirrored the policies of the administration. Carpenter Harold Miller recalled, "A lot of farmers came down from South Carolina [and Georgia]. They did their job, but prejudice. . . . You could cut the prejudice with a knife. There was this big commotion [and] everybody was walking in that direction. A guy in front of me said that a guy in front of him saw what happened. 'It was nothing; a guy fell down into No. 3 hold.' 'All the way?' 'Yeah, just a nigger.'"

Harold Miller remembered another situation:

> There was this guy, a shipwright, heavy, just getting fat, baby-faced and sort of swelled up. He sent Brown, one of the black helpers, to the commissary to get his coffee. Now it was 8:15 AM, and you couldn't go to the commissary after 8:00 AM, you had to be on the job by 8:00 AM. Brown went to the commissary and got six cups of coffee. When he returned, he told this guy, "Tell Allan his coffee is in the shipwright's shack." This guy took his hammer and said, "You fucking nigger, you don't call Allen, 'Allen.' I call Allen, 'Allen,' but you don't. If I hear you call him 'Allen' again, I'll put this goddamned hammer through your fucking thick nigger skull." Here is a guy taking a chance on losing his job by getting coffee for us, and he talks to him like that!

A final Harold Miller story falls into the "what goes around comes around" category:

> There was this laborer boss. If you didn't have enough helpers you wanted to carry some timber or whatever, you'd call him and say you needed some laborers. He'd say, "How many, where? I'll send you some good niggers." I was working in a bank some years later, and this same guy came in and said to me, "Goddamn white man can't get a job here anymore." The SOB hadn't worked since he left the shipyard. All he knew how to do was to send two niggers, three niggers, four niggers.

People of different races did sometimes work together at Southeastern, and it was not uncommon for positive relationships to develop between white and African-American workers. Burner Thelma Hodges had a helper, Sam Cotton, "who saved my life three times. Once I was working with goggles on—couldn't see very much. A gantry carrying a large steel plate moved too fast, and the plate swung. Cotton shoved me to the floor. It just missed." She would later have an opportunity to reciprocate.

As Hodges recalled, "Some black man was supposedly giving candy to a white woman worker. Candy was hard to get. These white males got upset and came looking for the black man to beat him up. They thought Sam was the man and came after him. I lit my torch and threatened them with it. They ran off. Sam wasn't the person they were looking for anyway."

The tension Hodges described—created because somebody said, saw, or heard something and the story about it was then passed along through several workers and embellished at each stop—was always boiling just below the surface. Rumors, no matter how farfetched, could quickly escalate into major confrontations.

Red Pitts found himself in the middle of a very serious situation caused by a rumor:

> At Southeastern, blacks were used as laborers. Now at the yard in Brunswick, I understand down there, they were welders. That caused a strike. They floated around messages that [the shipyard administration was] going to bring up niggers—they had to use the worst possible term—and they were going to take the women welders' places out there. . . . Wasn't a bit of it true, but all you have to do is tell that to one idiot, and it will go like wildfire and that's what it did.

When this incident occurred, Pitts was told by his supervisor not to put anyone to work and, later, to bring all of his workers up to the administration building. When Pitts and his crew got to the building, they found a large very unruly crowd of workers, all of the union business agents, and several members of the yard's management. The management team tried to talk, but no one was listening. "They just wanted to strike," Pitts said. "Man, they were raising Cain. You had a bunch of crazy people, and we didn't work. Well, they had a cure for that. The next evening when we went down to work, everybody that had a 53 or 74 badge wasn't even allowed to go down the hill. Couldn't get anywhere near the shipyard property."

The next day the workers met with the union bosses and the management team at one of the housing projects, but again the men were in no mood to talk, as Pitts described:

> Then Bridges, he was a welding foreman on the second shift. He was part Cherokee Indian, and he had plenty of guts. He told them that if they would shut up and let the man talk, we [would] get things straightened out. A couple of men made threats, and he said, "You ain't threatening me, son. I ain't scared of nobody, and you better believe that." They shut up, and it got straightened out and we went back to work the next day. That Bridges, he was something else. They were talking about lynching him, and he walked straight into that crowd. He said, "You don't scare me. . . . I'd like to see one of you come on and try something." Nobody volunteered.

Photo 14. "Spear Men." *Photo from the* Sou'Easter, *August 1, 1944*

The *Sou'Easter*, which so diligently supported women workers at the yard, also published stories about African-American workers that its editor must have considered positive. There is the November 1, 1943, article on "Uncle Cole," who at sixty-three had twenty-seven "livin' head of children" and "is one of best workers."[3] Uncle Cole's full name is never given in the article. Another issue contains a photograph of a smartly uniformed African American with an accompanying story that indicates the man was a bonded messenger–chauffeur who, along with acting as a driver, ferried mail and currency between banks, the post office, and the shipyard. "Those who come in contact with Nathan have a good word for his conscientious way of doing his job and his politeness," reads the caption. Other than Nathan not having a last name, this all sounds fine. But then there is the line, "Nathan reminded us of Eddie Cantor—minus the burnt cork."[4]

In the June 15, 1945, issue of the periodical, the three white employees stationed at the "Colored Time Gate," are praised, with one of the three described as having "had a good word to say about our Colored workers. They are a remarkable set of Colored people; we never have trouble with them coming to work under the influence of alcohol."[5]

Even the photographs in the *Sou'Easter* were segregated, with skilled white workers shown in one and helpers in another. In one issue, below a photograph of ten laborers and their leaderman, the title "Spear Men" appears. This photo's caption reads, "With burlap bags slung across their shoulders and short-handled

spears in their hands
these laborers patrol the
grounds picking up bits
of paper and trash."[6] On
the back cover of another
issue, the same job was
featured in a cartoon as
part of an effort to combat
absenteeism. An African
American is shown with
exaggerated white lips and
racing to pick up paper
while in the background
other employees are at
work building ships. Still
another cartoon shows
seven African-American
laborers, again with the
exaggerated white lips
and big eyes, shooting
craps. The caption for this
second cartoon reads,
"Come on you seven!
Baby needs ah new pair
of shoes and mah ration
board says, OK." Then
there is a third cartoon

Photo 15. Cartoon with dialect from the shipyard's in-house publication, the *Sou'Easter*. *The* Sou'Easter, *May 1, 1943*

with the same stylized laborer, this time very small standing in front of a very tall white supervisor, asking, "Boss, what kin I does fo u today?"[7]

Other examples of such dialect can be found throughout the issues of the official shipyard publication. The following anecdote appeared in the August 1, 1943, issue: "It is said that that certain dark complexioned workers on wanting to leave the yard ask for, 'one oh dem slip-out passes.'"[8] Add entertainment to the African-American worker's other duties of cleaning and carrying at the shipyard.

Beyond all of the problems of low pay, lack of access to skilled jobs and leadership positions, lack of respect, segregated facilities, the cartoons and dialect stereotyping institutionalized by the official organ of the shipyard management, the fear among African-American Southeastern shipyard workers that one was always physically in jeopardy because of rumor or whim was palpable. Still, hundreds of African-American workers went through

Photo 16. Cartoon in the shipyard's in-house publication, the *Sou'Easter*. *The Sou'Easter, August 1, 1943*

their Colored Peoples gate each day, did their jobs, and contributed to the war effort. They may not have liked the situation at Southeastern, but they tolerated it and understood how to survive it. As one former laborer, Walter Simmons, who was still a teenager when he worked there explained, "I grew up in a segregated society. I knew how to play the role." Besides, the African Americans figured, they were working, and the pay, while the lowest at the yard, was still higher than that for any work in the outside community. As Sam Williams said, "They were making more money than they had ever made in their lives."

There was another reason for African Americans to continue going to work to help build Liberty ships. They, too, wanted to see Germany, Italy, and Japan defeated. They, too, had fathers, sons, and brothers fighting and dying overseas, and many agreed with heavyweight champion Joe Louis when he told reporters, "There may be a lot wrong with America, but there is nothing Hitler can fix."

Many of Southeastern's African-American laborers cheered as much as anyone else when the first ships were launched in front of huge crowds of workers and guests. Those launchings elicited the same emotions of pride and patriotism in them as the launchings did in other workers. For some, including Sam Williams, however, such feelings were a luxury. "You didn't have the opportunity to think like that," Williams said. "If you are not being treated right, it will cut off any other thoughts you might have." He too, wanted America to win the war, but he could not accept things as they were at the shipyard. He was striving for the Double V, even though he did not remember ever hearing that term. That striving would lead to confrontations at the yard and problems for him. At one point, he was threatened with being drafted. "I guess I was the ringleader. I caused all of the problems," he would say fifty years later.

In 1945, after two frustrating years of trying to be recognized as being something more than a laborer and trying to bring about some changes at Southeastern, Williams quit the shipyard and went into business for himself selling wood and ice. Time may soften experiences for some. For Williams, however, his experiences at Southeastern remained bitter memories.

Chapter Seven

If You Don't Join, You Don't Work

One battle Sam Williams did not have to fight was with the unions. As a laborer, he was not allowed to join one.

Skilled African-American workers at shipyards in other parts of the country were constantly embroiled in struggles with the various craft unions. Begrudgingly allowed to join only auxiliary locals that were subordinate to white locals that controlled their policies and their treasuries. The only area of equality was dues, which were exactly the same for whites and African Americans.

Lawsuits filed in federal and state courts over labor conditions and representation were not settled in favor of the African-American workers until the spring of 1945, by which time many of the rights the plaintiffs had been fighting for had been granted by the unions. All of these problems were academic at Southeastern, where African Americans were not allowed to work in craft positions. "There was no pressure on me to join a union," explained cafeteria helper and truck driver Walter Simmons. "I don't think there was a union in the cafeteria."

In this one area African Americans may have been envied by some of their white colleagues. If you were a white worker at Southeastern, male or female, you joined the union. Each new employee at Southeastern who received a copy of Executive Circular No. 13, President William Smith's welcome to the shipyard, also received a second welcome from the eleven American Federation of Labor (AFL)–affiliated unions operating there. Article Four of the agreement between the company and the unions stated that all employees "shall be members and remain in good standing in the respective craft unions." New employees were told that they had fifteen days to become union members; if you did not join, you didn't work. As Robert Smith said, "It was automatic. You were there, you belonged to the union. You paid your dues and you worked."

To ensure that defense plants were closed shops, unions agreed to accept a basic wage freeze at a level set by the federal government and to abide by no-strike clauses in contracts for the duration of the war. The average worker was aware of this and saw little or no reason to join a union. Welder Joe

Williams, for one, did not want to pay his initiation fee, but "they finally got me. They told me to pay my fees, but I said, 'I never heard of you.' They just wanted the money, $50.00, I think." AFL initiation dues at that time ranged from $12.50 to $53.00, and monthly dues ranged from $1.25 to $4.50.

Williams continued: "That was a cost-plus job and wartime. You knew it wouldn't last. The union steward came out and questioned me pretty good and I said, 'Well, I just might leave.' It wouldn't get us any more money; the wage scale was set. The only way to get more money was to advance. Of course, I went and paid my dues. That's the last time I ever heard from them. That's all they wanted."

Others felt similar pressure. Seventeen-year-old Jeff Dukes was no match for the power of the union, recalling,

> One day I was working in the shop, and my boss said, "See that fellow standing over there? Leave this job and go over and see him." . . . First of all I knew he wasn't a Southerner as soon as he opened his mouth. He had a New Jersey accent. He didn't look Southern—tight curly black hair, small fellow. I knew he was tough, and he was not there to spend much time with me. I wasn't old enough, experienced enough, or tough enough to put up a lot resistance to that fellow, but I did manage to say, "Well, I don't believe I want to join the union." He said, "You've got to join because the union got you this job." I made one more parry: "Well, I believe Hitler and Mussolini got me this job, not the union." He smirked, shook his head, and walked away.

Dukes knew that this was not the end of it, though. The next day, when he came through the gate and reached for his card to punch the clock, it was not there. "There was a slip telling me to go to the personnel office," Dukes said. "I was really angry. They told me he could pull my card and, furthermore, I would pay my dues and join, or they were powerless to put my card back. That was my first exposure to labor relations. I felt beaten, but I went along to keep my job."

Southeastern was generally free of strikes for most of the war. In spite of the no-strike clause, however, there were two minor skirmishes. Sam Williams led a laborers' protest for higher wages and skilled jobs that lasted about an hour, and as described earlier, welders staged a one-day work stoppage because of the rumor that African Americans might replace women welders at the yard. Labor unrest finally took hold in the summer of 1945, when Germany had surrendered, the war in the Pacific was drawing to a close, and Southeastern had completed its Liberty ship contracts and shifted over to building smaller auxiliary ships designated AV-1s.

On the morning of Friday, July 20, 1945, four hundred members of the International Brotherhood of Machinists walked off the job. According to management at the shipyard, the union was seeking to negotiate an upward revision of the hourly rate and to establish a rate higher than that of skilled journeymen for men with exceptional qualifications. Three days later, with the machinists still out, shipyard officials posted the following notice to all employees: "Due to the continued absence of machinists in the plant and the mechanical condition created there-by, this shipyard will be closed effective 3:30 PM, Tuesday July 24."[1] This meant that some 750 workers would be out of work.

A meeting of the business agents of all eleven operating unions at the yard was called for 10:00 AM, July 24, by Herbert Skinner, president of the Savannah Trades and Labor Assembly. "I certainly hope that the meeting . . . will result in a solution to this situation and that the meeting will certainly avert the closing of the yard," Skinner was quoted as saying in the *Savannah Morning News*.[2]

The union's side of the dispute was aired in a story in the *Savannah Evening Press* on the 24th. Walter Jarvis, the machinists union's business agent, stated that the problem arose over management's handling of "a Form 10," which was the paperwork to establish a premium rate for a certain percentage of skilled craftsmen. While Southeastern managers had stated publicly that they could not grant a request for a premium rate, Jarvis contended "that this Form 10 was negotiated and signed by the management and the union eight months ago and it was at that time to have been submitted by the management to the War Labor Board for approval. . . . On July 5, management was asked if Form10 had been submitted to the WLB."[3]

According to Jarvis, the form was traced by management, and it was found that it had not been submitted. Shipyard officials then erased the original date and lowered the total number of employees eligible for the higher pay rate. The meeting on the 24th between union officials and shipyard managers did not resolve the problem, the machinists refused to return to work, and the yard was closed. The next day, representatives of the Maritime Commission, the U.S. Conciliation Service, and the International Brotherhood of Machinists arrived in Savannah to meet with local union officials and management but made no headway toward solving the problem.

On July 27 the War Labor Board sent a telegram to the union, stating, "This strike is seriously interfering with vital equipment needed by our armed forces and must be terminated at once. The National War Board directs all strikers to return to their jobs forthwith."[4] With WLB telegram in hand, Southeastern officials reopened the yard on July 28 but closed it after two hours when not only the machinists, but also the electricians, failed to report to work.

After a meeting with representatives of the ten unions that were not striking ironed out some differences, management reopened the yard for the second shift, still without the machinists, who had voted 359 to 0 to reject the ultimatum from the WLB. When asked how long his members would stay out, Jarvis replied, "We will stay out until management goes along with us on Form 10 or a joint petition to the War Labor Board."[5]

Southeastern's managers stated that they had no intention of doing either. On the tenth day of the strike, management announced the launching of an AV-1 and that the completion of thirteen others had been delayed by the strike. Admiral Vickery of the Maritime Commission notified the yard that unless assurances could be given that the ships called for in the AV-1 contract could be completed on time, action would be taken to have the ships moved to other yards for completion.

Further pressure was put on the union when another telegram from the WLB ordering a return to work the next morning was delivered. The machinists were threatened with having to defend their actions at a board hearing the following day in Washington, D.C. Undaunted, the machinists voted to report to Washington rather than return to work.

The WLB then got very personal: It ordered Jarvis to appear before them and explain why he had not ordered his men back to work. Apparently not wanting to face the board, especially by himself, and after twice refusing its direct order and realizing there was no support from the other craft unions, Jarvis faced reality. Thursday morning, August 2, he called a meeting, and the machinists voted to return to work on the second shift that day, thus ending the fourteen-day walkout.

Basically, nothing had changed. Having agreed to hear both sides after the men returned to work, the WLB scheduled a hearing. At 8:15 AM Washington time on the morning that the hearing was to be held, the first atomic bomb was dropped on Hiroshima. Three days later, a second atomic bomb destroyed the Japanese port city of Nagasaki, and by August 14, the war was over. Layoffs began immediately at Southeastern, and the primary concern of the machinists and every other employee of the yard was not a pay raise, but how long would they have jobs.

While the yard was in operation, however, pay was a significant factor in attracting workers to Southeastern. Patriotism motivated some, but most people came to the yard because the pay was good. In fact, for people coming out of the Depression, the pay was magnificent. Most production line jobs paid $1.20 an hour, and leadermen, who supervised ten to twenty workers, made $1.42. Quartermen, who oversaw five or six leadermen, earned $1.68 an hour. Nightshift workers earned more, and overtime was paid at time-and-a-half. Sunday work was paid at double time.

N̤ 683513

| EMPLOYEE'S NAME | | | | | WEEK ENDING | | |

| | | | | | MO. | DAY | YEAR |

M G HAMMOCK

1 0 1 7 4 3

WEEK	DEPT	BADGE	TOTAL HOURS	P. W. & PREMIUM	TOTAL EARNINGS		
4 2	7 4	4 1 5	6 4 5	7 4 0	1 1 3 0 0		
BOND DED.	O. A. S. I.	U. S. WITHHOLDING	OTHER DED.		NET PAY		
1 8 7 5		1 5 8 0			7 8 4 5		

DETACH THIS STUB

IT IS REQUIRED BY LAW AND SHOULD BE RETAINED AS A PER-
MANENT RECORD OF YOUR EARNINGS, DEDUCTIONS AND NET PAY

SOUTHEASTERN SHIPBUILDING CORPORATION
SAVANNAH, GEORGIA

Photo 17. M. G. Hammock's pay stub. *Courtesy of M. G. Hammock*

One female worker at the yard may have failed to appreciate how high her salary was, however. She received a paycheck one week for $00.00. Her earnings were $42.12, but $37.50 was deducted for a war bond, $0.42 was withheld for Social Security, and another $4.20 was withheld for income tax. The total deductions, then, were $42.12.

Many Southeastern workers had never been employed by a large corporation before, and at least one coworker of welder Nan Hiott, was particularly unfamiliar with payroll procedures. "He had never been paid by check before," Hiott recalled, "and didn't know he could cash the check. He told me that he had worked as long as he could for victory, but now he had to find a job to feed his family."

Shipyards, other defense industries, and military bases drew Savannah, and the American South in general, out of the long economic stagnation that had existed since the end of the Civil War. The average payroll at Southeastern during each week of full operation was $750,000, and the payroll for the first week in November 1943 reached $1 million, a Savannah record. For the total period of its operation, Southeastern pumped $112 million into the economy of Savannah.

By the end of September 1942 more than 5,000 workers were employed at the shipyard, and that number was increasing rapidly every month. The vast majority had never seen a ship, much less built one. If they were to become welders, burners, shipwrights, shipfitters, or any of the thirty-six different tradespeople required to build a Liberty ship, they had to be trained, and trained

Photo 18. Bob Fennel's badges. The medal on the right is
the Ships for Victory medal given by the U.S. Maritime
Commission. *Photo by the author*

quickly. Fortunately, new training techniques, and the relatively simple mass-
production methods developed by Henry Kaiser and others, reduced the need
for long apprenticeships and made it possible for inexperienced workers to be
hired, be trained, and begin constructing ships at a pace that would have been
totally unthinkable during peacetime. Training classes were set up at the new
vocational school on Bay Street, the number of drafting classes at Savannah
High School was increased and night classes were added, and training classes
were created at the shipyard that would eventually produce more than 6,000
welders and burners.

Chapter Eight

Doing the Same Thing
Over and Over

Southeastern was not the prewar type of shipyard, where thousands
of highly trained skilled workers built ships on the ways from the keel
up. Rather, it was an assembly plant, where, for the most part, hastily
trained workers following very simple instructions and doing the same jobs
over and over pieced together the more than 30,000 parts of a Liberty ship,
which were brought in on freight cars from 500 plants in 32 states.[1]

To avoid production conflicts with existing programs, parts for Liberty
ships were ordered from companies not normally involved in marine-
oriented production. Thus, engines were ordered from companies that
ordinarily made railroad locomotives, and compasses came from the Lionel
Corporation, which normally made toy trains. This was the production line
manufacturing pioneered by Henry Ford and adapted for the shipbuilding
industry by Henry Kaiser.

Large sections of each Liberty ship were put together on a concrete slab
in front of a ways and then lifted into place by huge cranes. When the hull
and superstructure were complete, the ship was launched and moved to a wet
dock for fitting out. During the fitting-out stage, some two hundred items
were added, including the guns and all furnishings and equipment. After
successful dock trials and a ten-hour sea trial, a ship was ready to be delivered
to the steamship company to which it had been assigned by the War Shipping
Administration (WSA).

Building ships by the Ford/Kaiser method was costly but quick. The average
cost per ship at Southeastern was $2.043 million, making Southeastern the
second-highest in terms of production costs among yards building a similar
or higher number of ships. The Maritime Commission paid this bill with little
complaint, though, because cargo ships were needed immediately and in large
numbers for the war effort. When challenged in 1946 during a congressional
committee hearing for wasting money, wartime commission chairman Adm.
Emory S. Land responded, "We did the best we could with the tools we had.
What we did, we did honestly. We built the ships and the war was won, and if
you don't like that, you can go to hell."[2]

Photo 19. The fabrication shop at night. *Photo from the* Sou'Easter, *n.d.*

The shipyard that built the *Oglethorpe* and eighty-seven other Liberty ships became the largest industry in Savannah (see Appendix D). On the ninety-six-acre Southeastern site, there were sixty-five buildings with more than half a million square feet of floor space. There was also eight miles of railroad track, on which ran five locomotives and sixty-nine flat cars. The company owned twenty flatbed and four pickup trucks. There were thirteen gantry cranes—each capable of lifting seventy tons—and twenty-one locomotive cranes. The cafeteria had a seating capacity of 1,000 and served an average of 3,000 cups of coffee and 150 dozen eggs every day. Sixteen tons of ice went into the water coolers throughout the yard daily. A central first aid station and two substations were staffed by three doctors and eighteen nurses. Southeastern's telephone switchboard could handle calls for a city of ten thousand and had four operators on duty during the day and three at night.

At the yard's peak in December 1943, 15,303 workers were employed on three shifts at Southeastern. In all, 46,766 workers punched their time cards there between 1942 and 1946.[3] Not only was Southeastern the largest manufacturing company in Savannah at the time, it remains the largest individual manufacturing plant in the city's long history. Given the current trend of downsizing major industries, the Southeastern Shipbuilding Corporation may well be the largest industry Savannah will ever see.

Photo 20. The Southeastern Shipbuilding Corporation, looking north, December 9, 1944. *Photo from U.S. Maritime Commission*

Most of the people employed at Southeastern during the war were capable, hardworking, and willing to do their part for the effort. Most were also very proud of what they achieved. Outside machinist Bob Fennel felt that pride as he watched the *Oglethorpe* slide down the ways. "I think that was a wonderful thing to watch that bunch of farmers and people from all walks of life come here, learn a trade, and build that first ship in one year," he said decades later.

Sheet metal apprentice Jeff Dukes was both proud and amazed: "I gained a terrific admiration for the fact that those people would take those piles of metal spread out all over everywhere and bring it together and build a ship. I had no idea that they were smart enough to do that. I was in awe of it."

For crane operator Wallace Beasley, working at Southeastern was the best of times. "Everybody thought that they were doing something important," Beasley recalled. "It was like one great family, and everybody seemed to work together in harmony. . . . Everybody worked, the pay was good, the job was good, the people were treated good, and they worked well." Dukes again had a similar recollection, saying, "As bad as war is in its ultimate sense, it can bring out the best qualities in people—sacrifice, devotion. It brings out the stamina to apply oneself. I saw all of this at the shipyard. Those people really worked." And there were few easy jobs at the yard.

Photo 21. A keel laid on the ways just after a Liberty was launched from the same ways. *Photo from the* Sou'Easter, *n.d.*

On Maritime Day, May 22, 1942, when the keels were laid for the yard's first ship, *Oglethorpe*, and the *Handley*, Savannah Mayor Thomas Gamble addressed the workers at the ceremony, saying, "You men who will lay keel after keel, who will finish ship after ship, are essential to victory. That thought will sustain you in fatigue, will lighten your work when it is heaviest, will cheer you in the hours of the night shift, will add joy to your toil in the thought that America and the world look to you as soldiers of industry, sounding the doom of tyranny wherever it has reared its ugly head."[4]

One has to wonder how many workers remembered and were sustained by that thought over the next few years as they labored in conditions that were often less than ideal. Most production workers at Southeastern worked out of doors in the steel yard, on the slabs, or on the wet dock. Bad weather rarely slowed down production, but during one particularly cold stretch one winter, working conditions became so hazardous that some jobs were suspended for a short period. Extremely high winds also delayed some launchings, but workers generally persevered through the cold, the rain, and the heat.

Welder Joe Williams remembered the cold in particular, saying, "We had to close down several times on account of ice. Ice would form on the steel decks, and it was almost impossible to get around." Freezing temperatures were also a problem for welder Nan Hiott, who said, "In cold weather we would get pieces of pasteboard to sit on to work. It was like sitting on ice on the steel."

Workers did whatever they could to stay warm during the winter months. On the ground workers burned waste materials in oil drums. Seventy feet up in the air in the cab of the gantry crane it was a bit cozier, according to Beasley.

Photo 22. First shift welders. *Photo from the* Sou'Easter, *n.d.*

"There was nobody but me and the oiler in that cab," he explained. "They built us some heaters out of half inch iron plate and a big old iron pipe. We had a box of coal in there, and that fire kept us warm in there."

At the other extreme, during the day in the summer, temperatures in Savannah reach the high 90s, with some days seeing readings of over 100° Fahrenheit. The heat in the yard was magnified by the sun beating down on and reflecting off all of the steel plate, and temperatures in confined spaces could reach 120° Fahrenheit. As welder Shorty Beasley recalled, "That steel in the summertime was so hot, and you're inside a hood, a pair of gloves, high top shoes, and a leather jacket . . . and there's all that smoke from the welding rod. They had some fans, but they were never on." Workers were advised to take the salt tablets available at all water coolers four times a day, and sixteen tons of ice went into those coolers—most of them, anyway—each day in an attempt to mitigate the high temperatures.

The paraphernalia that caused such discomfort during the summer also served as protection from some of the area's other hazards. The stretch of the Savannah River on which the yard was built was, and still is, prime mosquito and deerfly territory. Mosquitoes bred in prodigious numbers in the salt marsh across the river, and deerflies, while smaller than horseflies, bite just as hard and occur in much greater numbers. And these were not the only creatures the

Photo 23. Summers are hot in Savannah. This worker really could fry an egg on a steel plate. *Photo from the* Sou'Easter, *n.d.*

workers had to face. "The little sand gnats were terrible . . . and the wharf rats . . . big as squirrels almost," Joe Williams remembered. "They said, 'Why don't you get some cats?' Heck, those rats would have killed cats."

Then there was the noise. With thousands of people working at hundreds of different tasks, it was only during a change of shifts that the noise would die down to a dull roar. "I want to tell you," Jeff Dukes said, "the noise—metal being moved, hammering, drilling, pneumatic things banging down, heat welding, spot welding on metal. . . . You'd be down in a ship and hear all of the drills and hammers. The noise was unceasing. It was a horrible thing. People don't talk, they shout. From the time you came in, you shouted all day. And when the day's work was over and you came out, it took you some time to quit shouting."

Williams, too, was affected by the noise. He recalled that "you couldn't believe the noise. I lost a lot of hearing in my right ear. If you happened to be underneath the upper deck when a chipper was working above . . . that was one heck of a noise . . . about like those redheaded woodpeckers pecking on a hollow tree but magnified a million times. It would rattle your brain."

Photo 24. Bow section being lifted into place. *Photo from the Sou'Easter, n.d.*

Williams, Dukes, and many other production workers at Southeastern would not have understood the perspective of the office worker who described what she saw of the yard's activity from her office window in the April 1, 1945, *Sou'Easter*:

One expects action and noise in a shipyard, but its color can be thrilling and unexpected. Once in a while an artist captures this shifting panorama of raw color on canvas and produces something really notable.

A ship under construction is a maze of color—glittering lengths of galvanized sections against the deep orange bulk of ventilator pipes, the fluttering azure of great sheets of blueprints against the dead static black of plate sections and the bulk of a giant propeller seemingly made of gold.

White-hot rivets, tossed through the air to a man who casually catches them in a gadget that looks like a funnel, are like miniature comets, and a spray of white sparks gushes forth when a cutting torch gnaws through steel plate.

Mix all this against a background of rippling green water and a shipyard emerges with color unmatched by any other American industry.[5]

One has to wonder if very many production line workers noticed the "glittering lengths," the "fluttering azure," the "miniature comets," or the "gushing spray of white sparks." As for the "rippling green water," the Savannah River has a rich history and has been key to the economic and cultural life of the city, but the only time it has been any color other than muddy brown was when it was dyed green for St. Patrick's Day 1961.

Colors were important at the yard. According to Dukes, "Everybody wore hard hats, and you could tell by the color scheme whether somebody was a pipefitter, a sheet metal worker, or what." You could also tell who the bosses were. Executives wore white hard hats, while the protective headgear of leadermen and quartermen had white brims with the crowns painted the color of the wearer's department. The welder's color was orange, and the burner's color was dark green. Shipwrights wore light green hard hats, and pipefitters wore purple. Perhaps the most colorful hard hats were those worn by the electricians—dark blue with red sparks on the sides of the crown. In all there were some thirty-three color schemes for hard hats. At a change of shifts, with thousands of workers jammed together as they entered and exited the yard, the view from above must have been a veritable sea of colors.

The beauty of this spectacle, too, was probably lost on a production worker who had just completed a double shift, had worked seven days in a row, or had spent eight hours doing the same monotonous task over and over. Much of the work at the yard was repetitive. To produce the huge number of ships necessary to meet logistical requirements of America and its allies and to produce them quickly, prefabrication and the use of tens of thousands of inexperienced workers was essential. Training workers do only one or two relatively simple jobs and having them do those jobs over and over again made it possible for production quotas to be met. For some workers, however, spending eight or sixteen hours a day doing the same thing time and time again was boring.

Dukes said, "I was so bored, seventeen years old and doing the same thing over and over. I was the guy that would hold the other end of a piece of metal while another guy would shape it. The front office would send this chit that would say, 'Do sixty pieces of iron bar with an arch on the end.' We didn't know or care where that iron bar would fit, but we knew the specs. So we would roll it, cut it, twist it, turn it, whatever. It just absolutely ground me down."

The first job given to welder Ben McClendon working on the *Oglethorpe* was boring, he said: "The ship was built up enough so that they were putting the shell plates on. They must have picked up what metal they could find at other places that had been made for other ships because they had holes stamped out for rivets. My first job was welding those holes up. That was a monstrous job . . . 10,000 holes."

Photo 25. Southeastern officials J. F. McInnis, William H. Smith (president), and George A. Rentschler receiving the Maritime *M* pennant, September 27, 1943. *Photo from the* Sou'Easter, *n.d.*

Some Southeastern workers were bored because the nature of their jobs involved long periods of inactivity. Left to their own devices, these workers would come up with different and sometimes macabre ways of staying busy. "Fellows that didn't have anything to do, like watchmen, guys that had the fire watch, they'd be underneath the ship where they would set deadfalls and put bait underneath them," Red Pitts recalled. "When about a dozen rats would get underneath it, they'd trip it and squash them just to have something to do."

In spite of the hard work, the difficult conditions, and the boredom, morale at Southeastern was generally high. This was due in some part to the very effective official propaganda that emanated from the Maritime Commission. Early in the war the commission created a series of pennants to be given to shipyards that had met or exceeded their production schedules. These were presented with much fanfare at launchings and on other special days, with celebrities and officials from the commission on hand. With the pennants came a lapel pin and an award of merit for each employee. Later, when it was realized that some yards might not ever receive a pennant, criteria were loosened a bit so that reasons could be found for recognizing every yard.

Southeastern received the Maritime *M* pennant on September 27, 1943, during the launching of its twenty-fourth ship, the SS *William Black Yates*. Nine stars were added to that pennant, and a second pennant, the Maritime Merit Eagle, was awarded in December 1944. All of these awards were given even though the yard did not complete a single ship by its contract date and in spite of the fact that the cost per ship was higher at Southeastern than at all but one other comparable shipyard.

The recognition of special anniversaries was another means by which the Maritime Commission could recognize a shipyard and maintain pressure to improve production. For a shipyard located in Savannah, a city with a long and proud maritime history, there were a number of significant anniversaries from which to choose. The city could, in fact, boast the premier American maritime anniversary, National Maritime Day, commemorated every May 22, to celebrate the sailing from the city of the SS *Savannah*, which in 1819 became the first steamship to cross the Atlantic Ocean. Southeastern timed the launching of the SS *Francis Bartow* for that day in 1944, and Admiral Land gave the main address. Land used the occasion to urge workers not to let up for a minute, saying, "You have produced miracles and will continue to produce them. If our sons want to avoid war twenty years hence, let's keep up our merchant marine and shipbuilding."[6]

Another attempt by the commission to instill the "we are all in this together" spirit was the establishment at each yard of a Labor–Management Committee that had the mission of removing any bottlenecks that were holding up production. This committee was also given the responsibility of awarding war bonds to workers who came up with suggestions that would improve efficiency and save money. This proved to be one of the commission's most successful programs, and by October 1945 at shipyards around the country, some $25 million had been saved at a cost of just $22,000.

At Southeastern there were a number of bonds awarded. J. H. Nettles, a shipfitter quarterman, received a $75 bond for his suggestion. There was only one gantry on the slab where he worked, and it would often be tied up working in another area when he needed it. This was slowing down production, so, using scrap materials, he constructed a small revolving crane powered by two air motors and capable of lifting four tons. Shipwright quarterman J. A. McGraw created a holder for a steamboat jack that could be fitted onto the end of the bulkhead shores, thus eliminating the need for oiling cables on the bulkheads and padeyes to hold the cables. He received a $100 war bond.

Not all suggestions were accepted, however, and not all added to the $25 million saved. M. C. Nettles, the burner hired originally to help construct the Savannah Shipyards yard who then stayed to build ships with Southeastern, had watched a crew trying to lay railroad tracks on one of the ways. He said,

[The crew] had no electricity. They hadn't gotten power in yet, so they were using a crane handle to drill holes in the plates used to join the rails together. I told the foreman that that seemed like a slow way to do that. He said it was the only way without power, but I told him I could take my torch and burn a hole through it quicker. "Show me," he said. I burned a hole in the plate and stuck a bolt in and tightened it down. "Damn," he said, "this will get us out of here much quicker."

I got a $50 war bond for coming up with that idea. They got the tracks built, and the first time it froze out there during the winter, every one of those holes I burned cracked the plates in half. They had to do it all over again.

M. C. was asked to return the bond, but he told them that he had already cashed it and spent the money.

As part of the national campaign to promote patriotism and encourage the meeting of production quotas through the use of positive stories in newspapers and magazines and on the radio, the two Savannah dailies, the *Savannah Morning News* and the *Savannah Evening Press*, carried stories and photographs of every launching, every award given, and any happening of any significance at Southeastern. Southeastern's official publication, the *Sou'Easter*, was perhaps the shipyard's most effective means of conveying official propaganda to its employees. Published bimonthly, the magazine provided workers with all of the news that was positive to print. The publication openly stated that its raison d'être was to boost morale and provide pertinent information. With a peak circulation of 15,000, sixty-four issues were published, each carrying photos and articles about new facilities, families working at the yard, the successes of various skilled craftspeople, ideas from other shipyards, the outside interests of employees, information about ships' names and construction, and statistics and information from the Maritime Commission. There were also features on former employees, especially if they had joined the military or shipped out on one of the ships built at the yard; the company's athletic teams; war bond drives; new officials; and the tallest, shortest, oldest, and self-proclaimed ugliest employees.

Most issues of the *Sou'Easter* carried a center spread photo feature of the launches from the previous two weeks. There were also want ads, poems from employees, letters from dignitaries, and information on rationing. The goal of the publication was to be positive, cheerful, and as upbeat as possible, and to include as my photos and names of employees as possible.

Nothing that might in any way be detrimental to production, such as fatal accidents or union problems, was reported in the *Sou'Easter*. The only time minor accidents or absenteeism was mentioned was when that information could be used to admonish workers to do better.

By the end of the war, the *Sou'Easter* had become a very slick and professional publication. C. Winn Upchurch, a former merchant seaman and newspaper reporter, was editor and photographer for the last forty-seven issues. The staff artist and cartoonist was the former professional cartoonist Joseph Quadrella.

Southeastern sponsored a number of athletic teams that competed in communitywide leagues and intramural contests to bolster morale. The company's all-white baseball team, which featured the former Washington Senators and Cleveland Indians pitcher Monroe Mitchell, played against teams from other local defense plants and military bases. A confident Mitchell stated at the time that the Southeastern nine was as strong as the city's professional team, the Savannah Indians.

The company's intramural softball league featured such teams as the Burners, the Mold Loft Men, the Riveters, the Riggers, the Fab Shop Men, and the Wet Dock Men. Coming up with logos for the Mold Loft Men and the Wet Dock Men must have been interesting. The Mold Loft Men probably did not worry too much about that, however, as they won the league championship every year. Basketball, bowling, and golf teams participated in contests in the broader community, and the yard's annual golf tournament featured a first prize of $10 in war bond stamps.

Southeastern's boxing team was anchored by one of Savannah's boxing legends, featherweight Tommy Keane, and by heavyweight John Merritt, who known around the yard as "Joe Palooka." The yard also sponsored an African-American baseball team whose exploits were covered in the *Sou'Easter*, and a women's basketball team that was never mentioned in print.

Entertainment in various forms was also used to boost morale at Southeastern. Rallies and drives were held for a variety of organizations and purposes, and each had the stated goal of encouraging donations for the particular cause and the not-so-subliminal goal of fostering patriotism and increasing production. At one Red Cross rally held to encourage the donation of both money and plasma, more than $15,000 was raised. When an Army corporal originally from Savannah who had been badly wounded in the Pacific theater told of how blood plasma had saved his life, he was appealing for blood donations and also letting workers know how tough combat was and how important was their task of building ships.

The rallies also featured area military bands and civilian bands that were often made up of Southeastern employees. Marion Hall and his Georgia Nighthawks provided the music for the Red Cross rally at which the wounded corporal spoke, and at the Community War Fund rally held in February 1944, the music was performed by Reuben Ware and his Hillbilly Band, the Boston Jubilee Singers, and two African-American singing groups—the Heavenly Bound Glee Club and the Gold Star Quartet. All the members of each of the groups were Southeastern employees.

Photo 26. Workers at a rally at Southeastern. *Photo by Caroline Strang*

The shipyard also sponsored its own band, which provided music for launches and other special occasions. This band, made up entirely of employees and under the direction of Henry J. Applewhite, also gave lunchtime concerts for workers every Monday, Wednesday, and Friday. Some people who were then or who would become some of Savannah's finest musicians played in this band. Drummer Sandor Chan played for years with local bands such as the Jewel Casey Orchestra, as well as with Russ Peacock and pianist Ken Palmer. Southeastern band clarinetist Johnny Phillips would later front his own band, and Ed Wheeler played with the Russ Mooney Orchestra after the war and later with Jewel Casey.

Applewhite was, himself, one of Savannah's best-known musicians during the 1940s and 1950s, leading a number of his own bands and playing trumpet in many others. He was also was the longtime band director at Savannah High School. That he was also long-suffering was evidenced by the year he spent attempting to teach this author how to blow a bugle and how to stay in step in the Washington Avenue Junior High School Drum and Bugle Corps.

Perhaps the biggest events at shipyard were the war loan drives. Nationally known celebrities visited Southeastern to entertain and to encourage workers to purchase war bonds. Huge crowds saw Veronica Lake in the spring of 1943 and Columbia Pictures star Janet Blair in December 1944. Generally, the

Photo 27. Henry Applewhite conducting the shipyard band at the launching of the SS *Hamlin Garland*, July 6, 1943. *Photo from the* Sou'Easter, *August 1, 1943*

appeals worked. Almost every issue of the *Sou'Easter* carried stories of workers who had gone above and beyond in the buying of bonds. The January 15, 1944, edition ran a picture of Rogers J. "Robert" Lovett, an African-American worker who for years before the war been a waiter at the DeSoto Hotel. Lovett had bought a bond each month for the previous six months. Contributing to his motivation was the fact that he had two sons and a son-in-law in the military overseas.[7]

The *Sou'Easter* for August 1, 1943, reported that J. H. Whitten, a first-class shipfitter, had invested 71 percent of his wages in bonds for more than a year.[8] In the same issue, R. Outz, who worked on the night shift, was reported to have increased his bond buying from $25 to $100 each week. That must have been quite a sacrifice; even working overtime on the night shift, it is difficult to understand how Outz' salary allowed for a contribution of that size.

Most workers bought war bonds. As Dukes recalled, "Yeah, I bought bonds. We all did. It was just something you did. It helped win the war." During an interview with the author, Shorty Beasley sang the song that the Andrews Sisters recorded to encourage bond buying, "Any Bonds Today":

> Any bonds today?
> Bonds of freedom
> That is what I'm selling
> Any Bonds today?
> Scrape up the most you can
> Here comes the freedom man
> Asking you to buy a share of freedom today

Workers were not forced to buy bonds, but they did receive very strong encouragement. Beasley said that he was "invited" and "urged" to buy them, but "nobody was pushed into it." Walter Simmons, who was a teenager when he worked in the cafeteria and drove a truck for Southeastern, had a different experience. "I guess my pay was so low," Simmons said, "they didn't bother me." Carpenter Harold Miller felt a bit more pressured, explaining, "You couldn't escape them. Your life would be unpleasant if you didn't get in on a bond drive. I never questioned it, I just bought some—made a payroll deduction so the company could look good."

To limit the financial impact of buying bonds, many workers cashed them in as fast as they bought them. Williams remembered that a visit to the yard by actress Lauren Bacall convinced him to buy bonds, but the incentive to keep them left when she did. As Williams told the story, "Yes sir, you signed up for whatever. I cashed most of mine, but if I had known then what I know now . . . that interest rates kept going and didn't stop. . . . I missed my chance to get rich."

Workers may not have gotten rich off of the bonds, but several were glad they had bought them. "Both my mother and I signed up for bonds right from the beginning," said clerk-typist Sue Donahue. "When I left there I had $250 in bonds, which came in handy after I got married. They were just put away in the bottom of a cedar chest and forgotten about." M. C. Nettles bought his first

Photo 28. Movie star Veronica Lake at a Southeastern war bond rally. *Photo by Amelia Dreese*

house with his bonds, and the bonds Ruby Clifton purchased were also put to good use after the war. "Those bonds I cashed when [my husband] Pete came out of the Army are how we were able to go into business," Clifton said.

By the end of production in 1945, Southeastern had "bothered," "encouraged," "urged," and "invited" workers to buy bonds in the amount of $117,550.

As with the military, food at the shipyard could be a source of high morale. It was a missed opportunity at Southeastern, however. Unlike the facilities at other shipyards, where only executives or office staff would be served hot meals, the cafeteria at Southeastern was constructed to serve all workers. Well, almost all.

African Americans could work in the cafeteria, but they could not eat there. And most white workers did not. One hundred and twenty five people, mostly African Americans, were employed in the 12,000-square-foot building. Southeastern subcontracted the food service business to Crotty Brothers, Georgia, Inc., who would boast that the cafeteria served an average of 3,000 cups of coffee and 1,800 eggs every day. Five women working in the dish room washed some 3,000 plates and 3,000 glasses just during the day shift. They claimed that during peak employment, between five and six thousand workers were served each day. The cafeteria was located, however, next to the administration building, placing it about as far away from the yard's production areas as it could be without being in the parking lot. As a result, most workers brought their own lunches.

Creasy, for one, brown-bagged it because a lunch was included in his $5-a-week room rent. He did occasionally visit the cafeteria, though, because "they had drink machines and coffee machines." Welder Myrtis Hammock, on the other hand, never went to the cafeteria, recalling, "I know there was a cafeteria at the yard, but I imagine it was pretty expensive. They didn't hardly give you time to go to the cafeteria to eat. You just had a few minutes. The rich folks, the ones with the big jobs, were the ones that went there to eat. Us poor people, we didn't."

Williams also remembered that most workers brought their own lunches "until you moved up into a leadership position. Then you might have the time and the money to eat in the cafeteria. I ate there sometimes. That's where I ate my first horsemeat. It couldn't have been anything else the way it looked."

There were alternatives for Williams and his fellow workers. "Sometimes several of us would go up right across from where the Savannah Electric and Power Co. office is today," he explained. "Over on the hill was a restaurant called King's Kitchen. Boy! They put out the best shrimp you ever ate. And out in front of the gate they had a little concession stand that the top lifted up. We called it the 'Blowfly' because there were so many flies around it."

Two canteens were set up within the shipyard. One was on the southern boundary, about 250 feet from the No. 6 slab. The other was about one hundred feet from the wet dock. Simmons, who was a fifteen-year-old working at the yard after school, remembered, "Those men who worked on the waterfront and who could not make the trip up to the cafeteria, we provided meals for them by putting them in a container that kept them warm and hauling them down to the riverfront where we had young ladies who manned the food booths. I think there were two ladies in each booth. My job was to make coffee and drive the truck."

No one had to worry about Simmons' morale. For a teenager who had just learned how to drive, his job provided a tremendous thrill. "That was better than pay day driving that panel truck around," he said. "I would haul the food and the ladies down to the waterfront. I remember that the ladies would ride on the running boards, and the men would whistle at them."

Whether a worker bought lunch at the canteen or brought it from home, eating outside on the work site had its problems. "At lunch you had to watch the seagulls. They would bombard you, you know. You'd have to hide under the ways to eat," river catcher Jimmy Hodges said.

In spite of all of the efforts to boost morale and, thus, production, a few workers never got the message. In a company that employed as many people as Southeastern did, there would always be some who would take any opportunity to avoid work or, when working, cut corners to make their jobs easier. According to Pitts,

> It don't take long to pick out fellows who would do stuff like that. I saw a couple of them that started to put a slug in and weld over it. I said, "No you don't, you weld that damn thing."
>
> "Yeah, but look at that crack."
>
> "You are paid to weld. You're risking somebody's life when you do things like that."

When Pitts was working after the war at Savannah Machine and Foundry repairing Liberty ships built at yards around the country, he saw the results of this type of shoddy work. "One of my people went to weld an overhead, and somebody [during the construction of the ship] had filled in part of the thing with dirt and welded over it," Pitts said. "Sand started pouring out. The person who did that should have been shot."

Harold Miller related similar stories, saying, for instance, "These guys were making a welding pass on this shell strake, laying welding rods in it and welding over it. They made two passes, but it looked like seven. Some of those ships broke up and people died as a result of it." Southeastern did try to ensure that these types of problems were held to a minimum. "They issued one hundred

rods, and you had to turn in one hundred tips to get a hundred more rods,"
explained merchant seaman and dock worker Charlie Gross.

With the seemingly endless supply of materials and tools at defense plants,
theft was a major problem. Because the shipyard was working on government
contracts, the Federal Bureau of Investigation (FBI) was given jurisdiction in
matters of theft. A number of former Southeastern workers remembered a
particularly blatant case of attempted theft. Miller told the story:

> This guy was going to steal some electric cable. It must have been a
> considerable amount, maybe a couple of hundred feet. This stuff was
> unobtainable during the war, and he probably had a garage or something.
> He wrapped the cable around him under a jacket and started for the
> checkout gates. About halfway, [the cable] started settling down. It was
> really heavy. A couple of his buddies were with him and they got him by
> the elbows to steady him, but he collapsed. There was no way. He was
> done. The FBI made an example of him. He was sent to prison.

The FBI, however, did not catch everybody. "We used to tease the women in
the cafeteria about coming to the yard with these big pocketbooks. You know,
the flat kind? Simmons remembered. "Well, they wouldn't be flat when they
left. There'd be chicken or something left over from making salad in them."

Other problems were serious enough for the FBI to be concerned. On
October 3, 1943, the *Savannah Morning News* ran a story in which the special
agent in charge of the Savannah District, John R. Ruggles, warned that the
war effort was being hurt by pranks and horseplay that had the same effect
as sabotage—the slowing down of production. The article goes on to report
that one Cardell C. Saxon, a worker at Southeastern, had placed a penny in a
light socket and interrupted work at the yard for several hours. Ruggles noted
that in most case such as this, the person involved was motivated by personal
anger towards a supervisor, the desire for notoriety, or just the desire to create
mischief. The story does not report the motive Saxon had for investing his
personal funds in a light socket or the legal consequences of that activity, but
Agent Ruggles is quoted as saying that "the majority of persons convicted on
misdemeanor or malicious mischief charges state that they do not intend to do
any harm."[9]

Most pranks at the yard did not have the dramatic effect of Saxon's misuse
of a penny. Rather, they involved the normal practical jokes and teasing that
goes on in any workplace. The negative effects on production schedules were
minute, and, in some cases, the pranks may have been positive. Such activities
served to break the ice in work crews and helped workers relate to each other
and, thus, improve the work rate. Jimmy Hodges, however, might have had some

difficulty in finding a positive aspect to the actions of some of his fellow workers. "They'd take their cigarettes and stick them in my back pockets," he said. "I didn't have a pair of pants that didn't have a hole burned in the back. Mine weren't work pants. They were gabardine 'cause I didn't get dirty from what I did."

While practical jokes could be positive, loafing was not. In a radio address on March 24, 1942, Admiral Land called loafing one of the most serious problems facing shipyards in their attempts to meet production quotas.[10] An investigation begun that same month by the Maritime Commission determined that at most yards, workers could be found sitting around in the holds of vessels, standing in groups talking, and wandering aimlessly. One inspector said that he could always find men sleeping on ships any time of the day or night and craps games going on during working hours. Southeastern had just started operations when this investigation was done, so it is unlikely that the yard was inspected, but incidents such as those described did occur.

Supervisors at Southeastern had their own ways of dealing with the loafers Land admonished. Pitts recalled, "If they were in my crew, they worked. There was no loafing. There was this one fellow who thought he was bad, a real fighter. I caught him two, three times. He was supposed to be welding. I'd come by, and he'd be out on deck. Finally, I told him, 'Charlie, at knocking-off time if you're not through welding that escape trunk, I'm going to beat your behind all over this deck.' He got back in there and went to work. He got it done."

Another of Pitts' welders who was either afraid of his boss or thought that he could do better—or perhaps less—under another leaderman had to think again. "This old boy wanted to know why I wouldn't give him a transfer," Pitts remembered. "I said, 'Well, I'll tell you, most of these fellows, these other leadermen around here are my friends. If I ever find somebody I hate, I'll transfer you then.'"

Outside machinist Leon Judy's leaderman had another method of dealing with slackers. According to Judy, "We had one man in the crew that was very lazy. He would always be found in the restroom sleeping. One day the boss caught him sitting on the toilet sleeping with his pants down. He sprinkled some glass wool insulation in his underwear. About thirty minutes later, we saw him climbing up on top of the water tower. He jumped in with his clothes on."

Charles Wollenberg, in his book *Marinship at War*, reported that prostitution, drinking, and workers selling chances on cars and houses, running lotteries, and floating craps games were common at that West Coast shipyard.[11] Such activities were common at Southeastern, too. In an attempt to minimize these and other problems, Southeastern officials, with the approval of the Labor-Management Committee, established a set of rules and regulations and posted them throughout the yard. Listed under the category of causes for immediate dismissal were all of the problem behaviors already identified, as well as fabricating records; using the wrong badge; deliberately destroying property; sleeping on duty; possessing concealed weapons, explosives, or cameras; and giving or taking bribes as a means of obtaining advancement or retaining a position.

Workplace problems that would be handled on a case-by-case basis included habitual tardiness, absenteeism, loitering, deliberate violation of safety rules, leaving the job site before the final whistle, running, vending, and soliciting or collecting unauthorized contributions. While the rules were tough, they were never strictly enforced. Pitts recalled, "Coming to work on the second shift, if you got out there about fifteen minutes before your shift, you couldn't get in the place. There would be at least five hundred people at the gate already lined up to get out, waiting for the whistle to blow."

Harold Miller remembered seeing gambling both on and off the shipyard property, saying, "I was with this guy, we were eating lunch. He said, 'You hear that? They're going to roast in hellfire.' It was lunch hour, and they were shooting craps. 'Yes sir, they're going to die in hellfire.'"

With shipyard workers making so much money, it is not difficult to imagine how quickly places that had the sole purpose of relieving them of the burden of carrying that money around sprang up. "Fifteen thousand people and, boy, did they play those slot machines. Some of them put all of their money in the slot machines," Miller said.

At least one of the activities at Southeastern would most properly be classified under stupidity rather than morale-boosting or entertainment. According to gantry operator Robert Smith, there were a number of "self-appointed preachers" working at the yard. Often, a preacher would find a group of employees sitting around eating lunch, climb up on a piece of equipment and begin sermonizing. "There was this one that was going to walk on water down at the wet dock," Smith said. "He put up a sign saying he was going to it at a certain time. The riggers wanted to put a rope on him, but he said, 'No.' He went down on a float, put one foot in the water, and sunk about to his ankle. He couldn't understand that, so then he stepped off right there, and they had to pull him out with a rope."

Perhaps this preacher should have been charged with violation of Rule 8: Deliberate Violation or Disregard of Safety Rules, or Rule 9: Leaving the Job Site Before the Final Whistle.

Chapter Nine

You Can't Spell Victory
with an Absent "T"

One of the biggest problems at all shipyards, including Southeastern, was absenteeism. It was a problem that would continue throughout the war, and it was most acute in shipyards on the East Coast, where the average monthly rate of absenteeism was 12 percent.

Among the general public, chronic absenteeism by defense workers engendered the same outrage as avoidance of military service, and many felt that absentees should be jailed or drafted. Some workers did have legitimate excuses. Car problems were legion for the many people Southeastern employed who came from surrounding rural communities, who had to drive long distances on bad roads with old and patched tires. At harvesttime, some men had to help their wives and children bring in crops. Others faced the problem of trying to shop for their families when working hours coincided with the opening hours of shops and stores.

In towns and cities where new shipyards were built, they were built in areas where there were no established shopping areas. In Savannah the announcement of plans for construction of a five-store shopping center on the corner of Pennsylvania Avenue and Liberty Street, about equidistant between Tattnall Homes and Pine Gardens, was welcome news to the workers at Southeastern.

The average rate of absenteeism for Southeastern employees stayed between 10 percent and 11 percent. It was not unusual for a total of 1,500 or more workers to be absent from the three shifts on any given day. A January 1943 report from the special Senate Committee to Investigate the National Defense Program chaired by Harry S. Truman states that while "pretty good progress" was being made in building ships, absenteeism was very bad. Quoting the committee's report, the *Savannah Morning News* reported, "We received very discouraging reports on absenteeism. . . . It is very bad the way men are laying off the job. They don't seem to realize that every time they save up enough money to knock off a few days, that Hitler, Mussolini and Hirohito are not taking time off."[1]

Several months later, the Southeastern management announced a "house-cleaning." A large number of employees would be dismissed because of their histories of absenteeism and incompetence. Officials admitted that the problems were serious despite an organized campaign to combat them. A number of strategies had been utilized, including the placing of a large number of signs reminding workers that "You can't spell Victory with an absent *T*," using women employees with good attendance records to christen ships, and including admonitions to do better in almost every issue of the *Sou'Easter*. Individuals with impressive records were spotlighted.

H. H. "Pop" Hall, a machinist, had not been late and had been absent only once in the past year, the *Sou'Easter*'s editors informed readers before writing, "Let's all give three cheers for Pop Hall and then try to follow his example." The November 15, 1944, issue reported that Harry J. Reynolds, a leaderman in the paint shop, had worked 765 days without an absence.[2]

This shipyard publication also ran the following letter, which supposedly came from a former employee serving with the military overseas but sounds suspiciously as if it were written in the editor's office:

Dear Friends,

Remember me? When I was working at Southeastern with you I didn't think much about taking a day off now and then, but now I know what it means to the boys on the fighting front. Since leaving you I have seen good men die for lack of help a ship could have brought. I have seen men waiting with empty guns while the enemy closed in for the kill. I have seen strong men bleed, cry, curse, and pray for a chance to fight the foe on even terms.

I hear that an average of 1,288 of you are absent without reason every week day. I'm not much on figures, but I'll bet that many workers could build a ship alone in a few months if they really tried. That extra ship could save a lot of lives, a lot of needless suffering. It might even save your life if you have to go.

There are now over 1,900 of us former Southeastern workers on or serving the fighting front. At least there were that many of us— it's already too late to help some of them. Please remember us the next time you think of taking a day off. We're going to win this war, but we can lose it you know if we don't have the ships.

Yours,

X-Fellow worker[3]

One would think that if the letter writer could get all of this up-to-date information on the shipyard at the front, the man could also get a bullet or two. Most workers must have known where this letter originated, and, while it did make a point, it did not convince many readers to change their ways.

The next message from management was a bit more ominous. A small article appeared in the May 1, 1943, *Sou'Easter* that indicated that some chronic absentees might shortly be joining X-Fellow worker at the front. Under the headline "Draft Board Seeks Absentees," J. Reid Horne, the Southeastern official in charge of draft data, was quoted as saying, "In more and more instances the boards are granting deferments at our request. This is particularly true in the case of men with good attendance records. The boards want to know how often a man of draft age is absent from his work. If he has an absentee record of a day a week the chances are that we will not be able to hold him here, even though he might be a skilled worker."[4]

Later in 1943 the *Sou'Easter* published the results of a survey conducted by management regarding the reasons workers had for being absent. Forty-seven percent cited personal illness as the leading reason they missed shifts, 15 percent said family illness, 10 percent cited visiting family, 6 percent were drunk, 4 percent said they had no transportation, 3 percent reported a death in the family, 2 percent had been arrested, 1 percent were visiting the draft board, and 1 percent were shopping. The other 9 percent must have been made up of one-off excuses that would be interesting to know.

Even though the replies to this survey were anonymous, shipyard officials were suspicious. "Now if you believe that the stork brings little babies," the reporter wrote, "you accept that figure of 62 absences due to sickness out of every hundred [adding up the first two reasons given]."[5]

In June 1943 unexcused absences among Southeastern workers averaged 1,537 each day, not counting Sundays. That meant, given the percentages listed in the survey, that 705 Southeastern employees and 225 of their family members were sick each day. The Official Secrets Act must still be prohibiting the release of information about the Great Savannah Plague of World War II.

Excused absences were not listed in the survey, but included in that category would have been days lost because of injuries received on the job. This, too, was a serious problem at Southeastern, as it was at all shipyards. The process of building ships was dangerous, with extremely heavy pieces of steel being lifted and moved about over workers' heads and workers having to climb and move around high above the ground in constricted spaces. Cutting and shaping steel produced fumes, sparks, and splinters, while the moving parts of machinery were often exposed and tools were heavy, sharp, and hot. Ask a workforce that was for the most part inexperienced to confront all of these hazards, and injuries were bound to happen. "Most people I know who worked out there were first-time shipyard workers," Walter Simmons recalled. "There were a lot of accidents. They weren't used to that kind of stuff."

Early on, the Maritime Commission established a minimum code of safety standards and sent inspectors into its shipyards to ensure that the code was being enforced. Funds were provided for special studies on safety and health measures, and for medical staff at each yard. Statistically, the results of this effort were dramatic. Injuries in all shipyards dropped from 9.2 per 100 employees in 1942 to 4.9 per 100 in 1945. The actual number of injuries, however, was still very high. In 1943 and 1944, it was estimated that seven hundred workers died as a result of injuries in shipyards. During that same period there were 173,000 nonfatal injuries. More than one-third of the fatalities were the result of head injuries, and 7 percent were the result of drowning. Thirty-seven percent of the fatalities occurred among shipwrights, riggers, and welders and helpers to those craftspeople.[6]

Maritime Commission inspectors insisted on protective equipment and proper ventilation to combat two other major sources of problems for workers— injuries to the eyes as a result of welding flash or splinters, and respiratory problems caused by the inhalation of various fumes and gases. "I loved welding really," recalled Shorty Beasley. "I loved to see the melt of the metal. I think it just got to my eyes. My eyes got flashed a few times, what they call 'welding flash.'"

Two other common medical problems that concerned shipyard workers were studied in an attempt to discover causes and reduce anxiety. "Shipyard eye"—which was in reality pink eye, or conjunctivitis, and not peculiar to shipyards—spread through yards on the Gulf and West coasts during the winter of 1942–43. The consultants' task was to convince workers that shipyard eye did not come from welding flash or welding fumes. At the same time, it was determined by the U.S. Public Health Service that "welder's cough," which caused workers to spit up blood, was in fact a mild respiratory infection or the more serious, but still-temporary, arc welders' siderosis, caused by inhaling welding fumes, but not tuberculosis, as feared by many workers. These findings were not available until after the war, making it difficult to convince workers that they were not seriously ill.[7]

Exposure to the large amounts of asbestos used at shipyards did not appear be a problem during the war, so this did not contribute to absenteeism among workers. The asbestos used for insulation and pipe coverings on Liberty ships would become an extremely serious problem for many shipyard workers decades later, however. It is ironic and tragic that even though workers described the installation of asbestos in overhead panels as being like working in a snowstorm, such work was still considered to be clean and desirable. Jeff Dukes observed that "had we known what asbestos could do to you, I don't know that we would have been there doing what we were doing. We never gave it a thought. I didn't deal with asbestos, but other people did. We were all in the same area. Sometimes the stuff would come down—granular stuff. It was kind of fibrous and would get down your sleeves and down your collar and made life miserable."

Savannahian Charlie Gross sailed on a number of Liberty ships during the war and said that "the quarters, all the steam pipes, the radiators, all those lines were insulated with asbestos. They had asbestos in the ceilings, too. The room that we slept in was lined with asbestos."

A 1945 study found almost no cases of asbestosis owing to exposure in shipyards and concluded that the installation of asbestos was not a hazardous job. Few people were then aware that there could be a twenty- to forty-year incubation period for the disease, but in 1975 the U.S. government estimated that some 4.5 million shipyard workers had been exposed to dangerous levels of asbestos in the thirty-four years since the beginning of World War II. By 1982 more than six thousand lawsuits a year were being filed against Johns Mansville and other manufacturers of asbestos materials, alleging that the companies had been aware of the dangers since the 1930s. Hundreds of claims have been filed in Savannah by former Southeastern employees, and one legal firm there has dealt exclusively with these types of cases for many years.

Health and safety were taken seriously at Southeastern. Almost every issue of the *Sou'Easter* carried an article by the yard's medical director, Dr. J. L. Robak, stories of near-miss serious accidents, admonitions to wear protective clothing, or advice to drink plenty of water and take the salt tablets provided at every water fountain. The May 15, 1945, issue told of three riggers—leaderman T. C. Goodman, H. D. Lindsey, and W. H. "Sparky" Parrish—having a narrow escape. The men were supervising the hoisting of a 2.5-ton line shaft on the wet dock. The shaft was 150 feet above them when something went wrong, and it fell, crushing the heavy dock planking. The shaft missed Goodman and Lindsey by fifteen feet, and Parrish by just three. Lest readers miss the lesson, the article concludes with this: "The moral is, do not stand under a load that is being lifted. The three lucky riggers observed this safety rule and that's why they are alive today."[8]

Cranes were involved in a large percentage of accidents at Southeastern. Crane operators and oilers were given a three-page set of rules in an attempt to reduce the danger. The three riggers who escaped being hit by the falling line shaft were attempting to observe Rule No. 3: "Keep clear of moving loads and keep others from getting under any load." Another rule involved making sure that the track or roadway was clear before moving a crane, and not just relying on warning gongs and whistle blasts to get coworkers to move out of the way. Generally, when one of the tall gantries was being moved, a pusher or signalman walked ahead to clear obstructions, especially people.

Regardless of how comprehensive a set of rules might be, when there

Photo 29. Gantries at work at Southeastern. *Photo from the* Sou'Easter, *n.d.*

are large numbers people working under pressure, there are going to be accidents. As gantry operator Robert Smith described the situation, "There were people out there like flies, and I'm surprised there weren't more accidents. We were under stress all the time, picking up steel plates, moving them around over people's heads. We were swinging them, just missing the tops of their heads a little bit. There were hundreds of people down there, and you are bringing steel plates right over their heads. They were like a bunch of flies. One slip of the foot would kill half a dozen people. Man, today, they'd move everybody out of there. Then, they just didn't pay any attention to it."

Through March 1944 there were 1,367 crane-related accidents at Southeastern. The cause of every accident was not specified, but workers standing under a suspended load accounted for 233 of those accidents, while poorly rigged load hooks or slings accounted for 235. Another twelve involved someone operating a crane without proper authority or proper hand signals, and twenty-eight were caused by overloading.[9]

Surprisingly, the most spectacular crane accident at the yard did not cause any serious injuries. Late on the night of April 10, 1943, two large gantries were working in tandem to move a large section of inner bottom. Smith had operated one of those gantries during the day. "My gantry was one of the two involved, but it happened at night," he said. "Mine was on No. 2 way, and the other was on No. 3. They made these inner bottoms out on the slab, and they had to be turned over once in a while. What they would do is hook a gantry on one side and another gantry on the other. Both would reach out and pick this thing up. Evidently, he was boomed a little too far, or he was overloaded. When the gantry on No. 3 turned loose, it must have thrown all the weight on him and it just laid him over on his side."

The phrase "laid him over on his side" does not begin to describe the danger or excitement of a gantry as tall as an eight-story building falling over. The fall laid the eighty-five-foot gantry across the slab in front of the No. 3 ways and the boom across the Liberty ship nearing completion on the No. 2 ways. Red Pitts was there and saw it fall:

> I couldn't believe my eyes. I was sitting there with another fellow, and he said, "Look there." The gantry was falling over. . . . Those gantries are high up, and that long boom crashed on top of the ship on No. 2 way. It's a wonder that it didn't kill somebody because that ship was the hot ship—the next one to be launched— and it was covered with workers. It didn't hit a single one.
>
> The girl had just got down. They had this girl who would walk at the bottom of the gantry. She would sit on a seat to go along with the crane. The operator couldn't see what was down on the ground so they had the girl ringing a bell. Well, she was walking at the time. She was hysterical. She just knew that everybody on it had been killed.

Calls for ambulances were made to three funeral homes and half a dozen vehicles were dispatched to the scene, but, miraculously, no one had been killed. P. J. Thorpe, the operator, had to be helped out of the wrecked cab, but he was only bruised and badly shaken. Describing the accident for a *Sou'Easter* article, Thorpe said, "I felt the cab totter and then start going down. I called to [my oiler Royce] Ring and remember saying, 'This is it, we're goners.' Then I stepped back out of my seat. The next thing I knew we were on the ground in a cloud of dust. I don't remember the fall itself, but I was surprised when I found out all my joints worked."[10]

Royce Ring was on the platform outside of the cab when the gantry began to fall. He remembered hearing the cab door slam shut behind him as the crane tipped. The next thing he knew, he was picking himself up off the ground. Pitts told Ring's story this way: "The oiler, they couldn't find him. He was on the outside, and when it got near the ground, he jumped clear of the thing, and it didn't fall on him. They didn't know where he was and just knew that that he was under all that mess. Come to find out he was over at first aid. He ran all the way to first aid to get checked out."

Ring was described in the *Sou'Easter* as having minor injuries, but according to Joseph Williams, at least one of Ring's injuries did not occur during the fall. "The oiler nearly killed himself running to first aid," Williams recalled. "He ran into a post out there somewhere and nearly brained himself."

Other Southeastern employees also had narrow, if less-dramatic, escapes. The report of the crane tipping in the *Savannah Morning News* states that a large number of workers had been in the vicinity of the accident but that all had been accounted for and were unharmed.[11] Two riggers who had been directing the operation were at first feared to have been caught under the tangled wreckage, but they, too, escaped without being injured. According to Bob Fennel, one worker may have escaped physical injury, but his emotional state would probably never be the same. "We had this kind of elderly fellow driving an old Ford flatbed truck," Fennel said. "He was picking up scrap steel that welders and burners threw off the ships. That boom came down across the back of the bed of that truck and flattened it down. They were looking for him, thought he was in the cab of the truck, but he wasn't anywhere around. When they finally found him, he told them that he had crossed the Savannah River and didn't even get his feet wet."

Immediately after this accident, all workers then on shift were dismissed. According to Red Pitts, "They blew the whistle and knocked everybody off. They wanted only supervisors to stay. They told the rest of us to go." The extent of the damage to equipment, material, and the ship on the No. 2 ways was never revealed, but Wallace Beasely said, "I came in at 11:00 that night and picked up the pieces. It was a mess." The ship involved, the SS *John C. Breckenridge*, was launched twelve days later on April 22, on schedule.

Gantries did not fall over every day, but there were other dangers inherent in their operation. Beasely revealed one such risk when describing a job he and another gantry operator were given that involved climbing out on the booms. According to Beasley, "Those booms were 120 feet long on top of those gantries, and our job was to lubricate them. It was risky at times We had to climb out as high as we could, hold on with one hand, and use the grease gun to reach out as far as we could. It was very dangerous, but we were very careful and never had any problems." Others may not have been as careful, as fourteen accidents occurred while workers were oiling crane parts.

In spite of the dangers, gantry operators had a perspective of the shipyard that was very different from that of other workers and had a special role to play in accident situations. "I was eighty-five feet above the ground, and I could look around and see what was going on," Beasley said. "Others wouldn't even know someone had got hurt. When they would get injured, they would call an ambulance in. I would pick them up, sling them out and lower them down to the ambulance. With that crane, I could reach out and have access to places that the ambulance couldn't get to."

Smith also spoke about bringing out a number of injured workers, saying,

We had these litter baskets. When a man on the ship would give me a signal—crossed arms was the signal for the basket—I would swing around, tell the riggers what I wanted, and they would hook it on. In July one year, I brought seven people out of the holds in one day. We had these trash tubs, almost as big as the hold on the ship. I was hauling it out of the hold, and one of the riggers was riding on it to guide and another was on top flagging me. That rigger turned around, and when he did, he kicked a piece of pipe out of the trash tub. There was a man down below bent over. That pipe went through his head like an arrow. They gave me the signal to put the tub down and asked for the basket. Usually, by the time they got them out of there, the ambulance was there. When I set him down, the ambulance took him away. That same day, I hauled out six more. I think most were from heat exhaustion.

No records of the number of fatalities at Southeastern could be located, but there were a number of fatal accidents. According to Fennel, "I don't think we had over five or six fatalities in the whole time . . . more injuries than that. It's not bad considering the number of people that worked out there and the kind of work you were doing and the rush to get it done." M. C. Nettles said, "I think there were several people killed out there. One was a shipwright. There was a pneumatic drill drilling through these timbers, and it caught him and just pulled his clothes off. All his intestines came out with them. Killed him right there."

Bob Fennel was stationed in a garage in the same building as the fire station, and he recalled some fatal accidents. "They had this ambulance right there, next door in the same building," Fennel said. "They got some calls. We lost one man. He was working on something in front of one of the ship ways, and he got electrocuted—welding machine or something. I don't remember. Anyway, we lost him." In another situation Fennel remembered that, "on the wet dock they had these gantries, and this kid was an oiler on one. He poured kerosene in a coal stove. Set him on fire, and he jumped out of the crane into the water and died."

Smith was a lot closer to that deadly incident. He explained the reason for the accident this way: "Up in the gantry we had these little coal stoves, and the oiler had to haul coal up there in a bucket. One day the oiler was going to build a fire in the stove and threw some kerosene on it. I guess there were hot coals in there, and it flared up and caught him on fire. He jumped for the water, but on the way down, he hit some of the cables the ships were tied with and it spun him around and killed him right there. We had quite a few accidents, but they weren't publicized. A lot of people didn't know about them."

Most of the injuries at the yard could be dealt with at the infirmary or one of the first aid stations, but others required the more extensive medical facilities of the local hospitals. In 1943 some 376 ambulance runs were made to Southeastern, and that number increased to 544 in 1944.[12] Many of the former workers interviewed knew of other workers, sometimes friends, who had accidents that left them with permanent disabilities. According to Williams, "I have seen hands mutilated, fingers cut off. One of my friends lost a thumb one night. They had this plate wedged up so he could bevel both sides before it was welded. Somehow, the wedge slipped out, and the plate clipped off his thumb. We called him 'Nub' after that."

Harold Miller remembered another crippling accident: "There

Photo 30. Lifting an injured worker off of a Liberty at the wet dock with a gantry basket. Photo from the Sou'Easter, n.d.

was a man hanging there, and the gantry was coming in with a big piece of material, a fifteen-ton piece. He couldn't pull himself up, and he couldn't drop. It cut all of his fingers off. He dropped then."

FBI Special Agent Ruggles, who equated pranks with sabotage, would not have been happy with a prank played by Jimmy Hodges that caused an accident.

Hodges, who seemed to be always involved in something, had a problem with some riggers. He said,

They would eat their lunches on No. 4 way, and I'd go over there and eat with them. I would bring ham sandwiches and things like that, and they would take some of my lunch. One day they got upset with me, so they got hold of me and pulled my pants down and put that launching grease all over my privates. Man, I had a heck of a time trying to get that off.

A few days later, they were all sitting down there eating, and I was climbing on the scaffolding on the side of a ship above them. I had some water and poured it down on them. One guy, a real big boy, came after me. He couldn't get along the scaffolding like I could 'cause he was a big old heavy fellow.

I ran down underneath on the ways, and he was running after me. I turned and looked back. . . . This six-inch pipe was running across there, and he hit it . . . right just above the eyes. I mean, "Bam." He went down, and I said, "Oh, my God, we killed him." We got him and took him to the aid station and told them a piece of scaffolding fell and hit him.

One has to wonder if Hodges ate many more meals with the riggers.

More seriously, Fennel described a near miss that could have killed a number of workers and closed down the yard. "We had this English freighter that came in without a tugboat or a pilot," Fennel said. "It was a foggy night, and you could hardly see the light ahead. He must have thought we were the dock or something. He headed right up into the crane ways. Come right up to it. Didn't hurt a thing, just came, stopped, and backed off when they found they were in the wrong place. It could have been a catastrophe if he had come in faster."

The Maritime Commission's health and safety consultants tried to convince workers that shipyards were no more dangerous than any defense industry facility, but they were very dangerous places to work. Accidents did happen, injuries occurred, people were killed, and workers remained concerned. Dukes explained, "You always had to be careful. Somebody would strike an arc with a weld, and you might be nearby. I always wondered how they kept from starting a fire. I used to think, 'God Almighty, if a fire breaks out here, I'm not even sure which direction was out.'[a] Looking back on it now, it was a horror show."

Accidents and injuries were responsible for some absenteeism, but rarely did they slow down the construction of ships. Liberty ships were needed, and there were schedules to be met. As Miller stated, "It was expedient to get the work done and not let anybody or anything distract you. The work had to go forward."

The appeals to patriotism, the threat of dismissal, and fear of the yawning jaws of the draft board were all used in the attempt to reduce absenteeism. None were totally successful, and workers missing shifts would be a problem that would continue to plague all shipyards, including Southeastern, until the end of the war.

---

[a]According to a report in the October 15, 1945, issue of the *Sou'Easter*, during Southeastern's three-and-a-half-year history, the fire chief at the yard estimated that there were more than seven thousand fires, but none were serious and most were put out before they caused any material damage.

Chapter Ten

Who Are All These Chaps?

With all of the problems already described, it might seem that the launching of even one ship might have been extremely difficult. However, the vast majority of workers at Southeastern did come to work, were not late, were not dishonest, and did not spend their time gambling, goofing off, or playing practical jokes. They worked hard, and they worked well. And they would by late 1945 launch all of the Liberty ships Southeastern had contracted to build, plus a number of AV-1s. Not all of the AV-1s for the Maritime Commission originally requested were completed, but that was because the war ended and not because of problems at the yard.

When the first Liberty ships were launched and began to enter service with shipping companies, the initial impression was less than positive. Already branded "dreadful looking objects" by the president and "ugly ducklings" by the media, the ships were further criticized for being slow and expensive to operate. The Liberty ships' competition, vessels built in Japan during the interwar period, was bigger, faster by nine knots, and, since it was diesel-powered and carried almost 1,300 more tons of cargo, more economical to operate. Everyone who saw a Liberty ship had an opinion, and those opinions were generally low. William G. Schofield wrote in *Eastward the Convoys* that "nobody with even the lowest morals and sensibilities could be so crude as to have a love affair with a Liberty ship. . . . They had no soul, no spirit, no sex appeal."[1]

Similarly, John Bunker, in his book *Liberty Ships*, referred to the vessels as homely and unromantic, noting that a newspaper called them "Sea Scows with Blunt Bows. They were sitting ducks—too big to hide and too slow to run away."[2] A union official declared after an inspection of the first one, that from the standpoint of the black gang, the Liberty ship was unsatisfactory, and to the Germans, they were "Kaiser's Coffins." A British merchant marine officer stated that seamen did not want to sail in ships that had been stuck together.

The Libertys' wartime record would put paid to these criticisms, but initially, their one redeeming feature was that they were relatively simple to build, operate, and repair. Of the more than 2,700 built, the vast majority were exactly alike, all clones of the first. Everything was standardized, including hulls, boilers, engines, masts, booms, and funnels. A deck fitting on one ship would fit perfectly in the exact same place on another. This meant that Libertys could be built by inexperienced workers following simple directions and then crewed equally well by old salts who came out of retirement after twenty years and first-trippers who would need to be shown things only once. The ships' booms could be operated by stevedores throughout the world, and they could be repaired in any shipyard.[3] Like a row house in downtown Savannah, if a sailor returned to one late at night and worse for wear with drink, he might not realize that he was in the wrong one until the light of day.

In spite of the fact that Libertys were mass-produced at eighteen different shipyards, and each looked exactly like every other, each had a separate identity. The first indication of the identity would occur during a ship's planning stage, with the assignment of a Maritime Commission hull number. These numbers were assigned on the basis of the contract with the shipyard. If the contract for a particular yard called for twenty-five ships, the numbers assigned might be 751 to 775. Those for ships in the next contract would then begin with 776. In the commission's initial contract with Southeastern for twelve ships, the hull numbers ran from 341 to 352. Southeastern then assigned its own hull number, as well. The *Oglethorpe*—the first ship built at the new shipyard—was therefore USMC Hull Number 341, yard number 1.

With the laying of the keel came the second and most-public indication of a ship's separate identity, its name. This was where the fun began. Before the first Liberty ship was launched, the Maritime Commission decided that ships in the class would be named after deceased individuals who were outstanding Americans, eighteenth- and nineteenth-century heroes, and leaders in American history and created a committee to search for appropriate names. At first, with just three hundred ships authorized in the building program, finding names was relatively simple. As the program grew to more than 2,700 ships, however, the process became much more difficult, and, as Felix Riesenberg Jr. wrote, "never before had so many long-forgotten men and women had their biographies written up."[4]

Some sixty name lists were created for authors, athletes, abolitionists, painters, historians, scientists, reformers, university presidents, military heroes, diplomats, politicians, Native Americans, pioneers, and, towards the end of the war, Merchant Marine heroes. Names were suggested by politicians; religious, ethnic, and patriotic groups; and by schoolchildren involved in scrap drives, war stamp sales, and farm projects. Some Libertys were named for foreigners, and a few were named for things, such as the SS *Stagedoor Canteen*, SS *Pearl Harbor*, and SS *USO*.

The Libertys built for and named by the British all had the prefix "Sam,"
which either stood for Uncle Sam or, more likely, was an abbreviation of the
ship type—superstructure aft of midships. In many cases names important to
the state or community in which the shipyard was located were assigned to that
yard. As there were two shipyards in Georgia building Libertys, Southeastern
had to share regionally important names with the J. A. Jones yard in Brunswick.
Southeastern, however, with a head start in construction of several months, was
assigned most of the more well-known Georgia names.

The challenge for Georgia's most well-known name came not from the J. A.
Jones yard, but, strangely enough, from a shipyard in Texas. For some reason
the Maritime Commission included the name of the founder of the colony of
Georgia, James Oglethorpe, in a list of thirty-nine names assigned to ships being
built in Houston by the Todd Houston Shipbuilding Corporation. In a strongly
worded letter, Savannah Mayor Thomas Gamble insisted that the Oglethorpe
name be given to the first ship launched at the new shipyard in Savannah.
According to Gamble, the assignment of this name would make the launching
of that vessel an occasion for "the stimulation of patriotic fervor and national
devotion not only in Savannah, but throughout Georgia." The mayor went
on to stress that Georgia's history furnished a great number of distinguished
individuals whose names should be given to ships launched at Southeastern,
and he offered a list of these names. Gamble closed his letter with, "But do not
let the names of some of its greatest leaders and sons go to yards in other states
where they will not have the right meaning and the vital power of stimulation
they would possess here."[5]

Savannah's mayor apparently had a much better grasp of public relations
than did the Maritime Commission. Why, indeed, would anyone in Houston,
or in all of Texas, get excited about the launching of a ship named for the
founder of the state of Georgia. Gamble also knew how things worked in
Washington. He sent copies of his letter to Georgia senators Walter F. George
and Richard Russell, and to First District Rep. Hugh Peterson. Within a few
days George wrote back, saying the vessel in Houston would not bare the
name of Oglethorpe. Three weeks later, on Maritime Day, when the first keel
for the first ship to be built in Savannah was laid, a sign was placed at the
beginning of the ways that read,

S.S. James Oglethorpe

U.S.M.C. Number 341

Southeastern Number 1

The ship would never sail with that name on her bow or stern. It was painted
on only for her launching and painted over immediately afterward. A wooden

signboard would be hung on either side of her deckhouse when she was in port, but taken down before sailing. The names of Libertys were known only to their crews, the shipping companies, convoy commanders, and, strangely enough, often to the Germans.

Many of Gamble's suggested names were accepted by the commission, including the names of the three Georgia signers of the Declaration of Independence—Lyman Hall, George Walton, and Button Gwinnett. Other Southeastern-built ships bore the names of John A. Treutlen, Georgia's first constitutional governor; Josiah Tattnall, Revolutionary War hero, governor, and U.S. senator; James Jackson, another hero of the Revolution and statesman; and Casimir Pulaski, who was killed as he led the American cavalry at the Battle of Savannah in 1779. Many other Georgia political leaders and several from other states were honored by having ships named for them.

Artists and writers were honored. The SS *Hamlin Garland* was named for the Pulitzer Prize winning author of *A Daughter of the Middle Border*. The SS *Thomas Wolf* was named for the famed North Carolina writer, and the SS *Ruben Dario* for the South American poet. The SS *Jonas Lie* was named for the Norwegian-born painter whose works hang at the U.S. Military Academy and in many galleries in America.

Savannah Libertys were also named for religious leaders. For instance, the SS *George Whitfield* was named for the founder of the Bethesda Home for Boys, the first orphanage in America, and the SS *William Black Yates* for a South Carolinian who was chaplain for the Port of Charleston for forty-six years and the founder of the first floating maritime school in America. The SS *Harry Glucksman* was named for a leading figure in the Jewish Community Center Movement, and the SS *Josiah Cohen* for one of the founders of B'nai B'rith International.

Five ships were named for women: the SS *Florence Martus* for Savannah's famed Waving Girl; the SS *Juliette Low* for the Savanniahian who founded the Girl Scouts of the USA; the SS *Martha Berry* for the educator who established the Berry Schools near Rome, Georgia; the SS *Addie Bagley Daniels* for the wife of a former secretary of the Navy, personal friend of President Roosevelt, and author of the resolution for the carving of the Confederate Memorial on Stone Mountain near Atlanta; and the fifth ship honored Moina Michael, the "Poppy Lady," who created the silk poppies that were taken up by the American Legion and sold to raise many millions of dollars for the relief and rehabilitation of disabled war veterans.

Among the scientists commemorated were Charles H. Herty, a pioneer in the development of newsprint from pulpwood, and Samuel T. Darling, who was one of the foremost malariologists in the world. Crawford W. Long, a surgeon and pioneer in the use of anesthetics, and Robert Parrott, the inventor of the rifled cannon that bore his name,[a] were also honored with ships named after them.

Surprisingly, given that the ship's names were selected by a committee of the federal government, the names of a number of Confederates were assigned to several Libertys built at Southeastern. Namesakes included Confederate Secretary of State Robert Toombs; John C. Breckenridge, who served as vice president of the United States of America under President James Buchanan and then as secretary of war for the Confederacy; Confederate Governor of Georgia Joseph E. Brown; and Francis S. Bartow, a brigadier general in the Confederate army.

Labor leaders, too, were recognized, with ships named for Jerome K. Jones, a staunch supporter of public schools, free textbooks, and compulsory education; Robert Fechner, a Savannahian who became a national labor leader and director of the Civilian Conservation Corps; and Frank P. Walsh, one of America's foremost labor attorneys.

Nine Liberty ships were named for publishers and newspapermen. Those honored included Rudolph Kauffman, managing editor of the *Washington Evening Star*; Edwin L. Godkin, the creator of the *Nation*; Clark Howell, editor and publisher of the *Atlanta Constitution*; Floyd Gibbons, the war correspondent and commentator; and William L. McLean, the publisher of the *Philadelphia Evening Bulletin*.

Ships were named for Isaac S. Hopkins, who founded the school that later became the Georgia Institute of Technology; pioneering farmers James H. Couper and Charles A. Keffer; Ben A. Ruffin, a former president of Lions Clubs International; and Milton J. Foreman, who was a founder of the American Legion. The SS *Benjamin Brown French* was the first Liberty ship built to be sponsored by the Masons.

Finally, nine Savannah-built Libertys bore the names of Merchant Marine heroes. The SS *William G. Lee* carried the name of the former inspector of hulls in Savannah. Lee was also famous because he had saved a number of lives at sea, including that of a mule. The SS *James Swan* was named for the developer of the merchant shipbuilding program at the beginning of the war, and seven ships honored merchant mariners killed in the line of duty earlier in the war. One of those men, Earl Layman, was second mate on the SS *Stephen Hopkins*, the only Liberty ship to sink a German surface raider during the war.

The *Hopkins* had actually engaged two raiders, sank the more-heavily armed *Stier*, and was herself sunk. According to the citation that accompanied the

---

[a]Ironically, Parrott was not a name revered in Savannah. The first use of his cannon was by Union troops in the Civil War, firing from Tybee Island at the mouth of the Savannah River at the Confederate-held Fort Pulaski. The greater range and destructive power of the guns quickly reduced the fort's walls to rubble and forced its surrender.

Navy Distinguished Service Medal awarded posthumously to Layman, he was in charge of the two forward 37-mm guns and put shell after shell into the German ship, maintaining fire until all of his crew was killed and the gun platform was wrecked. As the *Hopkins* sank, only one very overcrowded lifeboat managed to get away. The *Sou'Easter* later reported that "Layman unselfishly and heroically remained on board and went down with his battered ship."[6] Layman's mother was presented with the medal at the ceremony during which she christened the ship that would carry her son's name.

Four of the Savannah Libertys were turned over to the British and given the names *Samcebu, Samdart, Samhorn,* and *Samvannah.* The *Samvannah* was launched as the SS *Louis A. Godey,* but she was renamed at delivery. Similarly, the *Bartow* was launched with that name but then assigned to the Greek government in exile and renamed the *Themistocles.*

There were no Benjamin Franklins, Alexander Hamiltons, or Thomas Jeffersons among the ships built in Savannah; those names went to other shipyards. Several Southeastern ships, such as the *Thomas Wolf* and the *Juliette Low* did carry names that would have been recognized throughout the country. There were also a number of names that any Georgia schoolchild would have known, and a few that residents of other states would have been proud to see. Then there were some that were household names only in their own households. When the author asked retired Royal Navy Captain Peter Wyatt if he recognized any of the names of the Savannah-built Libertys as being those of any of the ships involved in the convoys he escorted during the war, he replied, "Who are all of these chaps: Addie Bagley Daniels, William Black Yates, and Hoke Smith? It's interesting to see what a large proportion were male names, while ships are usually referred to as females. They usually behave like them."[7]

After the war, the Libertys that were sold to U.S. and foreign shipping companies for peacetime service invariably underwent name changes, and the original names were often forgotten. Still, if one knew where to look, the ship's original identity could be discovered. The ship's original name, hull number, and builder's name appeared on brass plates mounted on the deckhouse and in the engine room. One Savannah ship underwent nine name changes during her peacetime career, but to the men and women who built her, she would always be the SS *Thomas W. Murray,* Hull No. 88, the last Liberty to be built at Southeastern.

Chapter Eleven

Fifteen Minutes of Fame

When a Liberty under construction on the ways neared completion, she was referred to as a "hot ship," and she took priority over anything else in the yard. For about week before a hot ship was launched, crews were moved from other ships, and whatever the hot ship needed, she got. The date for the launching had been set, plans for the ceremony were set, guests had been invited, the tides in the Savannah would be at the right stage, and that ship had to be ready. According to gantry operator Robert Smith, "When we had a hot ship, we were just go, go, go! Take this off! Put this on!"

Other formalities would also be dealt with at this stage. Either the builder's certificate or the master carpenter's certificate for the ship declaring its value would be delivered to the U.S. Treasury Department. The WSA would have advised the appropriate steamship company that the ship had been allocated to it for operation, and the ship's official number and call letters would be assigned and registered with the collector of customs for Savannah. Also at this time, the steamship company was advised to have the officers and various members of the crew report on the appropriate dates (see Appendix E). The Navy, too, would be advised as to a tentative delivery date so that the Armed Guard commander and his gun crew could join the ship several days before it sailed to assist with the mounting of the guns and other Navy equipment.

Launch day was perhaps the most important day in the life of a Liberty ship. Sitting on the ways with her bow draped in red, white, and blue bunting and with strings of pennants streaming from her masts, the ship was accorded a primacy and importance that she would be unlikely to experience ever again. She was truly an individual then, and on that day, everyone knew her name.

The launch had been announced in the newspapers, and government officials and the hierarchy of the shipyard gathered to celebrate the ship's entry into the maritime world. Work in the yard may not have stopped, but when the big moment arrived, everyone in a position to see the spectacle would pause to watch as she slid down the ways into the muddy waters of the Savannah River. The launching gave each Liberty ship her fifteen minutes of fame, but as the tugs moved her to a berth at the wet dock, she slipped back into the anonymity of

Photo 31. The "hot ship"—the next to be launched. *Photo by Reese Shellman*

being just one of 2,710. Her bunting and pennants were furled and stored for the next ship's launching. The officials left to attend a breakfast or luncheon in honor of the sponsor, workers returned to their tasks, and the ways that were her home for six weeks were already feeling the weight of the keel plates of another ship.

There is a sense of mysticism involved in the launching of any ship. With the smashing of a bottle of champagne on her bow, a mass of wood or steel comes to life and becomes a vessel "with a character and a life of her own."[1] The champagne of modern ceremonies replaces the blood of a brave seaman or sacrificed maiden once used to appease the gods and bring good fortune to the fragile ship and its crew who will be heading into dangerous waters. The Vikings launched their longboats on rollers interspersed with bound slaves, and the blood from the crushed bodies coated the bottom of the ships. As people became more enlightened, the religious aspect of the launching ceremony, now Christian rather than pagan, continued, but the sacrificial human blood was replaced with the breaking of a bottle of red wine on the bow of the ship for its christening. Champagne, with its effervescence and vitality, gradually replaced red wine. Traditionally, ships were christened by men. Only since the late nineteenth century has this honor been reserved for women.

Hand in hand with the mysticism of the launch ceremony comes superstition. One superstition involves the breaking of the bottle of champagne. Supposedly a ship can have a successful sailing career whether she has been properly christened or not, but it is never considered a good sign when a problem occurs during the launch. The history of sailing and shipping is full of stories of the misfortune of ships whose launchings went awry because the christening bottle did not break. The SS *Timothy Pickering*, launched in California, broke free and slid down the ways fifteen minutes before her scheduled launch without being christened. She was hit by a bomb during the invasion of Sicily and sunk.[2]

Southeastern never let a ship get away without a proper christening, but there were several near misses. Lucy Heard George, the wife of Georgia's senior U.S. senator, did not set a great precedent by swinging and missing the bow of the first ship launched at the yard, the *Oglethorpe*. She was successful on her second attempt, but this was not a good omen.

A second launch glitch occurred on November 18, 1943, when the SS *Charles Herty*, anxious to begin her career, began moving down the ways ahead of schedule. Her quick-thinking sponsor, Mrs. S. M. Waldron threw the bottle of champagne, and it smashed against the *Herty*'s moving bow. Had she not been able to perform her duty satisfactorily, Waldron would have been doubly embarrassed. She was the sister of George Rentschler, chairman of the board of Southeastern. The *Herty* survived the war after a number of dangerous voyages across the North Atlantic.

The third near miss of a proper christening at Southeastern occurred on a warm afternoon in May 1944, when Jennie Fassett Nevin stepped up to the bow of the SS *Jacob Sloat Fassett*, named for her father, and swung the beribboned bottle of champagne. It did not break. Tied by a long ribbon to a point on the deck near the bow, the bottle hung against the hull as the ship moved down the ways. Nevin, the officials on hand, and the crowd of spectators stared at the receding ship and held their breaths. All knew what it meant for a ship to be launched without being christened. Carl B. West, a shipwright, riding his second ship down the ways, grabbed the ribbon and began slamming it against the hull. Each time, the bottle struck with a bang that could be heard throughout the yard.

"When we saw that the bottle didn't break," West told the *Sou'Easter*, "we all grabbed hold of the ribbon and started pulling it. I guess I had the best grip because everybody yelled to me, 'Break it, break it.' I had hold of the ribbon about three feet from the bottle and swung it seven or eight times. It was like hitting the ship with a sledge hammer. Finally, it broke"[3] just as the *Fassett*'s stern dipped into the river.

There was a tremendous cheer from the crowd, and Nevin and the Southeastern officials breathed a very big sigh of relief. The *Fassett* had a successful and relatively uneventful wartime career.

The number thirteen was the source of much apprehension in the shipyard, as it was in the broader community, and it was avoided wherever possible. According to Harold Miller, "The number thirteen was taboo. I think it was Liverpool in 1713 they launched a ship on Friday the 13th, and everything that could be done in the configuration of thirteen was done. The crew was thirteen by thirteen—they had thirteen officers and thirteen belaying pins around each mast. She set sail on the 13th and was never heard from again. We never launched a ship on the 13th."

There was, however, a Hull No. 13, the SS *Langdon Cheves*. Possibly to help assuage superstition in the yard, the *Sou'Easter* ran an article addressing those who worked on that ship, but aimed at all workers. "On the way to work you dodged black cats, kept a wary eye for ladders and all of the taboos connected with the number 13," the article read. "Maybe being on alert for trouble had something to do with it but the fact remains that Hull 13 constitutes our best record yet—for keel laying to delivery. . . . We're in favor of more superstition."[4] Thirteen proved to be no problem for the *Cheves*. She, too, made a number of successful wartime voyages and was sent to the National Defense Reserve Fleet at the end of the war.

There was one other launching superstition that was never broken throughout Southeastern's three and a half years of operation. No woman was ever permitted to ride a ship down the ways during a launching.

Photo 32. Mrs. Nonnie Skinner preparing to christen the SS *Thomas Wolf*,
December 15, 1943. *Photo courtesy of Ms. Evelyn Finnegan*

Launching a Liberty ship was not a simple operation. Preparation started twenty-four hours ahead of the scheduled launch time, with the shipwright foreman handing out detailed instructions listing each job to be done and the time each was to be done to the workers involved. In the hour before the launching, shipyard officials, visiting dignitaries, and the workers who would have some responsibility during the ceremony itself would gather on the platform built high off the ground against the bow of the ship. The sponsor and the maid or matron of honor, both wearing corsages with red, white, and blue ribbons, would be getting a bit nervous as launch time approached.

Actually, the maid or matron of honor had a pretty cushy job. Her role was to step in if the sponsor, for some reason, did not show up. No substitute was ever needed at a launch at Southeastern, but the position provided a means for honoring more people, engendering more goodwill, and attracting more publicity. The sponsor did, however, have a lot to think about. Would she swing the bottle at the right time? Would it break? Suppose it missed? Would she remember the traditional words to be said as she swung the bottle? There were just the three words, "I christen thee," plus the name of the ship, but who knew what would happen with all of the excitement and stress? Some sponsors admitted to practicing at home.

Photo 33. Mrs. Spencer Connerat christens the SS *Joseph Habersham* as shipyard official Harry Fair looks on, October 12, 1943. *Photo courtesy of the Georgia Historical Society*

Mrs. Spencer Connerat, who christened the SS *Joseph Habersham*, said, "I was hoping it would break. It would have been embarrassing to do it again and again." Connerat's sister, Mary Crisfield, was her maid of honor and was surprised at how suddenly the ship began to move. She was proud of the job her big sister had done. "She had to snap it up, but she did it perfectly," Crisfield recalled.

H. R. Mitchell, head porter in Southeastern's Administration Building, was also on the platform, having one of the most important responsibilities at each launch ceremony. It was his job to bring the ribbons, the flowers, and the bottle of champagne. At the proper moment, Mitchell would hand over these items then step aside to take "the best seat in the house for the launching."[5]

The ceremony itself varied depending on the circumstances of the occasion. Did the launch coincide with a major event such as Maritime Day? Were national officials present? Did the sponsor have celebrity status? Was the money for the ship's construction raised by some organization such as the Masons, the American Legion, or the 4-H Clubs that wished to have a large number of its members present? Including whatever and whoever could generate the greatest amount of publicity and propaganda value with the least amount of disruption of work was the axiom followed for designing launch ceremonies.

The first two launch ceremonies were major events. Southeastern was a new industry in Savannah, and the *Oglethorpe* was the first example of the company's product. She was also at that time the largest ship ever built on the southeastern Atlantic coast below Wilmington, North Carolina. Admission to that ceremony was by invitation only, but a very large number of invitations were issued. In order to prevent congestion, police were stationed some distance from the yard to stop and turn back automobiles whose occupants did not have invitations.

The launching of Southeastern's second ship, the *Handley*, was timed to coincide with the first anniversary of the attack on Pearl Harbor and was witnessed by thousands of workers and their families. A number of distinguished guests, including members of the company's board of directors and the chief executive officers of a number of America's major corporations, were also present. There was no major address, but Robert W. Groves, president of the Savannah Ports Authority, spoke briefly, congratulating the workers on a fine job, and Henry Dunn, a member of Southeastern's board and the company's attorney, served as master of ceremonies and gave a brief biographic sketch of the man for whom the ship was named. As noted, Groves' wife served as the ship's sponsor.

As the war dragged on and more and more ships were launched at Southeastern, the ceremonies generally became more routine, with no major speeches and only those workers in the immediate vicinity pausing to watch. During the thirty-day official mourning period after the death of President Roosevelt, ships were christened and launched without music and the other accoutrements of a normal ceremony.

Sponsors and maids and matrons of honor were selected on the basis of providing the greatest benefit to the shipyard and to the government in terms of publicity, improved worker morale, and expressing gratitude for services rendered. The list includes the wives of almost all of the members of the company's board of directors and senior officials, as well as the relatives of many of the men and women for whom the ships were named. Wives of prominent Savannahians, many of whom were prominent in their own right, shared the honors with the wives of outstanding workers on the production line and women employees selected by their departments because of their excellent work and attendance records.[a]

Several women participated in more than one ceremony, but the record holder was Mrs. J. R. Wakeman, who was the wife of the assistant to the president of the shipyard. She received two silver pins as matron of honor for the *Jackson* and the SS *Joseph H. Martin* and a gold pin for christening the *Godey*.

Some sponsors were allowed to select their own maids or matrons of honor. Mrs. Henry Dunn chose her sister, Mrs. Samuel Cann, and Mrs. P. L. Goldsboro,

---

[a]The sponsors and maids and matrons of honor for each Southeastern-built Liberty ship are listed in Appendix F.

the wife of an officer of the company, favored her daughter. Some chose friends. Patience Peterson, wife of Georgia's First District congressman, asked Mrs. A. S. Reid of Washington, D.C., to accompany her on the platform, and Abby Milton, daughter of a member of Southeastern's board, had her Foxcroft School roommate stand next to her as she christened the SS *Josiah Tattnall*.

The launching of the SS *Risden Tyler Bennett* in July 1944 was unique in that both a maid and a matron of honor attended the sponsor Mrs. Mary Bennett Little of Wadesboro, North Carolina. Little was the daughter of the U.S. congressman and, later, Confederate colonel for whom the ship was named, and she was described in a newspaper article reporting the launching as "a charming Southern woman prominent in the United Daughters of the Confederacy and the American War Mothers."

Charming and formidable Little did not travel light. Thirteen relatives from North Carolina and South Carolina made the trip with her to Savannah, where they were joined by Savannah-based relatives Mrs. W. A. Winburn, Mrs. Antonio Waring, Mrs. W. A. McCoy, and Randall Winburn. Little's niece served as the matron of honor, and her granddaughter served as maid of honor. During the ceremony Little presented the ship's master, Capt. Ernest Mountain, with a bible, a prayer book, a box of other books, and a portrait of her father in his Confederate uniform saying, "When you get in a tight spot, you can ask the Colonel what to do."[6]

Flowers were always presented to sponsors and maids or matrons of honor on the launch platform. Afterward, each woman was given a gift as a keepsake to commemorate the occasion. This tradition of gift-giving and the financing of postlaunch parties would be the source of much grief for the Maritime Commission during the war. When a private shipyard built a ship for a private owner, the launch celebrations and the value of the gifts was a private matter. The Maritime Commission, however, was a federal agency spending public money, and any funds used for such celebrations or gifts were going to attract scrutiny.

When the first ship was launched at the Kaiser yard in Portland, Oregon, the company wanted to serve Coca-Cola and other refreshments to workers at an open house. The yard wired the commission, asking for assurances that the costs involved would be reimbursed as part of the cost of the ship. Kaiser made the comment that "this is a goodwill program and will stimulate labor-employer relations and not a private party for a few select friends of the builder."[7] Many parties at shipyards, however, were for the select, and the gifts to sponsors reflected this. After the war, the Special Committee to Investigate the National Defense Program, which had been taken over by New York Senator James M. Mead, found that five women, all wives of government officials, received substantial gifts.

Early on, the Maritime Commission established a policy against reimbursing for gifts and set a limit of $500 for reimbursing expenses for any launch ceremonies other than a company's first one. Even this meager reimbursement was discontinued after Pearl Harbor, but photographs in newspapers of lavish parties and expensive gifts continued to cause serious public relations problems for the commission even though it was not paying a penny of the costs. A father whose son was earning $61 a month fighting in the Pacific wrote the commission noting that he had read about gifts of $2,000 bracelets to government officials and stating that "if this is true, I have purchased my last war bond."[8]

Photo 34. The 10-karat gold sponsor's pin presented to Mrs. Spencer Connerat at the launching of the *Habersham*, October 12, 1943. *Photo by the author*

Most shipyards, particularly the new emergency yards, gave much more modest gifts, rarely spending more than $25. At Southeastern, each sponsor was given a 10-karat gold pin in the shape of the Maritime Commission's Victory Eagle symbol with the ship's name engraved on the front and the sponsor's name on the reverse. Maids and matrons of honor received a similar pin in sterling silver. Sponsors were also presented with a framed set of six photographs of the launching, including one of the moment the bottle of champagne crashed against the bow of the ship; a newspaper clipping reporting the launch; a subscription to the *Sou'Easter*; and the broken bottle that had been hauled up on the deck of the ship and packed in an attractive wooden box. The company that bottled the champagne would completely wrap it in a number of layers of red, white, and blue ribbon, so that when it was smashed the pieces would stay together. All of the gifts were given at Southeastern's expense, not the Maritime Commission's and not the public's.

When it was time to launch, the sponsor, bottle of champagne in hand, was ready. The ship, too, was ready. All of the blocks, wedges, and cables that had held her captive on the ways had been removed. The ways had been cleared of all workers except for a dozen or so shipwrights and burners who waited quietly under the sponsor's platform for orders from the shipwright foreman. Two one-inch-thick steel sole plates, one on each side of the bow, were now all that held the device that would allow the ship to slide down the heavily greased ways. Laying flat and bolted in place at each end, each plate had a series of eight holes drilled across its middle. Burners, given the honor because of superior work and good attendance, stood ready with a torch to cut through each plate, burning from hole to hole. A backup stood ready with a lit torch to replace a burner or torch if a problem arose. Throughout the shipyard, construction on other ships continued during a launch ceremony. Gantries kept moving, welding torches kept popping, and all of the riveting, drilling, and hammering associated with shipbuilding providing a raucous background to the ceremony. Under the bow of the soon-to-be launched ship, however, there was silence. It was critical that the shipwright foreman be heard by the two burners and by the officials on the platform above. As the last wedge was knocked out and the last workers scrambled out from under the hull, the shipwright foreman, H. C. Smith Jr., who oversaw most launches, would holler out his first order: "Get ready! Burn out! Burn in!" This was followed after about five seconds with the order to burn the first hole.

As burner M. C. Nettles recalled, the process went like this: The foreman would order, "'Alright, burn one,' and you'd burn the first hole, both of you burning at the same time. He'd say, 'Burn two,' and you'd start from the other side and burn to the hole. Finally, when you got to the center, that metal would just stretch and pop. That's inch thick metal! You had a feeling of pride if you were selected to do that." Nettles must have been doubly proud, as he was selected as one of the sole plate burners for the launch of the *Oglethorpe*.

Timing was critical. The foreman had to watch the burners carefully, making sure that they were burning together. He might have to slow one down or speed the other up. Bob Fennel watched a number of launchings and was always fascinated by the skill of the burners. "That was something to watch, both of them pop at the same time," he said. "They had to be on the money." Joseph Williams loved to hear the noise as that last bit of sole plate stretched and broke, saying, "It just went 'Pow!' and a big noise. And down she went."

The timing on the sponsor's platform had to be perfect, too. Liberty ships seemed to have a mind of their own as to when they would begin their decent to the river. Some sat motionless, as if taking a few seconds to understand that they were no longer being held, like an animal might after a cage door is opened allowing access to freedom. One refused to budge at all. The launching of the *McLean* was delayed for two days because of weather and tide problems, but when conditions improved enough for the launch, the ship just sat in place. It was cold, and the grease applied to the ways had frozen. Even after all of the wedges had been removed and the sole plates cut through, the ship refused to slide down into the Savannah River.

Burners went to work to soften the grease, and other workmen mounted hydraulic jacks in an effort to break the grip of the congealed mass. Time dragged on, the tide began to turn, and another ten minutes would have meant further postponement when a worker shouted to ship's sponsor Mrs. Harold, "Better hit her!" Palmer swung with both hands, and as the bands played and workmen and launching party stood with bared heads in the winter air, the ship took to the water.[9]

Unlike the *McLean*, some ships just could not wait, backing down the ways immediately and forcing their sponsors to swing the bottle of champagne quickly before they got out of range. A standing joke around the yard went, "What's the fastest speed a Liberty ship [rated at eleven knots] ever travels? Sixteen knots, as she goes down the ways at her launching." That speed and the thousands of tons of steel sliding over the wooden ways created a loud groan that could be heard above the normal din of the yard.

Speed down the ways was also the cause of a good bit of anxiety among Southeastern officials leading up to the launch of the *Oglethorpe*. While some had had experience launching ships, no one had ever launched a ship this size in the Savannah River. They were not sure how fast the ship would travel down the ways or how far out into the river it would go. The stretch of the Savannah River on which Southeastern was situated was wide, but was it wide enough? Engineers were afraid that the *Oglethorpe* would run aground across the river on Fig Island. To guard against this, Fennel recalled, "they had some square concrete blocks. Must have been eight to ten feet cubed. And they hung them on the side of the [*Oglethorpe*] so they could turn them loose. If anything happened, they were going to drop those concrete blocks off the ship to drag it to a stop. They weren't needed, so they were never used again. It was just the first ship they were uneasy with."

What engineers did use as a potential safety break for subsequent launches was a sixteen-ton anchor called a "Sea Hag." Brought to the ways on a railroad flatcar, the Sea Hag would be picked up by a crane and carried to the river. Robert Smith, who had this duty more than once, remembered,

> I'd set it out as far as I could reach, and then the diver would go out and tie on to it. It would then be tied on to the ship. When the ship was launched, that sea anchor would take hold. When it ran to the end of its cable, that is what turned the ship upriver. Then the tugs went in, grabbed [the ship], and took it to the wet dock. The diver would then go down and unhook [the anchor], and I had to reach out as far as I could to hook on to the cable. When you lay a boom out like that, you don't have much lifting power. It was a strain to get that thing in.

A crew of workers always rode each ship down the ways. Some riders had

Photo 35. Southeastern President William H. Smith explaining launching procedures to young men from the Bethesda Home for Boys, August 6, 1943. *Photo courtesy of the Georgia Historical Society*

specific responsibilities during the launch, others were just there to enjoy the experience. "I rode down on one," said Jimmy Hodges. "I was up in the crow's nest as it went down. I got there early and got up there and watched the whole thing. It was really exciting."

On another occasion, riding a ship down the ways might have been too exciting. As shipfitter C. E. Lance said, "I was on a ship that was launched and the cables began to break. We thought it was going to turn over before it got to the water. I was on the top deck and saw it happening."

Employees at Southeastern never tired of seeing ships being launched. It was their moment of glory, too, the result of all of their repetitive, sometimes boring, and often difficult efforts. A small number of the workers, because their jobs required them to be working in a building or in a remote part of the yard, never saw a launching. Those who did, however, have never forgotten the spectacle. "It was a beautiful sight" recalled Nan Hiott. Her sister and fellow welder, Bertha Brown, said that watching a Liberty slide down the ways gave her "a great feeling." Jeff Dukes remembered that, too, saying, "There were visitors there—ladies with nice hats and fancy dresses and dignitaries up there. It was always a thrill to see it actually move down." For Ruby Clifton, launches were "very exciting. Everybody was whistling, yelling, and doing their thing."

Some launchings were special because of who the ship was named for and who was in attendance. Boys from the Bethesda Home for Boys were special guests at two launchings. Thirty residents of America's first orphanage watched the launching of the SS *George Whitfield* in August 1943. Two months later, they were invited back to witness the debut of the SS *Joseph Habersham*. Whitfield and Habersham's fathers were the founders of the orphanage. The boys were taken down to the ways after the launchings by Southeastern President William Smith and then treated to lunch in the shipyard's cafeteria.

President Roosevelt took special interest in the launching of the *Addie Bagley Daniels*. Roosevelt had served as an assistant secretary of the Navy under Mrs. Daniels' husband, Josephus Daniels, and when the ship was launched in September 1944, sent the following message to his old boss, who was present for the ceremony: "Eleanor and I are delighted that a vessel will be launched today bearing Mrs. Daniels' name. Realizing as we do, how pleased she would be to have her lifelong interest in the sea commemorated by one of the vessels that will continue in the best maritime tradition, it seems fitting to us that her honored name has been selected for a ship. I am confident that the S.S. *Addie Bagley Daniels* will have a distinguished service. I, for one, will follow her career with even more than my usual interest in our ships."[10]

On her own behalf, Eleanor Roosevelt sent a spray of yellow chrysanthemums to Elizabeth Bagley Daniels, the granddaughter of Mrs. Daniels, who served as a sponsor for the ship.

One launch carried particular significance for the people of Savannah. Southeastern's Hull No. 51 was named for Juliette Gordon Low, the Savannahian who founded the Girl Scouts of the USA. Hundreds of Savannah Girl Scouts were present in the large crowd that witnessed the launching on May 12, 1944. During the ceremony, Capt. W. F. O'Toole, newly appointed master of the *Low*, was presented with a flag by Low's cousin Irby Lasseter and a member of Troop 6. As she handed the flag to Captain O'Toole, Lasseter said, "May this flag wave unharmed and symbolize hope for a happier future for the ports of the Seven Seas." Lasseter's gift and good wishes may have helped the *Low* survive the war, but not without a few bad moments.

On one occasion the ship suffered buckled plates following a collision with another Liberty in the English Channel. The *Low* also escaped with no damage when a V-1 "Buzz Bomb" exploded off her starboard bow in the Scheldt River near Antwerp, Belgium. Peacetime was even more difficult for the ship. She suffered severe damage from high winds and seventy-five-foot seas while crossing the Atlantic in 1946, and she was involved in another collision later that year, sustaining more damage to her bow.

The end of the *Low*'s launching ceremony was not the end of her association with Savannah's Girl Scouts. The scouts continued to monitor her career as best they could in the face of wartime secrecy, and when Captain O'Toole visited

Savannah in November 1944 while the ship was loading in New York, the girls presented him with a copy of *The Life of Juliette Gordon Low*. When they realized that the ship would probably be at sea for Christmas 1944, the scouts collected papers, ribbons, shaving cream, stationary, and toothpaste to be placed in the crew's Christmas box. Christmas decorations were also included to help brighten what might be a dreary day at sea. More than 250 books were collected, including such titles as *The Life of Wellington* and *The Mystery of the Headless Debutant*, and given to the crew. O'Toole would later write to say that the ship actually spent Christmas in port, in Le Harve, France, and to

> extend a million thanks from each man aboard this ship to the Girl Scouts for the nice Christmas presents and decorations they gave us before we left; we were the only ship in port that had any decorations . . . and for the beautiful lot of books Miss Rusk gave us. I left 210 of them [including, one would suspect, the copy of *The Mystery of the Headless Debutante*] with the United Seaman's Service which had just opened up a place in Le Harve. While we were there they were caring for the crews of seven ill-fated American ships, and the books seemed to be very much in need.[11]

Many of the ships built at Southeastern were paid for through war bond drives organized by a variety of organizations. Funds for the SS *Jerome K. Jones* and the SS *Robert Fechner* were provided from bonds purchased by members of the Georgia Federation of Labor. 4-H clubs in Georgia, Tennessee, and South Carolina were each allowed to name a ship. The Masonic Lodge of Washington, D.C., raised $4.5 million through the sale of bonds to sponsor the *Benjamin Brown French*, and the Lions Clubs of Virginia were responsible for the sale of $10 million in bonds, five times more than was necessary to name a ship. The SS *Ben A. Ruffin* was their choice.

The reluctant *McLean* was the result of another successful campaign. Leslie Palmer, a fourteen-year-old newspaper carrier for the *Evening Times* of Sayre, Pennsylvania, sold more than 46,000 stamps to win the right to select the sponsor for the ship. He chose his mother, who christened the vessel that was named for the late publisher of the *Philadelphia Evening Bulletin*. During his remarks at the ceremony, the paper's business manager told Palmer, "You are the kind of boy for whose future this war is being fought . . . you are typical of our American youth."[12]

Palmer, in words that a Maritime Commission speechwriter would have been proud to claim, replied,

> When my schoolmates learned that I was to come to Savannah to see my

mother christen a Liberty ship, they gave me three cheers. I know that those cheers were meant for all the newspaperboys who are selling war stamps as part of their war job.

Boys my age can't wear the uniform of a sailor, a marine, or a doughboy, but we can do a lot of things which help a little bit to win the war. Someone asked me what my sales methods were in winning this honor. I said I had no sales method. The patriotism of my customers did the job of getting me to Savannah

When you carry a route on which every home displays a flag with one or more silver stars, it is easy to sell war stamps to people in these homes. War stamps mean more ships, more guns, more planes for their sons and other relatives.

This ship represents people who stayed on the job. I know I speak for all newspaperboys when I say that we, too, will stay on the job until the William L. McLean sails into Tokyo to bring supplies to the conquering troops.[13]

This ceremony and Palmer's speech were broadcast live over WTOC Radio in Savannah and recorded for broadcast the next evening in Philadelphia.

Every launching was covered by Savannah's two daily papers, providing reporters with magnificent opportunities to exercise their descriptive skills. When the SS *Button Gwinnett* was launched, "the vessel moved smoothly into the water flags waving in the stiff breeze while the round side of the ship reflected the rays of the bright early morning sun."[14]

The launch of the SS *Dudley M. Hughes* produced "the brilliance of the vari-colored lights and the streams of sparks from the worker's machines contrasted to the semi-darkness through which cranes, vehicles and numerous workmen moved about to form a backdrop for the viewing of the various procedures through which steel sheets are transformed into beautifully rounded 10,500 ton Liberty ships."[15] One has to be in shape to say that without taking a breath.

Sarah W. Wilkenson, writing in the November 26, 1943, issue of the *Savannah Morning News*, described the launching of the SS *John E. Ward* this way: "Floodlights, towering cranes, martial music and the odd blue flare of acetylene torches lent a carnival atmosphere to the huge ship-producing plant for the first night launching to be held there."[16]

The *Samhorn* was launched just before sunrise and afforded the night shift its first opportunity to witness such an event. While there is no byline on this story, it may well have been Wilkenson's as well: "Blue flames from acetylene torches stood out against the blackness of the sky to form an unusual background and the whistles and horns from machinery in the yard that accompanied the *Samhorn*'s motion toward the river were exceptionally enthusiastic."[17]

The efforts of these reporters may not have produced awards, but they do provide people today, many years later, with a glimpse of what it was like to observe the birth of a ship that was not a sleek destroyer or a powerful battleship, but a slow-moving cargo ship that would carry thousands of different items to friends, relatives, and allies fighting on the other side of the world. Perhaps the powers in Washington saw Liberty ships as utilitarian rather than beautiful or sexy, but to the workers who built them and the people in the communities where they were built, they had souls, they had spirit, they were loved, and each launch was special.

After each launch at Southeastern, workers who had been able to watch went back to work. Gantries began lifting the keel plates for a new ship onto the recently vacated ways, and the hull nearest completion became the next hot ship. Members of the shipyard band went back to their real jobs as welders, shipwrights, and carpenters, and the officials, dignitaries, and "ladies in nice hats and fancy dresses" moved on to an afterlaunch breakfast, lunch, or dinner.[18] If it had been a particularly significant launch, the postlaunch meal might be served in the Gold Room of the Hotel Desoto or perhaps in the Charlton Room or the Civic Room of the Hotel Savannah. On one occasion, after the luncheon, the guests were taken out to the home of Judge Arthur W. Solomon to view his azalea and camellia gardens.

As for the recently launched Liberty, her fifteen minutes of fame were over. Berthed at the wet dock with up to three other Libertys and with her name painted over, she anonymously began the next stage in her preparation for carrying vital cargoes through dangerous waters.

Chapter Twelve

Getting Ready for War

By the time Atlantic Towing Company tugs eased a newly launched Liberty ship into a berth at Southeastern's wet dock, the excitement of the launch ceremony was all but forgotten. The first brief voyage was just a couple hundred yards, as the wet dock was located just north of the No. 1 ways. The cheering of the crowd and the music of the shipyard's band were replaced by the noise of construction as workers and engineers clambered aboard to complete the work begun on the ways. When launched, Libertys were only 80 percent complete, and some two hundred tasks still had to be done at the wet dock before they could be delivered to their shipping agents to begin their wartime careers.

The wet, or fitting-out, dock at Southeastern was eighteen hundred feet long and wide enough to accommodate the double tracks of the huge gantry cranes and the rail tracks for the flatcars from which her equipment and supplies would be loaded. Four of the 441-foot-long ships could be berthed bow to stern while having their guns mounted and lifeboats, rafts, and deck machinery installed. The ship's cabins and galley would be finished, and the more than 50,000 separate items requisitioned for her deck, engine, and steward departments would be sent aboard from Southeastern's Warehouse No. 2. Everything a ship and its crew would need, from furniture, medicines, and cooking utensils to navigation instruments, spare parts, and linens came on board at the wet dock.

The linen list alone was enormous. When a Liberty ship sailed, there would be enough laundry on board for six months—2,160 bed sheets, 2,160 bath towels, 2,780 face towels, 1,380 pillow cases, and 118 blankets. Since no washing was done during a voyage, dirty linen would be stored until the ship was in an American port again.[1]

While all of this finishing and furnishing was being completed, the ship's engines were being readied for their first tests. While the engines were being run ahead and astern at different revolutions, pumps, motors, circuits, hydraulics, and plumbing would all be tested, and if everything checked out, the more rigorous official dock trial would be scheduled. During these trials the engines were run ahead at 68.8 revolutions per minute (RPM) for six hours and astern at 60.8 RPM for one hour. Data would be collected and recorded every half

Photo 36. The SS *Crawford Long* being moved to the wet dock after her launch.
Photo by Reese Shellman

hour and compared with that of operating Libertys. Also, all of the auxiliary machinery would again be tested, and its performance would be compared with existing standards.

Successful completion of the dock trials meant that the ship was ready for the next milestone in her career, her sea trials. "I remember the excitement the night before a trial run," said Walter Simmons. "We would work all night preparing food to go on that ship . . . cooking, preparing, and delivering stuff down to the ship. The cooks prepared dinners, not sandwiches, for these trial runs. A lot of people got to go on those ships. I guess they were dignitaries. As a fifteen-year-old boy, they all looked like dignitaries to me. Before a trial run I could see and feel the excitement when I drove that truck full of food to the waterfront."

Capt. Sam Prosser served as Southeastern's sea trial master for more than three years. At sixty-two, he had served as a lieutenant commander in the Navy during World War I, and he been at sea for a total of fifty years, holding a master's license since the age of twenty-seven. His was the honor to be in command the first time each Southeastern Liberty ship left the dock under its own steam.[a]

---

[a]Toward the end of the war, when Captain Prosser was asked about his plans for the future for a *Sou'Easter* article of January 7, 1946, he replied, "To buy a boat and retire on it."

Also on board for each sea trial were Maritime Commission inspectors, shipyard officials and their special guests, technicians, workers who were still finishing up various jobs, and the operating crew.[b] The Merchant Marine officers who would be operating the ship after she had been delivered would also normally be on board. When the SS *Clark Howell* first sailed down the Savannah River, her new captain, first mate, second mate, chief engineer, first assistant engineer, radio operator, and deck cadet sailed with her. So, too, did Minnie Overstreet, a nurse at the yard. While women were not welcome on board during launches, a nurse was required on sea trials.

During the ten-plus-hour trip down the Savannah River and out into the Atlantic Ocean, ten separate tests would be conducted to determine if the ship would meet the standards required by the Maritime Commission to be accepted for service. The ship would be accompanied by a tug that stood by in case of any problems, and it would be protected by a U.S. Coast Guard cutter, a blimp from the Glynco Naval Air Station in Brunswick, Georgia, and Army Air Force planes. When the first sea trials began at Southeastern, the period German U-boat captains referred to as the "Second Happy Time" because they were able to sink ships off America's East Coast almost at will had ended. That there was still a risk of attack, however, was evidenced by the flotsam and jetsam that regularly littered Georgia's beaches throughout the war.

No Southeastern Liberty ever had to face a U-boat on a trial run, but the crew and passengers on the *Gwinnett* were not really sure how close they may have come. Clifford Thomas, who had been assigned to the ship as second mate, recalled that as the *Gwinnett* was moving out into the Atlantic, it was passed by a Coast Guard cutter. A Coast Guardsman using a hailer yelled across to the *Gwinnett* that a submarine had surfaced at Buoy 6HI, off Hilton Head, South Carolina. According to Thomas, as the cutter passed, it was going in the opposite direction, into port. "I don't blame him," Thomas said. "He was just a converted private yacht. He'd have been blasted out of the water."

The *Gwinnett* had been heading north, toward the buoy, but changed course to the east. A short time later, the ship's lookouts sighted a small convoy with two escorts. Thomas, who was handling the signaling, explained the situation to the convoy and asked permission for the *Gwinnett* to join the convoy. A signal came back asking, "What is the code word for the day?"

---

[b]One member of the operating crew, J. P. Willis, sailed on all of the fifty sea trials conducted as of May 1944. The *Sou'Easter* reported on June 1, 1944, that Smith had spent six weeks on the ships and sailed fifteen hundred miles, but he had never really been to sea.

"Hell," Thomas remembered replying, "we don't have any code words. We just want to join the convoy." The *Gwinnett* was allowed to do so, and the ship returned safely to Savannah.[c]

Tests conducted during the sea trial included operating the anchor windlass to let out and take in at full speed the 8,400-pound anchor, checking the emergency steering gear located above the Armed Guard quarters on the ship's stern, and calibrating the ship's compass and radio direction finder. The ship would be run over a measured nautical mile as the wheel was swung hard to starboard and hard to port to see how quickly the rudder answered, and a crash stop was executed by reversing the engines from full ahead to full astern. Finally, there would be a six-hour run at full ahead during which technicians would take a wide variety of readings to determine the actual horsepower of each cylinder, the throttle pressure, temperature, vacuum, and fuel consumption. As the ship was being put through her paces, hull inspectors moved throughout the vessel, checking every installation, seam, and gasket. Anything not up to standard was noted and had to be corrected before the ship could be delivered.

As a ship sailed back up the river and passed the yard, workers, especially those who had helped build her, would pause and look to see if she was flying a broom at her masthead. The broom indicated a clean sweep, the passing of all sea trials. Of the fifty ships that had completed sea trials as of May 1, 1944, not one failed to hoist the broom.

When her sea trials ended and a ship returned to her berth at the wet dock, the dinner prepared by the cafeteria staff was served to those on board. This particular aspect of the sea trials concerned gantry operator Wallace Beasley. "The kitchens were loaded down with hams, turkeys, the finest food money could buy," he said. "When they completed the trip, the leftovers were just dumped overboard . . . and that was when there was rationing. I saw them do it!"

A clean sweep of sea trials did not mean that a ship was delivered free of problems. It was extremely difficult to inspect everything on a 441-foot ship during the ten-hour sea trial, and, inevitably, some problems would not show up until machinery and equipment had been run for much longer. In his first voyage report for the Southeastern-built *James Jackson*, Navy Armed Guard Commander Ens. Ray A. Dyke Jr. wrote that the ship was not in any condition to go to sea. Their first night out of Savannah, the *Jackson* could not be completely blacked out owing to defective equipment and poor construction. Blackout screens did not fit the ports, deadlights were not lightproof, and not all of the watertight doors fitted properly.[2]

---

[c]Just three months later, in the same area, the Liberty ship SS *Albert Gallatin* was struck by three torpedoes fired by *U-107*. According to Navy Armed Guardsman Frank Capobianco, who was serving on the ship during the attack, none of the torpedoes exploded, and the *Gallatin* continued her voyage with three dents in her hull.

Kenneth Strickland, who sailed on a number of Libertys, including Southeastern's SS *John A. Treutlen*, considered the ships to be good bulk cargo carriers
with very reliable engines. He also thought that they were thrown together.
According to Strickland, "There were too many things like boards left in pipes.
Somebody would tack weld a sewer pipe, put a board in it to hold it, and never
take the board out. Somebody comes along, welds a pipe to it, and then it's
gone. You get to sea, and there is no way to get that out. You'd have no cutting
torches aboard. It's very difficult to compensate for that."

At the beginning of operations at Southeastern, Libertys would spend nearly
three months at the wet dock. Later, when the yard was operating three shifts,
that time was cut to about twelve days. When a ship was completed, it would
be "delivered" to its owner. The Maritime Commission immediately transferred
title to its operating division, the WSA, and the WSA then assigned the ship to a
steamship company. Thirty-three different companies would operate ships built
at Southeastern, with the Savannah-based South Atlantic Steamship Company
assigned the greatest number, twenty (see Appendix G).

Once a steamship company had been given a tentative delivery date, it could
assign the ship's crew. The captain and the chief engineer were asked to report
at least two weeks before delivery, but most came for the launching and stayed
in order to make suggestions to the builder and become familiar with the ship.
The other officers and mates would join when necessary, and the ship's purser—
who was a combination office manager, clerk-typist, medic, and keeper of the
slop chest—would report ten days prior to delivery. Generally, the rest of the
crew would report three or four days before.

Because of the continuous work, the crew could not live on board while
he ship was at the wet dock. Generally, this was not a problem because
South Atlantic hired crews through the Seafarers International Union Hall
in Savannah, so most of the men were from the area and could stay at
home.[d] Men coming from other areas or crews working for other steamship
companies had to find lodging near the shipyard. These men received a per
diem of $4 to cover meals and lodging.

U.S. Navy Armed Guardsmen, the men assigned to the ship to man its
weapons, were also ordered to report to the ship several days before delivery
to assist with the mounting of the guns and the storage of ammunition. For
most of the Navy men recruited from around the country and for many of the
merchant crewmen, this would be their first trip to Savannah.

Newly appointed ship's master Capt. Norman Howe Jr. was a case in point.
The summer of 1943 was a busy one for Howe. In May he passed his examination

---

[d]The system of agents drawing most of their crews at a particular port meant that if a ship was lost,
that community would suffer heavily. Savannah was to become one such community.

for an unlimited master's license. On June 5, he was married, and a week later he sailed as first mate on a freighter to Europe. On his return, Howe's shipping company, the American Export Lines, appointed him as master of the soon-to-be-launched *Jerome K. Jones*.

Howe traveled to Savannah to join his new ship, but there was a problem. The *Jones* had been named for an outstanding leader of the Georgia Federation of Labor, a branch of the AFL. The WSA, with many other things to think about, had assigned the ship to the American Export Lines, which had ties to a rival union. With scores of top AFL officials invited to the launching, this would have become a major embarrassment, so the *Jones* was reassigned to the South Atlantic Steamship Company and the American Export Lines was given the next ship to be launched, the SS *Hoke Smith*. Howe's wife, Barbara, had also made the journey to Savannah. "We actually saw the *Hoke Smith* go down the ways," she said, "but did not know it was to be his ship."

The *Smith* was launched on September 16, ten days after the *Jones*, and it was not until later that day that Captain Howe was informed of his new assignment. His wife remembered, "At the time my husband took command of the *Hoke Smith*, he was the youngest master mariner in the United States. He had just turned twenty-six in September of 1943."[e] He would celebrate that birthday on the day his ship was officially delivered to his employer, September 27, 1943. In a letter to his parents, dated the day before, he wrote, "Had the trial trip today. Everything was OK and it was a peach of a day. She will be turned over tomorrow. Some birthday present to accept a two million dollar ship in the name of the American Export Line. I have to sign my name just as I used to sign it for, say an automobile part out at Jack Rose's in Pittsfield. Some business."[3]

The *Smith* spent just twelve days at the wet dock, but those were busy days for the captain. In the same letter to his parents, Howe wrote that the ship's first mate and third mate had been assigned and that the second mate and the engineers would arrive on the 27th. "The Mate will be OK, I think. He must be about 45 and has been at sea for quite awhile and holds a master's license. He is a Dane, I believe."[4]

Those twelve days were also a busy time for Lt. (jg) Howard A. Bloom and his twenty-eight-man crew of U.S. Navy Armed Guardsmen. During the week prior to the ship's delivery, these men brought on board and stored all of the Navy gear that would be needed for the ship's dangerous cross-ocean voyage. On the day of delivery, they supervised and assisted in mounting the ship's guns, which consisted of a 3-inch, .50-caliber Mark XXII antiaircraft gun on the bow, a 3-inch, .50-caliber Mark XXII Model II on the stern, and eight

---

[e]Capt. E. W. "Dick" Braithwaite, the first master of the Southeastern-built SS *John E. Ward*, was actually younger. He received his master's license in December 1941, and he was just twenty-five when the war ended.

Photo 37. Boiling crabs on Whitemarsh Island, Savannah, before the launching of the *Smith*. Pictured, from the left, are Adele Fleetwood, Barbara Howe, Norman Howe, Purser William Fleetwood, and a Mr. Glass. *Photo courtesy of Barbara Howe*

20-mm antiaircraft weapons mounted in tubs on the bow, the stern, and the ship's superstructure. Bloom and his gunners also stored more than five-hundred rounds of ammunition for the big guns, and almost 41,000 rounds of 20-mm ammo in the ship's three magazines.

Howe and his wife did have some time to enjoy Savannah. They had become good friends with the ship's newly assigned purser, Savannahian William Fleetwood, and Fleetwood's wife, Adele. "The Fleetwoods took us out to some friends of theirs yesterday to a cottage," Howe wrote to his parents. "Went crabbing and afterwards cooked and ate them. Must have caught about thirty. They were very good, but [we] ate them out doors. Do not know who had the best meal, us eating crabs, or the mosquitoes eating us, especially, Barb. She had twenty bites on one leg and fifteen

Photo 38. Capt. Norman Howe Jr. aboard his ship, the SS *Hoke Smith*. *Photo courtesy of Barbara Howe*

Photo 39. A lifeboat drill aboard the *Smith* under direction of Chief Officer Norden. *Photo by Norman Howe, courtesy of Barbara Howe*

on the other and that's no lie."[5] Most Savannahians would think that Barbara Howe had gotten off lightly. In a letter to the author, she wrote, "I must say that Adele and Bill Fleetwood played a big part in our very enjoyable time in Savannah."[6]

After being formally handed over to the shipping company, the *Smith* left Southeastern, moved up the Savannah River, past the rows of office buildings overlooking River Street, past city hall, and past the vocational school where scores of potential shipyard workers were learning trades. The ship would spend ten days at a loading berth taking on general cargo, and then, at 3:30 PM on October 7, Howe gave the order to let go lines. With a full merchant crew and the twenty-nine-member Armed Guard contingent on board, the *Smith* began her maiden voyage to New York and then across the North Atlantic to Hull, England. Barbara Howe and Adele Fleetwood watched from the roof of the thirteen-story Realty Building as the ship sailed past the city and down the river.

The Armed Guard crews assigned to the ships being built in Savannah, like the merchant seamen, could not stay on board their ships prior to sailing. Galleys were not operating, and the round-the-clock noise of construction and loading would have prevented any sleep. Some Navy men were billeted at the Naval Receiving Barracks in Savannah. Seaman First Class Dean Cain, who served on the SS *Rudolph Kauffman*, recalled that "not much happened at the base. We ate there, slept there, and went to some movies. They took us by bus to the ship. We put in supplies and got the guns mounted. They had women working on the ship. Things went fine, and the ship looked real good." Considering that he remembered that nothing much happened at the base and that women were on the ship, one might infer that Cain looked forward to the bus ride every morning.

Photo 40. Liberty at the docks on Hutchinson Island across the river from downtown Savannah. *Photo by G. C. Hopkins, courtesy of the Turecamo Towing Company*

John B. Taylor, a gunner assigned to the *Handley* was put up in a hotel, but SI/C Thomas Mischler and the rest of his crew were not so lucky. They had to stay at the YMCA. While merchant crewman had to use their $4 a day to stay wherever they could, their officers fared a bit better. Howe and his wife, for example, spent three weeks at the Savannah Hotel. The British crew sent to Savannah to pick up the newly completed *Samvannah* were also given more luxurious accommodations. They enjoyed three weeks at Savannah's finest hotel, the Desoto.

Most of these men interviewed for this book had fond memories of their brief stay in the "Hostess City." Fred Goddard, a seaman on the *Treutlen*, thought Savannah was a beautiful city. Ian Gorrie, a member of that British crew of the *Samvannah*, stated that "we had a good time during our stay in Savannah and appreciated the hospitality we received from a family on East 48th Street."

For one Navy man ordered to join the *Thomas Murray*, memories of the city would be very different. Clement N. Meadows was seriously injured, and his shipmate George O. Sims was killed, when the car they were driving in struck a palmetto tree on the road to the beach on Tybee Island.

After delivery, some Southeastern Libertys began their maiden voyages in ballast, sailing for Jacksonville, Florida; Charleston, South Carolina; New York;

or Philadelphia, where their cargoes would be loaded for the voyage through the line of U-boats waiting in the North Atlantic. A few took a southerly heading, loading in Gulf ports and then making the trip through the Panama Canal and out into the vast expanses of the Pacific Ocean. Many others loaded bombs, tanks, airplanes, and other cargo in Savannah before heading north to join the convoys forming off New York.

Loading ammunition was a task that had to done carefully and slowly. The holds of the ship would have to be cleaned, and then a solid wood deck had to be laid over the steel inner bottom deck. Wooden bulkheads also had to be constructed and attached to the insides of the hull so that there would be no steel surfaces that the metal-cased ammunition could come in contact with and create sparks. Bombs without detonators would be strapped to wooden pallets that had heavy timbers at each end, with the bombs fitting into circular cutouts in the timbers. When the pallets reached a certain height in the hold, a new wooden deck would be laid out to distribute the weight evenly, and then more bombs would be loaded onto that deck.

Any spaces were blocked to keep the cargo from shifting horizontally, and heavy timbers called "Toms" were wedged between the top cargo and the upper deck to prevent vertical shifting.[7] Harold Miller left his job in the mold loft at Southeastern after a number of months to take a job on the docks. "I was working on the docks as a carpenter loading bombs and crates of ammunition," Miller explained. "We would have to shore in between the crates . . . wedge wood in so there would be no movement."

The ammunition docks in Savannah were located west of the city, where the East Coast Terminals are today. As Clifford Thomas recalled, "We loaded five-hundred-pound bombs right here in Savannah. They went in the lower holds. The 'tween decks were packed with troops. You couldn't do that with animals. It was against regulations to carry animals and bombs together, but you could carry troops and bombs." Savannah was more at risk from an accidental explosion of American bombs—as happened in other ports—than from bombs dropped by German planes.

Getting ships loaded and out to sea was a priority, and work on the loading docks went on around the clock. "I had to work all day Saturday and all day Sunday, which was double time," said Miller. "You know you can't do that. We just had to lie down. Sometimes during the night, we lay on the deck and dozed off, dog tired."

Miller helped to load a lot of Libertys, and more cargo was put into some than the ships were designed to carry. According to Miller, "At the bow there were numbers recorded up to thirty. And when those ships left, you never saw the "30" because it was way down under water. You'd have to dive down to get to that thirty-foot marker." A Liberty was designed to carry a cargo of 9,149 tons with a full load of fuel. This was the equivalent of the capacity of three hundred freight cars. A Liberty's holds had space for 2,840 jeeps, 440 light tanks, 230 million rounds of rifle ammunition, or 3.4 million C-rations.[8]

Once a Liberty's five holds had been filled, additional cargo would be loaded on her deck. The deck was deliberately designed to be relatively free of obstructions, and this made it possible for the ship to carry an extra load of tanks, crated aircraft and machinery, locomotives, or, in the case of one Savannah Liberty, the SS *Robert Toombs*, tugboats. Few Liberty ships made the thirteen- or fourteen-day trip across the North Atlantic without a deck cargo, as Miller noted:

> They put these tanks on the decks and fastened them down with cables. They then put cargo on top of the holds. The holds had this frame where you'd insert these hatch covers. They were about four feet by two feet and had a place scooped out in the corners where you could get a hold of them. They were pretty heavy.[f] They put a canvas top on top of that, then more cargo on top of the cover. When they got through, we carpenters would build a walkway from the bow right across the cargo—wooden, about four feet wide, with rails on each side. [The walkway] rested right on the cargo. When they unloaded, they had to tear that down.

As well as the relatively normal cargoes of ammunition, equipment, and general war supplies, several docks in Savannah were set up to handle horses and mules. Merchant seaman and dockworker Dave Williams described the animal loading this way:

> We loaded them right here. . . . Well, we didn't load them. They brought these cowboys from Oklahoma to care for the horses and herd them. They had to rest them here after the long trip across the country in rail cars. I think it had to be three weeks or something before you could load them. These were regular cowboys. Stalls were built on the decks, and they kept horses down in the holds, too. Those ships carried extra crew for feeding and cleaning up after [the horses], and veterinarians, too. The stalls had to be built just so wide and long, and they had to be cushioned because the ship would roll and pitch the horses headfirst or tailfirst. Those ships would roll 30 degrees with those horses.

In the process of preparing any Liberty ship for its wartime duties, one last

---

[f]It is unusual today to find a restaurant on River Street in Savannah that does not use hatch covers as table tops. Many were supplied by former Southeastern employee and merchant seaman Nick Creasy.

Photo 41. A Liberty ship with mule stalls on its deck at No. 14 berth, Central of Georgia docks, Savannah. *Photo from the Strachan Shipping Company*

problem had to be dealt with. Guns had been mounted to defend against enemy aircraft, ships, or surfaced U-boats. Torpedo nets were also installed, but rarely used, to protect the ships from that deadly weapon. These measures still left the ship vulnerable to underwater mines, however.

Prior to World War II most mines were contact mines, meaning a ship would actually have to strike one of the horns of the weapon to set it off. During the early stages of the war, a new type of mine was developed that would explode when it detected the magnetic field of a ship. Ships constructed of steel have a certain amount of built in magnetism, a situation compounded by all of the electrical wiring running throughout the vessel. In order to avoid the danger of proximity mines, a ship's magnetic field would have to be neutralized using a degaussing process. Liberty ships had a built in degaussing system consisting of a network of cables running around the ship inside the hull that could be energized from a panel on the bridge. Deperming, a second method of neutralizing a ship's magnetic field, involved wrapping the outer hull with cables and running the ship over a grid of electrically charged underwater cables.

For most Savannah-built Libertys, deperming was done at the Charleston Navy Yard in South Carolina as the ships made their way up the East Coast to join their convoys. One ship was needed so desperately that the port director in Savannah was advised that the ship should sail without deperming. In a memorandum for file, dated March 30, 1943, the Maritime Commission stated that the SS *George Walton*, Southeastern's fourth ship, was "urgently needed for loading in Savannah for a trip to the U.K."[9] Since the direction that a ship is pointing when she is built determines the residual magnetic field she will have, and since the *George Walton* was built on the same ways as the *Oglethorpe*, which was parallel to those on which the *Handley* and the *Jackson* were built, the range readings for those vessels would be used.

Mines accounted for a large number of the merchant ships sunk or damaged during the war, and one has to wonder how Capt. George R. Ellis and his crew on the *Walton* felt about sailing through potentially mined waters during the height of the war with a cargo of ammunition while using only estimated magnetic field range readings. The ship's voyage to Liverpool was, however, uneventful.

Chapter Thirteen

New York to Great Britain

By March 1943 Southeastern had been in full production for several months. Six ships—the *Oglethorpe, Handley, Jackson, Walton*, SS *Lyman Hall*, and SS *John Milledge*—had been launched. Six ways were in operation, and on each, the hull of another ship was taking shape. Two, the *Toombs* and the SS *Robert M. T. Hunter*, would be launched before the end of the month.

That March, Savannah with its large Irish-American population was preparing for St. Patrick's Day. Unlike prewar celebrations this one would be subdued in an attempt to keep people on the job and maintain the sorely needed high levels of production. It would be the second year in a row that there would be no parade in Savannah.

In New York, just before midnight on March 8, the *Oglethorpe* was moving out of the Hudson River and into the Upper Bay on her way to join Convoy HX.229. With her holds filled with steel, cotton, and foodstuffs and her deck cargo of trucks, tractors, ambulances, and aircraft, all loaded in New York, the ship was riding low in the water. The white number "30" painted on her bows to indicate a draft of thirty feet was definitely out of sight. James Thomas "Tommy" Moore, who had signed on with the *Oglethorpe* as a mess man in Savannah, could not see the number. "The ship was loaded so heavy we were drawing over thirty feet," he said. "The Libertys weren't made for speed, but you could keep putting and putting material into them, and we had plenty."[1]

The *Oglethorpe's* scheduled time for departing New York Harbor was planned to allow her to take up her proper position in the convoy. Generally, the ship carrying the convoy's commodore would leave first and take up a position so as to be the lead ship in the center column. The ships that were to lead columns on either side of the commodore's column would leave next, with the others falling into their assigned slots behind. Convoy HX.229 was to have eleven columns, seven with four ships each and four columns with three ships each (see Figure 1). Ships were assigned positions according to their destinations, and as most of the ships in the convoy were destined for Glasgow, Scotland, or Liverpool, England, the ships were assigned to slots from the port column inward. With the exception of the commodore's ship, the MS *Abraham Lincoln*, those bound for Belfast were given positions in the starboard column and inward.[a] After crossing the Atlantic this convoy would sail up the west coast of Ireland and around Malin Head, County Donegal, move through the North Channel between Northern Ireland and Scotland, and then down into the Irish Sea. At that point the columns could then veer off to their respective destinations without having to cross through each other.

The *Oglethorpe* was to take position 94, which meant it would be the fourth ship in the ninth column. The news of their position assignment would have been of great interest to Moore and his fellow crewmen. Ships in the outside columns, and particularly those in the "coffin corners"—the last ship in either of those two columns—were considered to be most in danger. The *Oglethorpe* was not in the best position. While she was in the third column in from the convoy's starboard flank, she was also the last ship in her column. Being last in a column in this particular convoy meant extra responsibilities and, as it turned out, extra dangers.

Because of the large number of loaded vessels in New York waiting for convoys sailing eastward, Convoy HX.229 was forced to sail just three days behind the slower SC.122 and less than a day ahead of HX.229A. Normally, convoys leaving New York would sail at eight- or ten-day intervals. The ships of HX.229 and HX.229A were originally assigned to one convoy, HX.229, but because of the presence for the first time of so many "fast" merchant ships on the western side of the Atlantic, it was decided to split the convoy in two and add more vessels. When these three convoys with their 129 ships left New York, the pressure there for dock space was greatly reduced, but the sailing so close together of the groups of ships meant that their fortunes were to be inextricably intertwined.

The "HX" designation of a convoy indicated that it was a fast, nine-knot, eastbound convoy originating in the United States. "SC" was the designation for slow, seven-knot convoys, again eastbound from America. The "HX" and "SC" prefixes came from Halifax, Nova Scotia, and Sydney, Cape Breton Island, Nova Scotia, which had been the ports of origin in Canada for convoys before the United States entered the war.

As the *Oglethorpe* and the other ships moved out of the lower harbor, crews strained to get a final look at the shore. Those with a clear view would have seen a darkened Coney Island and then Long Island on their port side. Sandy Hook, New Jersey, with perhaps a few lights in Asbury Park, would have been visible to starboard. For many, this darkened east coast of America would be their last glimpse of land for two weeks. For some, it would be their last glimpse of land.

---

[a]In most convoys, tankers and ammunition ships were assigned to the middle, and supposedly more-protected, columns regardless of their destinations.

Figure 1.

The Formation of Convoy HX229 on Leaving New York, March 8, 1943

	Position			
	4	**3**	**2**	**1**
1		SS *Empire Knight* Flag: Great Britain Destination: Glasgow	SS *Robert Howe*[a] Flag: United States Destination: Liverpool	SS *Cape Breton* Flag: Great Britain Destination: Glasgow
2		SS *Stephen C. Foster*[a] Flag: United States Destination: Liverpool	SS *William Eustisa*[a] Flag: United States Destination: Glasgow	SS *Walter Q. Gresham*[a] Flag: United States Destination: Glasgow
3	SS *Matthew Luckenbach* Flag: United States Destination: Great Britain[b]	MS *Canadian Star* Flag: Great Britain Destination: Great Britain[b]	SS *Kaipara* Flag: Great Britain Destination: Liverpool	SS *Fort Anne* Flag: Great Britain Destination: Loch Ewe
4		MS *Antar* Flag: Great Britain Destination: Liverpool	SS *Regent Panther* Flag: Great Britain Destination: Great Britain[b]	SS *Nebraska* Flag: Great Britain Destination: Liverpool
5	SS *Empire Cavalier* Flag: Great Britain Destination: Liverpool	ST *Pan Rhode Island* Flag: United States Destination: Liverpool	MT *San Veronica* Flag: Great Britain Destination: Liverpool	MT *Belgian Gulf* Flag: Panama Destination: Liverpool
6	SS *Kofresi* Flag: United States Destination: Liverpool	SS *Jean* Flag: United States Destination: Liverpool	SS *Gulf Disc*[c] Flag: United States Destination: Glasgow	MS *Abraham Lincoln*[d] Flag: Norway Destination: Belfast
7	SS *Margaret Lykes* Flag: United States Destination: Liverpool	SS *El Mundo* Flag: Panama Destination: Liverpool	SWh *Southern Princess*[e] Flag: Great Britain Destination: Glasgow	SS *City of Agra* Flag: United States Destination: Liverpool
8	SS *Tekoa* Flag: Great Britain Destination: Liverpool	MT *Nicana* Flag: Great Britain Destination: Liverpool	SS *Coracero* Flag: Great Britain Destination: Liverpool	SS *Irénée du Pont* Flag: United States Destination: Liverpool
9	SS *James Oglethorpe*[a] Flag: United States Destination: Liverpool	MT *Magdala* Flag: The Netherlands Destination: Belfast	SS *Nariva* Flag: Great Britain Destination: Liverpool	SS *Clan Matheson*[f] Flag: Great Britain Destination: Loch Ewe
10	SS *Terkoelei* Flag: The Netherlands Destination: Belfast	SS *Zaanland* Flag: The Netherlands Destination: Belfast	MT *Luculus* Flag: Great Britain Destination: Belfast	SS *Elin K* Flag: Norway Destination: Belfast
11		SS *Hugh Williamson*[a] Flag: United States Destination: Belfast	SS *Daniel Webster*[a] Flag: United States Destination: Belfast	SS *Harry Luckenbach* Flag: United States Destination: Great Britain[b]

[a]Liberty ship   [c]Escort oiler   [e]Standby oiler
[b]No city was specified   [d]Convoy commodore   [f]Vice commodore

During the early hours of Tuesday, March 9, the ships of HX.229 steered an easterly course to gain some sea room before turning to the northeast toward Newfoundland. Steaming at between nine knots and ten knots, the ships did not zigzag. Almost three years of war and convoy experience had taught the British that zigzagging was a waste of time for convoys traveling at less than twelve knots. Once it was well clear of land, the convoy changed course to the northeast, passing 180 miles off Cape Cod, Massachusetts, and then sailing east of Cape Sable Island, Nova Scotia, at about the same distance off shore.

Providing protective cover for the merchant ships was the Western Local (South) escort group consisting of two Town-class destroyers, the HMS *Chelsea* and HMCS *Annapolis*, which were both ex-American World War I–vintage "four stackers" and among the fifty destroyers that had been exchanged with Great Britain in return for bases in the Caribbean. Also protecting the convoy were the more-modern destroyer USS *Kendrick,* which was on temporary assignment to the Western Local escorts, and two Flower-class corvettes, the HMCS *Fredericton* and the HMCS *Oakville.* The *Annapolis* did not begin the voyage with the convoy, but did join later. Additional protection was provided by U.S. Army and U.S. Navy air patrols since the convoy was still relatively close to American and Canadian shores. Lookouts were maintained around the clock on the merchant ships and the escorts, but at this stage of the voyage, U-boats were not considered to be a threat.

A year or so earlier this would not have been the case, as U-boat captains found themselves enjoying the inexperience of the Americans who had just entered the war. The begrudging acceptance of the convoy system, the organization of a system of air patrols, and the blacking out of cities and towns on the East Coast put an end to Admiral Karl Dönitz's Operation Paukenschlag. German submarines would become a major problem later in this voyage, but on March 9, the closest U-boat was some 1,400 miles from New York.

One of the first problems to arise for the crew of the *Oglethorpe* was station-keeping—the attempt to keep a 441-foot, 10,500-ton ship from crashing into other, often larger ships that were sailing in close proximity and, hopefully, in the same direction. During the early hours of the convoy, officers and men on the bridge had to study and become very familiar with their new neighbors and their various and particular idiosyncrasies. With ships' different sizes and shapes, different engine performances, and different propeller pitches giving each its own handling characteristics, learning to keep station was a matter of trial and error.

This problem was compounded for the *Oglethorpe*'s men because she was a new ship and the crewmen were still having to learn the ship's own eccentricities.

The challenges were mitigated to some extent because the *Oglethorpe* was last in her column. At least there was no danger of backing into a ship astern in an attempt to avoid the ship ahead that, for reasons known only to her crew, was slowing down. Some captains actually liked having their ships assigned to a coffin corner since there would be only one ship ahead and one other on a single side. While there were no radiotelephones on the merchant ships and all communication with other ships was by signal lamp or flags, skippers could be very vocal using these methods when a collision was imminent.

Fog and a heavy snowstorm caused problems with station-keeping and determining position the first couple of days out. Second Officer Joseph Duke was responsible for navigation on board the *Oglethorpe*. Each day he was to take a noon position and send it to the convoy commodore by signal flags. The commodore would take the positions sent by each ship, average them, and, thus, determine a position for the convoy. His ship had to be watched carefully for signals regarding change of course, possible contact with U-boats or German aircraft, or changed position assignments within the convoy. Merchant crewmen served four hours on and eight hours off in normal situations, with three lookouts assigned to each four-hour watch—one to the bow, one on the bridge, and a third on standby in the mess hall. Every hour and twenty minutes, these men would rotate stations so that each could remain alert.

For the men of the Navy Armed Guard assigned to man the *Oglethorpe*'s guns, the routine was similar, with watches of four on followed by eight hours off. Lt. (jg) James E. Bayne, a Michigan native, would call his crew to general quarters just before sunrise and just prior to sunset each day. If the situation was quiet, general quarters would be secured about an hour later. During a typical day the Navy men would conduct gun drills, conduct fire and boat drills, clean the guns and their quarters, and paint. Painting was certainly a necessity on a steel ship in a salty ocean, but to some of these men, the task must have seemed like breaking big rocks into little rocks.

For both the merchant crew and the Navy crewmen, off-duty hours were spent playing cards, acey-ducey, poker, pinochle, or other games. Reading was also a popular way to spend downtime. The merchant crews of most ships were given at least a few books and magazines by organizations at their home ports or by the individuals or groups that had been involved in sponsoring the ship. Some crews were given fairly extensive libraries.

The captain of the port where the ship was launched issued recreation equipment to the naval gun crew. Typically, this included a set of boxing gloves, a punching bag and inflator, a cribbage board, fishing gear, decks of cards, a puzzle, two sets of checkers, a Red Cross comfort kit for each man, a phonograph, twenty records, and two packs of phonograph needles. One can imagine how some members of the crew began to feel about those same twenty records during a long voyage. While the *Oglethorpe* had a radio in the merchant crew's mess, the radio could not be used in dangerous areas. Also, no private radios were permitted, as it was thought at the time that the amount of reradiation given off by these sets might enable U-boats to get a bearing on the convoy.

Generally, the ship became very quiet after 8:00 PM, as the crew tried to get as much sleep as possible. The men of the *Oglethorpe* slept with their clothes on and their life jackets and rubber zoot suits hanging close by. Nights were nervous times in a North Atlantic convoy. Every crew member, whether on his first or fiftieth crossing, knew that night was U-boats' favorite time to strike.

On Wednesday, March 10, the British ship SS *Clan Matheson*, bound for Loch Ewe, Scotland, signaled the commodore that she could not make convoy speed. At about 2:00 PM convoy time,[b] and with the vice commodore on board, she dropped out of line and turned to head back to Halifax to await a slow convoy.[c] The Royal Mail Lines refrigerated freighter SS *Narvina* moved up to position 91, becoming the lead ship in the ninth column, and assumed the role of vice commodore's ship. This meant that the *Oglethorpe* also had to move up, to position 93. She was still last in line.

On the 12th, HX.229, now with thirty-nine ships, reached the Halifax Ocean Meeting Point (HOMP). As there were no ships to be diverted to Halifax and none joining there, the convoy proceeded on its course of 70 degrees east northeast. That evening the *Chelsea* left the convoy and headed for St. John's, Newfoundland. Wednesday, March 12 had been a routine day, one without incident, or so the men of HX.229 thought.

Earlier in the day, just after noon, the Royal Canadian Navy had sent a radio signal to the convoy commodore, ordering a minor change in course. Within two hours that signal had been picked up and decoded by B-Dienst (German Intelligence) and forwarded to U-boat headquarters. This short signal gave Admiral Dönitz the position, course, and speed of the convoy. Several days earlier B-Dienst had intercepted another message giving the sailing date, route, stragglers route, and positions of the Halifax and St. John's meeting points for convoy HX.229A. The escort commanders of both

---

[b]There is a five-hour time difference between eastern standard time and Greenwich mean time, so the convoy would pass through five time zones while crossing the Atlantic Ocean. Crews would change their clocks as they moved into each new time zone. To avoid confusion, however, convoy time will be used throughout the report of this voyage.

[c] Her inability to keep up may have saved the *Clan Matheson* on this occasion, but she would be damaged later in the war by bombs at Calcutta, India.

HX.229 and SC.122 had both exchanged signals with New York regarding route diversions and escort joining points. These signals, too, had been intercepted and decoded,[d] so the Germans knew that two convoys had sailed, the complete route of one, and a very accurate idea of the rates of progress of HX.299 and SC.122 between New York and Newfoundland. However, the Germans did not yet realize that there were three convoys en route.[2]

When a signal from New York ordering HX.229A onto a more northerly course was intercepted, U-boat headquarters ordered one of the three packs of U-boats patrolling the North Atlantic south of Greenland, the Raubgraf (Robber Baron) Group, to move north to intercept. This order was countermanded two days later when a new signal giving a totally different position for convoy HX.229 and directing that convoy to take an easterly course was decoded. Not realizing that the intercepted messages were directed to two separate convoys, Dönitz decided that the first message was a ruse and sent the Raubgraf Group south to meet HX.229. On the 14th, B-Dienst identified SC.122 and was able to give U-boat headquarters the information that the slower convoy would turn to a course of 67 degrees east northeast as soon as it reached a certain point. So much for "loose lips sink ships."

Convoy HX.229 was only a little more than a day behind SC.122 on March 14, and that morning, another ship was forced to leave the faster convoy. The SS *Stephen Foster*, a Liberty ship built at the Todd Shipbuilding Corporation in Houston, developed cracks in the welding joints of her hull and began to flood. At 10:30 AM she was diverted to Halifax with the *Oakville* in company. Notably, the *Foster* had been sailing in an all-Liberty ship column with the SS *William Eustis* and the SS *Walter Q. Gresham*. The *Eustis*, which was in position 22 and directly ahead of the *Foster*, had also been built at Houston. The two ships had consecutive hull numbers, and they were both launched in January 1943. All three of these Libertys in the second column were carrying sugar, and all were making their maiden voyage. Not one would deliver its cargo to Great Britain on this voyage.[e]

About half an hour before the *Foster* left the convoy due east of Newfoundland, ocean escorts relieved the local escorts to provide cover for the convoy for the rest of the voyage. The new escort group was seriously understrength, however. Its leader was Commander E. C. L. "Happy" Day, an officer with fourteen

---

[d]In 1936, during the Ethiopian Crisis involving Italy and Britain, the Germans monitored the majority of British navy signals. This gave B-Dienst three years before the beginning of World War II to break the codes. Not realizing that their codes had been broken, the British continued to use them unchanged until the spring of 1943. Once the new codes were introduced, B-Dienst was rendered basically ineffective.

[e]The *Foster* was repaired and continued to sail throughout the war. She was scrapped in Oakland, California, in 1961.

months of experience with escort groups in the North Atlantic. Unfortunately, Commander Day's ship, the *Havant*-class destroyer HMS *Highlander*, was in dry dock at St. John's, having serious leaks repaired and a new ASDIC dome fitted. Thinking that the repairs to his ship would delay sailing by only one day, the commander asked that the convoy be ordered into Newfoundland's Placentia Bay to wait for his escort group to be made ready.

This request was denied, and to add to Day's problems, another of his destroyers was undergoing refitting, two of the group's six corvettes had suffered damage in storms and were not available, two others were still escorting another convoy, and the corvette HMS *Pennywort* was going to be delayed because of engine trouble. This left only the Town-class destroyer HMS *Beverly* and the Flower-class corvette HMS *Anemone* available for duty. To quickly bolster the ocean escort for Convoy HX.229, the HMS *Volunteer* was switched from another group, and the V and W–class destroyer HMS *Witherington* and the Town-class destroyer HMS *Mansfield* were added. Both the *Witherington* and the *Mansfield* were World War I ships with very limited fuel capacity. Used mainly to reinforce convoys within six hundred miles of St. John's, these ships did not normally make full Atlantic crossings.

Thinking that he would be able to catch up with the convoy quickly, Day decided to stay with the *Highlander* and to turn temporary control of the escort group over to Lieutenant Commander Gordon James Luther. Captain of the *Volunteer*, Luther had little escort experience. He had sailed with only one convoy, and that had crossed without incident. He was a prewar qualified antisubmarine specialist and had until recently served as staff antisubmarine officer with the Royal Navy's Home Fleet. Among the rest of the *Volunteer*'s crew, only the first lieutenant and about a quarter of the sailors had any experience escorting convoys. HX.229's ocean escort, then, consisted of four destroyers built for World War I—the *Volunteer, Beverly, Witherington*, and *Mansfield*— and the corvette *Anemone*. The HMS *Pennywort* would join later, as would the *Highlander* with the escort group's commander—but not until March 19.

As if HX.229 did not have enough problems, there would be one more that would prove to be extremely serious during the week ahead. Masters were told at the convoy conference in New York that no dedicated rescue ship would sail with the convoy and that the last ship in each column was to serve as the rescue ship for that column. The crew of the *Oglethorpe* knew all too well the dangers of stopping next to another ship that had just been torpedoed, shelled, or bombed in order to pick up survivors. They must have also been looking over their shoulders and asking who serves as the rescue ship for the last ship in the column.

At dawn on Monday, March 15, the *Oglethorpe* and the other ships of HX.229 were just one hundred miles southwest of SC.122, or about half a day's sailing behind. At 8:00 AM, HX.229 was overtaken from behind by a severe storm. The storm initially measured between 9 and 10 on the Beaufort scale, meaning winds gusted up to sixty-three miles per hour and seas increased to twenty-nine feet. Within two hours the gale had reached force 11, and Luther, concerned about damage to deck cargoes on the merchant ships and the impossibility of refueling the escorts, radioed New York to request that the convoy be allowed to head for a latitude 53° N, longitude 25° N on a course of 69 degrees east northeast. This would allow the ships to avoid some of the heavy seas and would shorten the period the convoy would be without air cover. Flights from Newfoundland had a range of 450 miles, and HX.229 had sailed beyond that limit and into the 800-mile, 4-day gap where no planes could cover them. That was the bad news. The day did bring some good news, however, as the HMS *Pennywort* was able to join the convoy and take up station just after noon. This brought the escorts strength up to six.

It was to stay at that level for less than one hour. At 1:04 PM the *Witherington* was forced to heave to because of damaged deck plating. About three hours later, she was spotted briefly by *U-91*, the southern most of the Raubgraf boats searching for the convoy. With visibility so poor, only 1,500 to 3,300 feet, the U-boat lost contact and was not able to reestablish it. The *Witherington* would ride out the storm without further damage, but she was not able to find the convoy again and had to return to St. John's.

Meanwhile, the Admiralty, which had received Luther's request for the course change, radioed New York supporting this request. There was, however, no response from New York. After waiting five hours for an answer, the temporary escort commander ordered the course change himself. There was no way for him to know the serious consequences that would result from that order.

The storm continued throughout the day and into the night, worsening as time passed. Even with the course change, ships were having a difficult time. The Liberty ship *Gresham*, in the convoy's second column, was hit by a wave that carried away a lifeboat, ripping the boat's davits out of the deck in the process. On the SS *Coracero*, the crew was facing a similar situation.

"Shortly before midnight we passed through the center of the storm, when for approximately half an hour there was very little wind and only heavy seas running," the *Coracero*'s third mate, R. McRae, later reported. "Then at the end of the half an hour the wind resumed its full force from an opposite direction. . . . Shortly after midnight we hit and shipped a mountainous sea which swept down our starboard side and broke amidships, smashed No. 3 lifeboat, and reduced it to matchwood, which the following sea smartly removed and nothing was left."[3]

On the *Oglethorpe* the No. 1 lifeboat was completely destroyed, and the No. 2 boat was carried away. Boatswain's Mate James H. Adams was injured by shifting deck cargo. "I was trying to lash down some deck cargo when a heavy tractor shifted against me and broke two ribs," he told the *Sou'Easter*.[4]

During the early morning hours of Tuesday, the 16th, the *Oglethorpe's* convoy, making better time than the Germans thought possible because of the strong winds from astern, passed the southern end of the Raubgraf patrol line unseen. Convoy SC.122 had earlier accomplished this same feat. Neither convoy, however, was home free. With one line of U-boats now behind them, another even more imposing group lay some three hundred miles ahead. The eighteen boats of the Stürmer (Daredevil) Group and the eleven U-boats in the Dränger (Harrier) Group were strung out twenty miles apart in a line three hundred miles long, running from north to south.[f]

Both convoys were now deep inside the air cover gap, that area of the North Atlantic that could not be covered by planes from America, Canada, Iceland, or Great Britain. Perhaps, if their luck held out and they could remain undetected for just a bit longer, the *Highlander* could catch up, and the HMS *Viking*, which was undergoing repairs in Iceland, would have time to join. This, however, was not to be a lucky convoy.

---

[f]U-boat groups on lines of interception were constantly being formed and reformed with different names when they changed positions to engage convoys and when replenished boats joined and those whose patrol time was ending left to return to base.

Chapter Fourteen

It Sounded Just Like a Two-Inch Firecracker

Before dawn on Tuesday, March 16, U-boat headquarters had released five of the Raubgraf boats to return to base because of low fuel reserves or other problems. *U-653*, one of the released boats, was having a variety of problems. It had only one torpedo left and that was defective. It was low on fuel, and its starboard diesel engine was not operating properly. In addition, an officer and four lookouts had been washed overboard in a storm and one of the boat's petty officers was very ill.

Lieutenant Gerhard Feiler, *U-653*'s captain, would not have been pleased with the boats successes on this patrol. On February 24 he had attacked three ships in Convoy ON.166, but only the Dutch motor ship *Madoeza* had been hit and damaged. According to German sources, *U-653* then sank the Liberty ship SS *Thomas Hooker* on March 12.[1] If she did, she wasted a torpedo. The *Hooker* had suffered severe storm damage and was breaking in two when her crew had abandoned her a week earlier. Two other sources indicate that this Liberty ship sank because of the wide cracks that developed during the storm.[2]

Regardless of what actually happened to the *Hooker*, *U-653*'s dismal, disappointing, and difficult patrol was about to become the most successful of her career. And she would not even have to fire that last defective torpedo.

Having left the Raubgraf line, *U-653* was moving in a southeasterly direction in order to join up with one of the Milchkuhe (tanker) U-boats to take on enough fuel to reach Brest, France. Moving on the surface between 3:00 AM and 4:00 AM on March 16, Obersteverman Heinz Theen was in command of the bridge watch. He later reported that "the wind was very strong and it was very dark, I saw a light directly ahead, only for about 2 seconds. I think it was a sailor on the deck of a steamer lighting a cigarette. I sent a message to the captain and by the time he had come up on the bridge we could see ships all around us. There must have been about 20, the nearest was on the port side between 500 meters and half a sea mile away."[3] The U-boat crash dived, allowed the ships to pass above, then surfaced after about two hours and began to shadow the convoy. At 5:25

AM convoy time U-boat headquarters received *U-653*'s sighting report: "BETA, BETA, BD1491 GELEITZUG KURS 70."ᵃ Convoy HX.229 had been sighted.[4]

In their makeshift operations room in Berlin's Hotel am Steimplatz, Admiral Dönitz's staff was elated. The eight remaining U-boats of the Raubgraf group, plus two boats that had just finished refueling from tanker U-boats to the south, were ordered to chase the convoy at top speed. The eleven southernmost boats of the Stürmer line were also directed to attack the convoy the next morning. Thinking that the convoy sighted was SC.122, the Dränger boats were told to stay on course to catch HX.229, which they thought was farther south. Unfortunately for SC.122, its position was between the Stürmer boats and HX.229.

No one in the convoy had seen *U-653*, and at 3:00 AM on the 16th, no one on watch on board the *Oglethorpe* knew anything at all about Raubgraf, Stürmer, or Dränger. The Allied crews knew that there were probably U-boats about, but their most pressing problem at the moment was keeping station in a bad storm.

Dawn found the convoy in winds that had calmed somewhat but still having to push through strong seas. Three ships were missing. Two were in sight well behind the convoy, the third the Liberty SS *Hugh Williamson*, was not seen again by the convoy. Sailing a straggler's route, she did eventually arrive safely in Belfast.

Shortly after 7:00 AM the crews of convoy HX.229 began to learn of the dangers ahead. The Admiralty advised Lieutenant Commander Luther that shore-based radio stations had picked up signals from the area indicating that U-boats were shadowing the convoy. The *Volunteer* was also beginning to receive these signals.

At 8:37 AM, *U-758* became the first of the Raubgraf U-boats to catch up with the convoy. She would shadow the merchant ships all day, waiting until evening to close in. During the day, six other Raubgraf boats were able to make contact with HX.299. At 11:42 AM the *Volunteer* picked up a strong signal that lasted long enough for a bearing of 353 degrees north northwest to be taken. Since she was the only escort with HF/DF (high frequency direction finding, more commonly called Huff Duff), no cross bearing could be taken in order to get an exact fix. All the *Volunteer*'s crew knew was that somewhere on a line at 353 degrees, a U-boat was signaling. The U-boat was probably *U-653*, which was sending convoy course and speed information every couple of hours.

ᵃBETA, BETA was the standard U-boat signal prefix. "BD1491" was the convoy's position on the U-boat charts, and "GELEITZUG KURS 70" meant "Convoy course 070."

Figure 2.

The Formation of Convoy HX.229 just before the first U-boat Attack on March 16, 1943

	Position			
	4	3	2	1
1		SS *Empire Knight* Flag: Great Britain Destination: Glasgow	SS *Robert Howe* Flag: United States Destination: Liverpool	SS *Cape Breton* Flag: Great Britain Destination: Glasgow
2		SS *Matthew Luckenbach* Flag: United States Destination: Great Britain[a]	SS *William Eustisa* Flag: United States Destination: Glasgow	SS *Walter Q. Gresham* Flag: United States Destination: Glasgow
3		MS *Canadian Star* Flag: Great Britain Destination: Great Britain[a]	SS *Kaipara* Flag: Great Britain Destination: Liverpool	SS *Fort Anne* Flag: Great Britain Destination: Loch Ewe
4		MS *Antar* Flag: Great Britain Destination: Liverpool	MT *Regent Panther* Flag: Great Britain Destination: Great Britain[a]	SS *Nebraska* Flag: Great Britain Destination: Liverpool
5	SS *Empire Cavalier* Flag: Great Britain Destination: Liverpool	ST *Pan Rhode Island* Flag: United States Destination: Liverpool	MT *San Veronica* Flag: Great Britain Destination: Liverpool	MT *Belgian Gulf* Flag: Panama Destination: Liverpool
6	SS *Kofresi* Flag: United States Destination: Liverpool	SS *Jean* Flag: United States Destination: Liverpool	ST *Gulf Disc* Flag: United States Destination: Glasgow	SS *Abraham Lincoln*[b] Flag: Norway Destination: Belfast
7	SS *Margaret Lykes* Flag: United States Destination: Liverpool	SS *El Mundo* Flag: Panama Destination: Liverpool	SWh *Southern Princess* Flag: Great Britain Destination: Glasgow	SS *City of Agra* Flag: Great Britain Destination: Liverpool
8	SS *Tekoa* Flag: Great Britain Destination: Liverpool	MT *Nicana* Flag: Great Britain Destination: Liverpool	SS *Coracero* Flag: Great Britain Destination: Liverpool	SS *Irénée du Pont* Flag: United States Destination: Liverpool
9		SS *James Oglethorpe* Flag: United States Destination: Liverpool	MT *Magdala* Flag: The Netherlands Destination: Belfast	SS *Nariva*[c] Flag: Great Britain Destination: Liverpool
10	SS *Terkoelei* Flag: The Netherlands Destination: Belfast	SS *Zaanland* Flag: The Netherlands Destination: Belfast	MT *Luculus* Flag: Great Britain Destination: Belfast	SS *Elin K* Flag: Norway Destination: Belfast
11		Straggler[d]	SS *Daniel Webster* Flag: United States Destination: Belfast	SS *Harry Luckenbach* Flag: United States Destination: Great Britain[a]

[a]No city was specified   [c]Vice commodore, replacing the SS *Clan Matheson*

[b]Convoy commodore   [d]The U.S. ship SS *High Williamson*, bound for Belfast, had fallen out line.

Ten minutes after intercepting the signal, Luther ordered the *Mansfield* out on the bearing to search for the U-boat. Luther asked the convoy commodore to make an emergency 90-degree turn to starboard to a new course of 118 degrees east southeast. Just after noon the convoy slowed to eight knots, to allow the stragglers to close up. It took them six hours to reform their columns.

Meanwhile the *Mansfield* had moved fifteen miles out on bearing 353 degrees north northeast, but she had not located the U-boat. Not wanting to separate his ship any further away from the convoy, the *Mansfield*'s captain set a course to rejoin. Unfortunately, he had not been informed of the convoy's 90-degree emergency turn, and the ship was not able to catch up with the convoy until 9:00 PM, leaving just four escorts to cover the thirty-seven ships.

Hoping that he had lost the U-boat the *Mansfield* was searching for, the escort commander then asked for the convoy to be brought back onto course 28 degrees north northeast. The two stragglers caught up at 6:37 PM, and the convoy moved back up to a speed of 9.5 knots. At 7:05 PM, the Navy in New York finally responded to Luther's course change request of the day before, approving the change to 55 degrees east northeast. Twenty minutes later the convoy was once again sailing this course, the most direct route to Great Britain.

By 8:00 PM on that Tuesday evening it was almost completely dark. The convoy was steaming at 9.5 knots with seas of between 6 and 8 feet and a north wind at force 2. There was a full moon, but illumination was intermittent because of cloud cover. Still, visibility was excellent, and ships could be recognized from the conning tower of a U-boat at up to nine thousand meters.[5] The *Volunteer* was on the port bow of the convoy with the *Beverly* on the starboard bow. The two corvettes were covering the flanks, with the *Anemone* to port and the *Pennywort* to starboard. The *Mansfield* was desperately trying to find them all.

Six of the seven U-boats in contact with the convoy were Type VIIC Atlantic boats that were 221 feet long and displaced 769 tons on the surface. Their top speed on the surface was 17.7 knots. Submerged, their top was 7.6 knots, a speed that could be sustained for about an hour. These boats could dive officially to 309 feet, and they carried 12 torpedoes that could be fired from four forward tubes and a single stern tube.

After seven weeks on patrol *U-603* had only four torpedoes left. All four were loaded in her bow tubes as she began to make her approach between the starboard bow and starboard quarter of the convoy. The approach was easy, with only four escorts to protect the convoy there was a gap of almost 10,000 meters (6.5 miles) between the *Beverly* and the *Pennywort*. At 8:00 PM and at a range of three thousand meters, Oberleutnant Hans-Joachim Bertlesmann began what was to become a very one-sided battle when he gave the order to fire a spread of the four remaining torpedoes at the two ships in the starboard column, the SS *Harry Luckenbach* and the SS *Daniel Webster*.

Neither was hit, but five minutes after the torpedoes were fired, the lead ship in the next column in, the Norwegian SS *Elin K,* was hit in her aft hold on the starboard side. That ship's crew managed to sound four blasts on her siren, fire off two white rockets, and light the red masthead light—all indicating that the ship was under attack—before having to take to the lifeboats. Within four minutes the ship with its cargo of wheat and manganese had sunk.

The *Elin K's* white rockets were seen by the escorts, but since no explosion was seen and the ship sank so rapidly, Luther was not certain a ship had been attacked. A sweep was ordered anyway, and the *Pennywort* spotted the *Elin K's* two lifeboats while nearing the end of her sweep. All forty *Elin K* crewmen were picked up by the corvette. The experienced, primarily Norwegian crew had behaved well, and the only loss of life suffered was that of a kitten belonging to one of the seamen. "I was most impressed by the calmness and efficiency of the Norwegians," said the *Pennywort's* Sub-Lieutenant L. M. Maude-Roxby. "Their seamanship and general conduct was much to be admired. I'm afraid I cannot say the same of some of our later survivors but I would prefer not to enlarge on that."[6] Maude-Roxby's last comment will cause some concern later.

The *Pennywort* now had forty survivors on board who should have been picked up by the last ship in column 10, but that ship the Dutch *Terkolei,* had sailed right past the *Elin K's* lifeboats. This incident was the first indication of the seriousness of the problem caused by there being no rescue ship assigned to the convoy. Throughout what would come to be called the Battle of St. Patrick's Day, escort captains repeatedly had to make the decision of whether to stop and pick up survivors or go after U-boats. The situation was going to get much worse.

At 9:15 PM the *Pennywort* completed its rescue operation and turned to catch up with the convoy. Commodore M. J. D. Mayall of the Royal Naval Reserve, contrary to normal practice, did not order an emergency turn in the direction from which the U-boat had turned away. Perhaps he, too, was not certain that a ship had been attacked. Whatever the reason, he had the convoy maintain course, which meant that the *Pennywort*, instead of being able to angle back, had to try and catch up from more than seven miles directly astern. This left the starboard flank of HX.229 wide open.

The situation was quiet for more than an hour after the torpedoing of the *Elin K,* and crew members on the *Oglethorpe* and the other ships in the convoy may have begun to hope that just maybe they had been lucky and the Norwegian had been sunk by a loner that had been driven off by the escorts' sweeps. This was definitely not a lucky convoy.

U-758 had been the first of the Raubgraf boats to catch up with HX.229, making contact at 8:37 on the morning of March 16. Built by K. M. Werft in Wilhelmshaven and commissioned on May 5, 1942, *U-758* had yet to achieve any great success. On her first patrol she had been part of a wolf pack that had attacked Convoy HX.217. In three different attacks, the U-boat had fired torpedoes at four tankers, claiming to hear detonations and heavy explosions, and in one case observing a column of fire on one ship. In fact, all of her torpedoes had missed.

This second patrol, begun a month earlier, had also been frustrating for Kapitanleutnent Helmut Manseck and his crew. Eight torpedoes had been fired with no results. As Manseck began to make his approach on the starboard side of the convoy, he, too, had only four torpedoes left. With good visibility and no escorts to concern him, the young U-boat commander was able to take his time.

Manseck explained that

> I had shadowed the convoy all day keeping at extreme range on the starboard side, just keeping the smoke and tips of the masts in sight. I remember that the ships were doing well and not making much smoke, we had been about 12 miles out during the day and came in to 4 or 5 miles at dusk.
>
> When I came in to make the attack, I found that I had misjudged the speed of the convoy and that we were almost level with it but decided to attack from there rather than to try to get ahead again; we came in from just ahead of 90 degrees. I could see six, eight, ten ships and selected a solid overlapping target of the third ship in the starboard column.[7]

Actually, there was no third ship in the starboard column. That was the position of the *Williamson*, which had become separated during the storm and was at that moment sailing alone toward Belfast. When Manseck fired his first torpedo at 9:23 PM, it was probably at the Dutch SS *Zaanland*, the third ship in the next inboard column.

At one-minute intervals, *U-758* fired torpedoes at what its captain described as a seven thousand–ton freighter and an eight thousand–ton tanker immediately astern of the freighter. After a gap of seven minutes, the U-boat's last torpedo was fired at another freighter. The frustrations of the crew of *U-758* were about to end.

Just after 9:30 PM the *Zaanland* and the *Oglethorpe* were hit almost simultaneously, each in the starboard side by one torpedo. Now low on fuel, with no torpedoes left, and thinking that he had sunk two ships and damaged two others, Manseck decided that it was time to quit the area. He turned his boat sharply to port and ran out, later setting a course to rendezvous with a tanker U-boat, before making the return voyage to his base at St. Nazaire, France.

The *Zaanland*, a refrigerated ship carrying a cargo of meat, frozen wheat, textiles, and zinc, was hit just abreast of her mainmast and began to slowly settle. The ship's master, Captain Gerardus Franken, could hear water rushing into the engine room with great force, and fuel oils began pouring out of the ship's tanks below and flooding the deck. He quickly fired off white distress rockets and ordered his crew to abandon. After some initial trouble with the lifeboats, they did so in good order. The *Zaanland* sank stern first.[8]

Earlier, when the *Elin K* had been hit, general quarters was sounded on the *Oglethorpe*, and the crew had gone to their stations. *Oglethorpe* messman Tommy Moore recalled that "when the first ship in the convoy was hit, we got a general alarm, and I went topside. I saw a ship hit in such a way that it went down stern first and I said to myself, 'This is the real thing.'"[9]

Capt. Albert Long immediately put the *Oglethorpe* on a zigzag course, but he maintained the ship's position in the convoy. Shortly before they were hit, a lookout spotted a U-boat on the surface some distance astern. This was reported to Long, but for some reason, he ordered the naval gun crew not to open fire. Being the last ship in the column and firing astern, there was no danger of hitting another merchant ship. Perhaps he was hoping that the U-boat had not seen the convoy or that if his ship did not antagonize it, the submarine might continue on and attack some other ship. In any case, Lt. (jg) James E. Bayne, the *Oglethorpe*'s armed guard officer, was given no opportunity to engage. It had been decided during the convoy conference in New York that the decision to use the ship's guns would be left to the merchant captain. There would also be no time to report the sighting.[b]

The *Oglethorpe* was hit in her No. 1 hold on her starboard side, and a fire broke out in the bales of cotton stowed there. Crewmen on the ship remembered the instant she was hit. "When the torpedo struck there was a jarring feeling. I thought we had collided with another ship. Then there was a loud explosion and I knew that we had been torpedoed," said Savannah native James H. Adams, who was the boatswain's mate on the ship.

Another Savanniahian, Tommy Moore, did not remember the explosion as being very loud. "When the torpedo hit us there was no great jolt," he said. "Only thing, it made a great geyser of water, like a waterfall. We could smell the awful gunpowder. It nauseated us, but it sounded just like a two-inch firecracker."[10]

Twenty-five year old William Ford, a deck cadet from St. Petersburg, Florida, was on the starboard wing of the bridge when the ship was hit. As Ford recalled, "The vessel settled with a slight starboard list and went down a little by the head. The engines were not stopped at this time, but I was told by Mr. [Wayne]

---

[b]The U-boat sighted could not have been *U-758*, as she was making her approach from the *Oglethorpe*'s starboard flank.

Fajans, the engine cadet, that the first assistant engineer [forty-two-year-old Gilbert B. Parks from Beaumont, Texas,] had gone down below after the first alarm and ordered the others on watch to go up on deck. When the torpedo struck, the first assistant engineer released steam from the boilers. However, the vessel had considerable headway for some time."[11]

Either because the rudder had been damaged or the helm had been abandoned, the *Oglethorpe* began making wide circles to port. The fire in the No. 1 hold was put out within fifteen minutes, the engine was not damaged, and the ship showed no sign of sinking. Long decided to try and save her. Apparently, not everyone agreed with his decision. "I know the captain did not give us orders to abandon ship. From the bridge he told us not to lower the boats. However, I do know that two of the boats did get away," said Ford.[12]

The *Oglethorpe* carried six lifeboats, unlike later Libertys that would carry only four. Boats No. 1 and 2 had been lost in the storm the day before, and according to Ford, the No. 3 and No. 4 boats were not lowered while he was on board. After the torpedo from *U-758* struck the ship, there was a great amount of confusion. It was cold and dark, the smell of the explosion and the fire in hold No. 1 permeated every recess of the ship, and men were afraid. A rush for the boats began. It is not known which crew member or members started it, but one source indicated that "two of the three mates were soon ordering boats and rafts away," and many merchant seamen and members of the Armed Guard crew assumed that Long had given the order to abandon ship.

"We started taking on water and sinking at the bow," recalled Moore. "A half an hour after that the captain, Captain Long, ordered abandon ship. A fire broke out in No. 3 hold but the men stopped fighting it at the 'abandon ship' call."[13]

In spite of having conducted a number of boat drills earlier on during the voyage, crew members had problems during the actual emergency. Ford was close by No. 6 lifeboat. He said, "I know that lifeboat No. 6 fouled while being lowered; however, she did get clear of the ship. After No. 6 was lowered I went over the side following the chief mate. In No. 6 boat were eight of the crew beside myself.[c] I should judge that this boat left the ship's side about half an hour after we were torpedoed."[14]

A tenth crewman, Engine Cadet Richard M. Record, tried to get into this lifeboat. Ford again: "I was informed by [Fireman/Watertender William J.] Brantley that he had seen this man attempt to get into No. 6 lifeboat while she was being lowered. He tried to grab the gunwales but missed and fell into the water. As the ship was still under way, he disappeared from view."[15]

---

[c]The other crew members in this lifeboat were Chief Mate Otto Lechner, Third Mate Jack C. Chapman, Boatswain's Mate James H. Adams, Oiler Leonard E. Hodges, Clerk Rupert J. Hunt, Able-Bodied Quartermaster Thomas C. Napier, Ordinary Seaman Henry Lanier, and Fireman/ Watertender William J. Brantley.

Crew members attempting to lower the No. 5 lifeboat had had even more trouble. Adams had originally intended getting off into that boat. "I went to my room and got my raincoat and some cigarettes and a flashlight," he told a reporter. "I went to the boat deck and found that No. 5 lifeboat had been swamped with five men holding on to it. They were swept into the sea. I went to No. 6 boat and slid down the net into the water and some men pulled me into the boat."[16]

Many more than five crewmen had been in boat No. 5 when she first began to be lowered. According to regulations no more than two men were supposed to ride it down, but more than thirty piled in as it hung on its davits. Fajans was the next-to-last man to enter the boat, and as it was being lowered the weight was too much. Either the crewman on the forward fall could not hold it, or the rope broke, causing one end of the boat to drop, dumping more than thirty crewmen into the sea. Moore had been one of the first two to get into this boat. "When the boat got halfway between the main deck and the sea the forward part gave way somehow and we were all thrown into the water," he recalled. "It was completely dark. We formed a human ring of hands with about a dozen boys in it."[17]

The North Atlantic, in the best of times, is not a great place to have to spend a long period in the water. On the night of March 16, conditions were miserable. Ford indicated that at the time these men were in the water, the wind had picked up to force 6, and the sea was rough with heavy swells. Some crewmen, Moore included, had had time to prepare and had put on their warmest clothes. He said, "I put on my heavy clothes because the weather was very cold and I put on my lifejacket, but I didn't put on that rubber suit they gave us. We couldn't swim in it and it took too much time and trouble to put on."[18]

After the No. 5 lifeboat fell, Fajans saw a number of men struggle in the water, eventually give up, and just drift away. Deck Engineer Woodrow Huggins, Wiper Clyde Reed Jr., Oiler Thomas W. Welsh, Fireman/Watertender Leroy Jernigan, and Second Mate Joseph Duke—all from Savannah—and Ship's Radio Operator Harry Kweit of New York were in this group. So, too, was fifty-two-year-old Chief Engineer William N. Tiencken, who with Captain Long, had been on the *Oglethorpe* longer than anyone.

Ford said, "Mr. Fajans told me that he had been informed by [Leroy] Jernigan just before [Jernigan] was lost, that he had seen the chief engineer in the water near No. 5 lifeboat. The chief engineer went down and his hat floated away on the surface."[19] Tiencken left a wife and three children at the Isle of Hope in Savannah.

Information regarding the fate of another seaman, Second Cook Thomas McDaniel of Bethlehem, Georgia, was also passed on to Fajans. "One of the Navy gunners informed me that he had seen this man in the water," Fajans said.

"He gave his light to one of the crew nearby, wished him good luck, and then disappeared."[20] McDaniel was just nineteen years old.

There were others lost in this incident, but Fajans could not remember their names. Meanwhile the No. 5 boat was righted, and twenty-one merchant and Navy crewmen who had managed to remain afloat and close by climbed in.

Four lifeboats from the *Zaanland* and two from the *Oglethorpe* were in the same area. For the wet, cold, and, in some cases, injured men in these boats, there was the prospect of being left in the middle of the North Atlantic. The last ship in the *Zaanland*'s column, the Dutch SS *Terkoelei*, again steamed past without stopping. Because the *Oglethorpe* was the last ship in column 9, there was no other ship to stop for her survivors. Adding to the problems of the men in the lifeboats was the danger of being run down by the *Oglethorpe*, which was in the process of making a number of wide circles through the area.

The *Zaanland*'s chief officer, P. G. van Altveer later described what it was like to be in one of the boats:

> Suddenly I saw a ship heading straight for us and I feared that she would overrun us. The accommodation ladder was hanging over the side and I thought we should get jammed underneath the spur [lower end] of the ladder. Most of my lifeboat's occupants rose from their seats to be ready for jumping overboard but I shouted, "Sit down, do sit down." I feared the boat might capsize. It was a very exciting moment. She passed us on her port side at no more than five yards.
>
> Then we saw a man floating on the sea. Apparently he had left that ship by way of the accommodation ladder but it was risky for us to pick him up. Firstly it was necessary to get clear of the turning circle of that ship and secondly my boat was very deep in the water, even overloaded. Furthermore, the condition of the sea and the weather did not allow me to take an extra risk in turning around. I would have had to take the bow away from the sea and high swell and incur the risk of being turned over or capsized by a cross-sea. I decided to stay on my course although it was a very painful decision. I feel sorry for that man but I could not risk all the lives of the men in the boat.[21]

There is no way to determine which crewman from the *Oglethorpe* had to be left to drown. This was another of those chance situations where a number of lives were spared while one was lost. The *Oglethorpe* nearly rams and drowns a boatload of Dutch seamen, but narrowly misses, and a member of the American ship's crew drowns when the lifeboat cannot return to pick him up. Fate was still at work. The out-of-control circling of the Liberty ship figured in the saving of another seaman. The *Zaanland*'s second officer was in one of the Dutch ship's lifeboats that was nearly run down by the *Oglethorpe*. He said,

> While I was trying to get out of the path of that American ship, I saw for a second the flicker of a red light.[d] I kept the bearing in mind and as soon as I was able to, I tried to get to that spot. After a while we came upon a black mass in the water; it was a body. The bos'n thought it to be a Negro and still alive. With difficulty the sailors got him aboard. He was covered by fuel oil, heavy and slippery. He uttered a few words and the boatswain shouted, "He talks Dutch, damn it, he's our captain."[22]

Messman Tommy Moore and several of his fellow crew members from the *Oglethorpe* were still in the water. An escort came in close, and Moore could hear her commander calling to them. "He said, 'Drift in toward us,'" Moore remembered. "As we were doing that a strong wave came toward us from the stern of the ship. We needed our hands to tread the water of the wave. [About twelve men had been holding on to each other in a circle.] We were covered in oil and when we tried to connect again, we couldn't hear each other. . . . It was a long time before I saw the outline of that ship and I swam to it."[23]

Moore, Fajans, Second Assistant Engineer Thomas Edison Bridges of Kentucky, and Utilityman James Bergh Henley of Savannah were finally picked up by the destroyer *Beverly*. The *Beverly* was also able to rescue either from the ocean or from the No. 5 lifeboat, seventeen of the *Oglethorpe*'s Armed Guard crew—Coxswain Harold Oliver Hawk and seamen Robert Dowling, Charles Lee Ehlert, Alred Donovan Ditton, Paul Raymond Day, Irvin Richard Dalen, Alfred Randall Davis, Homer James Dickenson, Henry George Woodham, Tolly William Brown, Fred Aller Dubois, Freeman Gene McCombs, James Lewis Barnwill, and I. J. Brown.

The nine merchant crewmen in the No. 6 boat had fared somewhat better and had been picked up earlier. "I and the others in No. 6 lifeboat were picked up about midnight by the British corvette HMS *Pennywort*," said Ford. "After a search was made for survivors, we left the vicinity about 2:00 AM, March 17. That was the last I saw of the *James Oglethorpe*."[24]

Adams, who was also picked up from the No. 6 lifeboat, remembered his last view of the ship: "The *Oglethorpe* was listing badly, but I did not see her go down. We were in the lifeboat two hours before the corvette picked us up. I did not see the sub, but some of the crew members said they saw it."[25]

---

[d]Life jackets had red lights attached to them so that seamen in the water could be seen more easily.

Chapter Fifteen

St. Patrick's Day, 1943

The *Oglethorpe* had not gone down. Captain Long and the other merchant and Navy crewmen who had stayed on board had gotten steam up and had the ship under control again.[1] She was listing slightly but had not settled anymore, probably because the cotton in No. 1 hold had swollen and prevented the hold from being totally flooded. Lieutenant O. G. Stuart, the Canadian captain of the *Pennywort*, closed with the stricken ship and talked with Long. The *Oglethorpe*'s master stated that he was going to attempt to get his ship back to St. John's, Newfoundland, some nine hundred sea miles to the west. Stuart already had more than a hundred survivors from three ships on board his small warship, having picked up the entire crew of the *Elin K* and the *Zaanland* and nine survivors from the *Oglethorpe*.

Stuart reported by radiotelephone to the *Volunteer* that he intended to turn over all survivors to the *Oglethorpe*, then he tried to persuade the nine crewmen of that ship to return. All refused. "I did not learn until after daylight that morning that the master and about thirty others had stayed aboard the ship," William Ford stated later. "The chief officer informed me of this. I was also told sometime during the night when I was on the corvette, the captain had asked for volunteers to return to the ship. If I had known this I would have joined the captain."[2]

No survivors from either of the other two torpedoed ships were willing to be transferred to the *Oglethorpe* either. Shortly afterward the *Pennywort* had to leave the American Liberty ship, as she was ordered back to the convoy, which was having its own troubles.

At 11:30 PM, *U-435* torpedoed the Liberty ship *William Eustis*, which was carrying a cargo of sugar. The ship did not appear to be in serious trouble, but her crew abandoned. Again, the last ship in the column, the American *Harry Luckenback*, sailed past without stopping to pick up survivors.

The crew of the *Volunteer*, which had to break off their search for a U-boat in order to pick up the men of the *Eustis*, were not pleased with either the *Harry Luckenbach* or with their first sight of the *Eustis'* survivors. Most were in their rubber survival suits with their best clothes on underneath—one with highly polished shoes, and many with full suitcases. The *Eustis'* captain had also left all of the code books and confidential papers on board a vessel that showed no indication of sinking.[a] The captain of the *Volunteer* did not have the time to try and convince the *Eustis'* crew to return to their ship, so he closed with the Liberty and fired four depth charges under her hull in an attempt to sink her. She survived this attack and would stay afloat to become involved in the next chapter of the *Oglethorpe's* story.[3]

The convoy was unprotected for almost two hours while escorts picked up survivors. The *Mansfield* finally rejoined at 12:30 AM, March 17, after its long search for HX.229. Seven minutes later *U-91* torpedoed the *Harry Luckenbach*, which quickly sank. Three of the *Luckenbach's* boats managed to get away, but because of some confusion on the part of the escorts, no survivors were rescued. The whole crew of this ship was lost.

Before dawn three more ships were hit—the American freighter SS *Irénée du Pont*; the British refrigerated ship *Narvina*; and the largest ship in the convoy, the British tanker SWh *Southern Princess*. The *Irénée du Pont* and the *Narvina* remained afloat after their crews abandoned. Once again, the designated rescue ships, the Dutch MT *Magdala* and the American SS *Margaret Lykes*, failed to stop. The New Zealand ship SS *Tekoa* did, however, picking up a number of crewmen from the *Irénée du Pont* and the *Southern Princess*, which sank several hours later.

It was still dark on the morning of St. Patrick's Day when the *Oglethorpe* and her seriously depleted crew came upon the *Eustis* somewhere astern of the convoy. This was not to be a propitious meeting. There was another vessel in the area.

At 5:00 AM Kapitänleutnant Heinz Walkerling in the Type VIIC boat, *U-91*, sighted a burning wreck with a freighter approaching on the wreck's starboard side. The *U-91* was on her third patrol, having sunk a destroyer in September 1942 and the *Luckenbach* just hours earlier. Later in the day the U-boat would apply the coup de grâce to the *Narvina* and the *Irénée du Pont*, but in the early hours of Wednesday, Kapitänleutnant Walkerling could not believe his luck. At 5:39 AM *U-91* fired a spread of three torpedoes at almost overlapping targets at a range of 3,200 meters. After a run of three minutes and twenty seconds, two German torpedoes struck the *Oglethorpe* astern and amidships. The stricken Liberty stopped, poured out white smoke, acquired a heavy list, and slowly began to settle.

The already abandoned *Eustis* was hit ten seconds later. She was just 150 meters away from the *Oglethorpe*. There was a huge explosion, then leaping flames and

---

[a] British seamen, many of whom did not have a very high opinion of American merchant crews, thought that the Americans were anxious to abandon a ship that had been hit, but was not sinking, in order to collect a survivor's bonus. There was no such bonus.

heavy smoke. The *Eustis*, too, began to settle and would sink at 8:13 AM.

The *Oglethorpe*, hit by three torpedoes in less than ten hours, stubbornly stayed afloat for almost four more hours, finally sinking at 12:00 PM, convoy time.[4] None of the thirty or more crew members still on board the first ship to be launched at Southeastern in Savannah were ever seen again. At exactly the same moment in Savannah, which would have been 9:00 AM eastern standard time, the celebration of the St. Patrick's Day Mass began in the upper church of the Cathedral of St. John the Baptist. Msgr. James McNamara and the congregation offered up a prayer to Almighty God invoking His aid for a speedy victory for this country and lasting peace and justice for all.[5]

Thirty or more seamen lost their lives attempting to sail the crippled *Oglethorpe* to safety. As indicated earlier, it is impossible to determine which merchant crewmen and Armed Guard sailors were still on board the ship, but among those still aboard or in the small group who drowned earlier, were nine more Savannahians. Assistant cook George W. Hayman Jr., who had lived on West Broad Street and who had a brother working as a welder at Southeastern, was in this group, as was Ordinary Seaman Melvin Kiley, a graduate of Armstrong College. Able-bodied Seaman Dowse Bradwell Deloach Jr., of a 36th Street address and who had been a merchant seaman for seven years was among the missing.

There was a Fireman/Watertender Letheridge Reginald Bustin of Palm Avenue, who, had the ship been able to complete the voyage, would have been able to visit the country where he was born, and there was also Messman Charles William Groover, who lived on Waters Avenue and who had joined the merchant navy only eight months earlier. Anthony "Andy" Von Dolteren had signed on this voyage just to find his young son and keep him from sailing with the Navy to a war zone. He, too, was included on this list. Missing as well was Danny A. Dix who had lived in Savannah before his parents moved to St. Petersburg, Florida.

Fifty-one-year-old Able-Bodied Seaman Bruno George Schiebolt had one of the more interesting backgrounds among this group. An expert ship rigger who had turned down several job offers from local shipyards in order to return to sea when the war began, Schiebolt was described as the "saltiest" member of the *Oglethorpe's* crew and was affectionately referred to as "Popeye." A native of Germany, he had served in the German navy during World War I, been captured, and been sent to America as a prisoner of war. After the war Schiebolt became a U.S. citizen and had lived in Savannah for twenty-four years, sailing as a merchant seaman with the Ocean Steamship Company many of those years. What thoughts must have been going through his head when his ship was torpedoed by a German U-boat? Popeye Schiebolt was never seen again.

Finally there was Ordinary Seaman Robert Ray "Bill" Wilson, a native of

Aylesworth, Oklahoma, who had moved to Savannah to work as a welder at Southeastern. He had begun work on the *Oglethorpe* the day her keel was laid, and he stayed with her through her launching and stay at the wet dock. Just two days before the ship was sunk, this short prayer for their first ship was published in the shipyard's magazine, the *Sou'Easter*: "May God sail with her and protect her and Bill Wilson who sailed with her."[6] Wilson, who had been with the *Oglethorpe* longer than anyone, probably died with her on March 17, 1943.[7]

The nine *Oglethorpe* survivors aboard the *Pennywort* were unaware at that point that had they rejoined the *Oglethorpe* they would not, in fact, be survivors. They and their twenty-one crewmates picked up by the *Beverly* still faced a number of problems and considerable danger. The two small and now very overcrowded escorts still had a fight on their hands trying to protect the convoy. England was still five days away, and the U-boats were not finished with the ships of HX.229. In addition, convoy SC.122, 120 miles northeast of HX.229, which had so far managed to elude the Germans, was spotted by boats of the Dränger group just after midnight on St. Patrick's Day.

Realizing that they were in contact with two convoys in close proximity, the U-boats became involved in a feeding frenzy that would begin to ease only when very long range (VLR) Liberators of the Royal Air Force's Coastal Command, flying incredible distances from bases in Northern Ireland, appeared over the convoys, and additional escorts, including the *Highlander* with HX.229's original escort leader Commander E. C. L. Day, were finally able to join.

The VLR bombers were a very unpleasant surprise for the U-boat captains, who had previously been able to operate in that part of the Atlantic without fear of air attacks. Although their time over the convoys was limited and their appearance intermittent, the RAF planes were able to force a number of U-boats to submerge, frustrating approaches and attacks.

When the four-day battle finally ended later in the afternoon of March 20, the results were catastrophic for the Allies. Convoy HX.229 had lost 13 ships, totaling 93,503 gross tons, and SC.122 had lost 9 ships of 53,094 tons.[b] More than 161,000 tons of badly needed cargo had been sent to the bottom. The sugar lost on the *Eustis* alone would have provided three weeks rations for all of Great Britain. The tractors, trucks, and aircraft on board the *Oglethorpe* never made it to the Eastern Front. Two hundred ninety-two merchant seamen, fifty-one U.S. Navy Armed Guardsmen, seventeen British gunners, and twelve passengers lost their lives.

---

[b]On the positive side, the twenty-seven ships of HX.229A, whose course the Germans learned through decoded signals, but confused with that of HX.229, took a more northerly route and reached Great Britain with just one casualty. The 15,000-ton British tanker *Svend Foyn*, was sunk not by a U-boat, but by an iceberg. The Germans never actually learned of HX.229A, but the convoy's presence did confuse the Germans enough to give HX.229 and SC.122 a little extra time before their fateful confrontation with the three U-boat groups.

The American system of signing merchant crews from particular ports resulted in major losses for several communities. In this battle, forty-two men living in the New York area were killed. Savannah lost fifteen seamen, including one who was not on board the *Oglethorpe*. Ens. Boyce Norris had sailed, against his better judgment, as a passenger on the ill-fated *Irénée du Pont*. Assigned to various naval posts in England, he and several other officers had sailed on that ship in an earlier convoy, but the *Irénée du Pont* had been forced to return to New York because of serious cargo-shifting problems. The group Norris was traveling with had not wanted to sail on a merchant ship originally, and after this abortive voyage, they went to the operations room of the commander of the Eastern Sea Frontier for reassurance that such a voyage was indeed safe enough. An officer told them that they had absolutely nothing to worry about. Not convinced, Norris made one last effort to find a seat on a plane or a "shelf" on the *Queen Mary*, but to no avail. He was again assigned to the *Irénée du Pont* and was killed when she went down.[8]

Against the staggering Allied losses, the Germans suffered just one casualty. *U-384* was sunk during the latter stages of the battle in a depth charge attack by a Sunderland flying boat. Altogether in the month of March 1943, the Allies lost 108 ships, totaling 627,377 tons, against German losses amounting to seven U-boats. The despair felt by Allied naval commanders was expressed in a December 1943 report quoted by Dan van der Vat in *The Atlantic Campaign*: "The Germans never came so near to disrupting communications between the New World and the Old as in the first twenty days of March 1943. It appeared possible that we should not be able to continue [to regard] convoy as an effective system of defense."[9]

The Germans, on the other hand, were elated over their successes during the month, but there was also a sense of foreboding after the attacks on HX.229 and SC.122. The appearance of Allied VLR aircraft signaled the closing of the mid-North Atlantic air gap. Foreseeing this eventuality, Dönitz had written earlier that such a development would result in the destruction of large numbers of U-boats and a reduction in their successes. "There are now no prospects for the successful conclusion of the U-boat war," he wrote.[10]

The survivors of the *Oglethorpe* had ringside seats for the rest of the Battle of St. Patrick's Day. The *Beverly*, with twenty-one *Oglethorpe* crewmen aboard, conducted a number of depth charge attacks against U-boats and was herself the target for four torpedoes, all of which she was able to avoid. The *Pennywort* also carried out several attacks and continued to pick up survivors, and the men of the *Oglethorpe* assisted. Tom Napier, an able-bodied seaman from the *Oglethorpe*, described the attempts to rescue crewmen from the Liberty ship *Walker Q. Gresham*:

One survivor, each time the wave brought him high enough for us to reach him, would grab the rescuer's arm. And when the wave moved out from under him, he would fall back into the sea. Then the same thing would happen again; he would be a little further toward the stern each time he was close enough to grab, but at last he was hauled aboard. There were two survivors next. One was holding a raft with his left hand and another man with his right. As they drifted alongside we could see the one he was holding was dead: his head was leaning back and the life jacket pushed up under his chin. His mouth and eyes were open and as each wave broke over him his eyes and mouth did not move.[11]

The *Pennywort* and the other escorts were crowded with survivors, putting a great strain on food supplies and accommodation space.[c] Some of the rescued men pitched in to do what they could to ease the situation. According to the British naval crews, the Dutch and the Norwegian survivors were generally hardworking and helped. Others became problems. One oil-soaked group picked up from a British ship refused to clean up their assigned quarters on the *Anemone* until they were paid; they were not fed until the quarters were clean. On the *Pennywort*, American survivors created a problem by refusing to work unless they were paid overtime. The corvette's captain, Lieutenant Stuart, locked the Americans in an ammunition locker until they agreed to cooperate.[12] Nine of the forty-nine Americans on board were from the *Oglethorpe*, the rest were crewmen from the *Gresham*. Since the malcontents were not identified, it is impossible to determine if any *Oglethorpe* crew members were involved.

On Sunday, March 21, the *Pennywort*, now moving into the Irish Sea, was detached from the convoy so that the 127 survivors on board could be landed as soon as possible. She docked on the 22nd at Gurock, Scotland, on the Clyde, near Glasgow, where a rescue station had been set up to deal with convoy survivors. Some of the men taken ashore were housed on an old Clyde paddle steamer, while the others were put up in a workhouse converted for the purpose. All were fed and given money and clothes. Those picked up by the *Beverly* were landed at Londonderry, Northern Ireland, on the same day. The local agent for the South Atlantic Steamship Company provided clothes for the merchant seamen, and the seventeen Armed Guardsmen were taken to the nearby U.S. naval base.

The two groups of *Oglethorpe* crewmen—one in Londonderry and the other in Gurock—thought that they were each the sole survivors of the sunken Liberty. Neither had any idea that the other existed. As William Ford later reported, "I learned later that Wayne D. Fajans, Thomas E. Bridges, James B. Henley and James T. Moore had been picked up by the British destroyer, *Beverly* and taken

---

[c] The number of survivors on the *Pennywort*, 127, was almost one and a half times that of her Royal Navy crew of 85.

to Londonderry."[13]

It would be some two weeks before the men landed at Londonderry would learn that others had survived. "Then we heard that an American destroyer [British corvette] had picked up nine men," Tommy Moore told a reporter after the war. "They were on the only lifeboat which was successfully launched. We met them and we all came back on the *Queen Elizabeth*."[14]

Moore's group was sent first to Belfast, then on to Glasgow to join the others. There, the thirteen merchant crew survivors were put on a train to London, where they boarded the *Queen Elizabeth*. The converted luxury liner sailed on April 6 and arrived in New York exactly one week later. For these survivors of the *Oglethorpe*, the trip home was much quicker and infinitely quieter than the voyage across.

The first news of the attack on the *Oglethorpe* that was received in Savannah came by way of a secret registered letter dated March 22, from the Navy to Raymond Sullivan at the South Atlantic Steamship Company:

> We regret to inform you of advices received from the Navy Department indicating the loss of the SS *Oglethorpe* as a result of enemy action.
>
> The SS *Oglethorpe* in convoy from New York to UKAY was torpedoed and sunk between 2215Z March 16 and 0508Z March 17 in position approximately 50 degrees 38 minutes North—34 degrees and 46 minutes West. We have not yet received details regarding survivors or if casualties have occurred as a result of this action. . . .
>
> In the event loss of life should occur as a result of this attack, Mr. R. H. Farinholt of the Coast Guard will attend to the notification of next of kin. Should it become necessary to notify cargo interests, etc., as a result of this action, it will not be necessary to notify shippers of Army, Navy or Lend-Lease cargo. Also, for security reasons, pleas omit any reference as to details and location of attack.[15]

Only twenty-five days earlier Sullivan and other South Atlantic and Southeastern officials had watched the *Oglethorpe* sail down the Savannah River to begin her maiden voyage.

The Navy's *Daily Serial No. 25* for March 26 included the information that the *Oglethorpe* had not sunk after the first torpedo attack: "Survivors *Oglethorpe* state vessel still afloat no danger to machinery or lines in engine room torpedo struck No. 1 hold forward. Captain and 30 men still on board trying to reach St. Johns. Rescue ship went alongside unable to make transfer of survivors. Last seen 0200/17 March attempting to get upsteam."[16]

That same day, R. H. Farinholt of the U.S. Coast Guard sent telegrams to the next of kin notifying them that their relatives were missing. Twelve families and one close friend in Savannah received the telegrams.[d]

Bertie Von Dolteren had had a premonition about her husband, and when the telegram arrived at 216 W. 43rd Street on the evening of April 19, she was afraid to open it. Thirteen-year-old Dorothy Von Dolteren, with her brother and two sisters standing next to her, opened it and read it aloud:

> The Navy Department deeply regrets to inform you that your husband Anthony Joseph Von Dolteren is missing and presumed lost following action in the performance of his duty and in the service of his country in the American Merchant Marine. The Coast Guard appreciates your great anxiety and will furnish you further information promptly when received. To prevent possible aid to our enemies please do not divulge the name of the ship.[17]

Bertie Von Dolteren's premonition had come true.

At this point the men lost in the *Oglethorpe* were officially listed as "missing and presumed lost." This gave a glimmer of hope to families who were understandably having trouble coming to terms with their loss. Almost every family immediately wrote the Coast Guard, asking for additional information. Minnie Jernigan wrote asking about her son, Leroy, and requesting help in relaying the information about his situation to her other

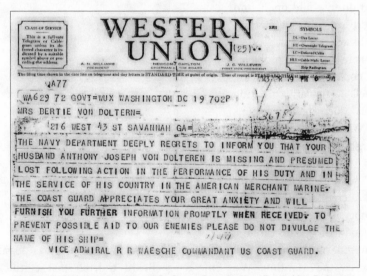

Photo 42. Telegram from the U.S. Coast Guard telling Bertie Von Dolteren that her husband, Andy, was missing. *Courtesy of Dorothy Wise*

---

[d] Bruno George Schiebolt had no family in America and had listed his best friend in Savannah as the person to be notified.

sons overseas. She concluded her letter by stating, "If there is any insignia for the Merchant Marine Gold Star Mother or other remembrance of this sacrifice, I would be grateful for it."[18]

Each piece of correspondence was answered with a letter answering as many questions as possible, but indicating that there was no new information regarding the writer's relative. Each Coast Guard response ended with the sentence, "The United States Coast Guard appreciates your deep anxiety in not having more definite information concerning your husband/son/brother and you may be assured that we will notify you promptly if further information is received."[19]

For the families of mer-chant or Navy crewmen who were missing and presumed lost, where no body was recovered, there was no sense of finality, no feeling that at least one knew that their relative was dead and the period of grieving could begin and would at some point dissipate to the degree that lives could go on. With the missing, there was always the feeling that one day the front door would open, and Albert or John or Francis would walk in.

There were legal problems that could not be dealt with, as well, particularly collecting wages due, making claims for War Risk Insurance or against insurance policies with private companies, and settling accounts with banks, creditors, and family members. Legally, unless the body of the deceased is

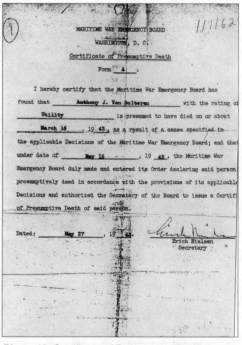

Photo 43. Certificate of Presumptive Death for Andy Von Dolteren. *Courtesy of Dorothy Wise*

recovered, no death certificate can be issued. Acting as quickly as possible, however, the Maritime War Emergency Board ordered that certificates of presumptive death be issued for the *Oglethorpe's* missing crewmen on May 15, 1943.

Bertie Von Dolteren's major problem was that of being left with five children aged three to fourteen at home but with no monthly allotment check from her

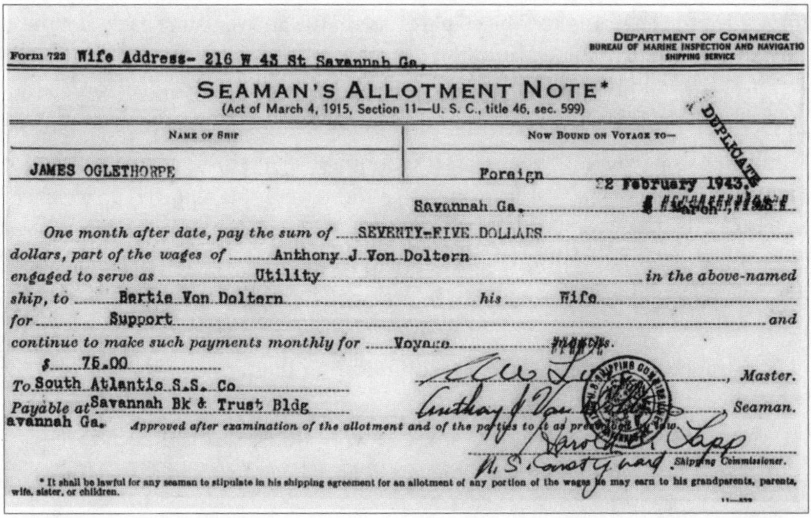
DEPARTMENT OF COMMERCE
BUREAU OF MARINE INSPECTION AND NAVIGATIO
SHIPPING SERVICE

Form 722 Wife Address- 216 W 43 St Savannah Ga.

SEAMAN'S ALLOTMENT NOTE*
(Act of March 4, 1915, Section 11—U. S. C., title 46, sec. 599)

DUPLICATE

NAME OF SHIP	NOW BOUND ON VOYAGE TO—
JAMES OGLETHORPE	Foreign

22 February 1943.
Savannah Ga.

One month after date, pay the sum of SEVENTY-FIVE DOLLARS
dollars, part of the wages of Anthony J Von Doltern
engaged to serve as Utility *in the above-named*
ship, to Bertie Von Doltern *his* Wife
for Support *and*
continue to make such payments monthly for Voyage *months.*
$ 75.00
To South Atlantic S.S. Co
Payable at Savannah Bk & Trust Bldg
Savannah Ga.

, *Master.*
Anthony J Von Doltern, *Seaman.*
Approved after examination of the allotment and of the parties to it as prescribed by law.
Harold Lapp
U. S. Coast Guard. Shipping Commissioner.

* It shall be lawful for any seaman to stipulate in his shipping agreement for an allotment of any portion of the wages he may earn to his grandparents, parents, wife, sister, or children.

Photo 44. Andy Von Dolteren's seaman's allotment note. *Courtesy of Dorothy Wise*

husband's salary. Andy had specified that $75 was to be sent to his wife each month. Mrs. Von Dolteren's sister wrote to Congressman Peterson, asking that he help to get Joseph Jr., then serving with the Navy in the Mediterranean, out of the service so that he could help out at home. Within just a few weeks, Joseph was out of the Navy and home with his family. Andy Von Dolteren had signed on with the *Oglethorpe* to try and find Joseph and get him out of the service. He would never know that he had succeeded.

With the issuance of the certificate of presumptive death, most families, even if they harbored the tiniest spark of hope, accepted that their loved one was gone. Others, however, refused to give up. The family of the *Oglethorpe*'s first assistant engineer, Gilbert B. Parks, continued a correspondence with the Coast Guard for more than nine years, hoping to find some indication that he might somehow still be alive. Parks' mother in Beaumont, Texas, had the Fraternal Order of Eagles in Savannah write a letter requesting information about her son. She was informed then that there was no further news. The engineer's sister wrote next and received a reply indicating that nothing further was known and giving her the names of three survivors whom she could contact for firsthand information. Since Parks was one of the crewmen who had probably remained on board the ship, none of these three contacts could have given Parks' sister any real news other than that they had not actually seen him die.

On May 19, 1943, the Parks family's insurance company wrote for information about Gilbert's status, but also received the reply that there was no new information. The sister wrote again, this time to Naval Intelligence, which forwarded the letter to the Coast Guard. Again the answer came back that there was no additional information and that Park's name was not on any prisoner of war lists, official or unofficial. It was then the turn of Parks' fiancée, who wrote in October 1943, and received the same reply. Almost a year passed, but the family had not given up hope. The sister inquired again in August 1944, and, in answer to her question, was informed that there were "no reported prisoners of war from the vessel on which he was employed."[20]

In September 1945, after the war ended, Parks' sister wrote once more. This time she was told,

> No information has been received indicating that any members of the crew of the Oglethorpe were taken prisoners of war by Germany. It is believed that if any members of the crew of this vessel had been taken prisoners of war the information would have been received at this time.
> . . .
> There is no record of any unidentified merchant seaman now in hospital suffering from loss of memory. . . .
> It is deeply regretted that there seems to be little basis for the hope so long entertained by you that your brother may have escaped death.[21]

When the fiancée, who had continued to hope for nine years, wrote one last letter in July 1952, she received a two-paragraph response stating that no further information had been received and concluding with the sentence, "On May 15, 1943, the former Maritime War Emergency Board issued a Certificate of Presumptive Death in the case of Mr. Parks."[22] After such devotion, one has to hope that this woman and Parks' family were able to find some happiness in their lives.

Survivors and their families and the families of men lost were asked by the Navy Department not to give out the name of the ship that had gone down. As the crewmen rescued from the *Oglethorpe* began to return to Savannah, however, it did not take long for the word to get around that the ship had been lost. Even if nothing was said, the fact that some men were back and others were not raised questions, and the families of the men who did not return could not be expected to carry on as if nothing had happened. Throughout April 1943, the Savannah newspapers carried the obituaries of the crew members from Savannah and those known to people in Savannah, but the name of the ship was never mentioned. Typically, there would be a headline such as, "More Seamen Are Reported Missing," and a first paragraph that would read, "Nine local seamen of the Merchant Marine have been reported missing in the line of duty according to information received here by their families."[23]

The first announcement in Savannah of the sinking of the *Oglethorpe* appeared in the January 1, 1944, issue of the *Sou'Easter*: "James Henry Adams, 66.075, splicer on the wet dock was one of 17 surviving crew members of the SS *Oglethorpe*, the first ship built at Southeastern, when she was torpedoed by an enemy sub March 16, in the North Atlantic."[24] Four days later the *Savannah Morning News* carried the story and stated that its article was the first public announcement of the sinking since the censorship ban on making public the fact that survivors were working at the shipyard, in place for ten months, had been lifted.[25] The families of survivors were then free to talk about their loved ones and the ship, and public memorial services could be conducted to remember and honor the lost crewmen.

St. Lukes Episcopal Church in Hawkinsville, Georgia, conducted a service for Chief Engineer William Tiencken and a navigator who had served in the U.S. Army Air Force. As an offering, Effie Caldwell sang "Say a Prayer for the Boys Over There." Later, at City Hall in Savannah, Mary Della Tiencken received the Mariners Medal awarded posthumously to her husband. Admiral Land sent a letter to be read at the ceremony, which referred to the chief engineer as

> One of those men who today are so gallantly upholding traditions of those hearty mariners who defied anyone to stop the American flag from sailing the seas in the early days of the Republic. He was one of those men upon whom the nation now depends to keep our ships afloat upon the perilous seas—to transport our troops across those seas; and to carry to them the vitally needed material to keep them fighting until victory is certain and Liberty secure.
>
> Nothing I can say or do will in any sense, requite the loss of your loved one. He is gone, but he has gone in honor and in the goodly company of patriots. Let me in this expression of the country's deep sympathy, also express to you its gratitude for his devotion and sacrifice.

Bertie Von Dolteren received a letter and a medal, too. All of the families of the Savannah men who died on the *Oglethorpe* received letters and medals at the same ceremony. In other cities all across America, similar ceremonies were conducted.

The *Oglethorpe*, too, had gone in "the goodly company of patriots." Six new Liberty ships began the voyage to Great Britain in convoy HX.229. Only three survived to deliver their cargoes. The *Oglethorpe* had faced the largest concentration of U-boats ever gathered in one area for a single operation. She and most of her crew were lost in the greatest convoy battle of World War II. This had been a battle "that featured none of the zest and glory, prestige and

Photo 45. Certificate from the City of Savannah presented to Mary Tiencken. *Courtesy of Jimmy Hodges*

Photo 46. Mariner's Medal for William N. Tiencken being presented posthumously to his wife, Mary, at Savannah City Hall. *Photo from Jimmy Hodges*

honors of tank warfare on land, or the stabbing thrill of battle in the air. For most of the men, most of the time, it was a cold, wet, miserable and hellish business."[26]

There would be no opportunity to paint swastikas on the *Oglethorpe's* funnel. She could not claim to have sunk a surface raider or a U-boat, or to have shot down an enemy plane. All that could be said about her was that she had tried to do a job, a job that it had taken three torpedoes to prevent her from doing. The men and women at Southeastern were proud of her. They had cheered mightily when she was launched, and again when she sailed past the yard to begin her only voyage. They would be too busy building other ships to formally mourn her loss, but there would be a sadness. The *Oglethorpe* was special. She was the first ship to be built at Southeastern, and she was the first to be lost.

Chapter Sixteen

A Submarine's Torpedo
Ended the Career of . . .

Whe n the *Oglethorpe* went down on March 17, 1943, work at the Southeastern Shipbuilding Corporation was just swinging into high gear. During the next two years, the men and women at the shipyard would construct and launch eighty-seven more Liberty ships, as well as eighteen of the smaller AV-1s. Two more of their ships would be lost to enemy action. One of those, the *John A. Treutlen*, was torpedoed in the English Channel on June 29, 1944. As one of that ship's Armed Guardsman, Seaman First Class Gerald Gormley, recalled, "We were about three hours from Cherbourg when we were attacked by a German sub. Three ships were torpedoed, then we were hit. I was on the 5-inch, .38 [caliber]. I had one projectile in the gun and one in my hand, but the explosion blew me about fifteen feet in the air. I came to about an hour later in a lifeboat."

Gormley's gun captain, Gunner's Mate Second Class Leo Usselman, added, "The gunnery officer announced over the phone to flex our legs, and at that moment we got hit. When I woke up there were 5-inch shells all over the deck. I couldn't stand, so I told one of the gunners to throw the ammunition overboard. I passed out, and when I woke up again, two of the biggest gunners were taking me to a lifeboat."

Usselman and Gormley's ship was hit by a torpedo fired by *U-984* as she was crossing the English Channel on her way to Omaha Beach. Still on her maiden voyage, the *Treutlen* had successfully crossed the North Atlantic to Glasgow with a cargo of ammunition and had sailed again on June 28, 1944, carrying engineering equipment and machinery to be used on the Normandy beachheads.

Many of the *Treutlen*'s crew were Savannahians, as she was another ship assigned to the South Atlantic Steamship Company and had crewed up out of the union hall in Savannah. Five of these men were former Southeastern employees. Fortunately, Savannah did not suffer as it had when the *Oglethorpe* went down. None of merchant crew of the *Treutlen* died when she was torpedoed, and only one was injured. The torpedo struck near the stern on the starboard side under where Gormley, Usselman, and the rest of the 5-inch,

Photo 47. The SS *John Treutlen* down by the stern after being torpedoed by *U-984* in the English Channel, June 29, 1944. This picture was taken by a *Treutlen* crew member in a lifeboat. *Photo by John Pettry*

.38-caliber gun crew were stationed. Seven other Navy men were injured; one was reported to have later died from his injuries.

The *Treutlen* was severely damaged. Two large holes had been blown in her hull, and the hull had buckled, her propeller shaft was broken, and holds No. 3 and No. 5 were flooded. The crew abandoned, but as the ship was still afloat, sixteen merchant crewmen stayed aboard to wait for a tug to take them in tow. Bored while waiting during the night, these men entertained themselves by doing something all had probably wanted to do since signing on. "We stayed there all night and shot at buzz bombs as they passed over," explained purser Kenneth Strickland. "We fired 20-milimeter, and we fired the 5-inch, .50 [caliber] off the bow, too. We saw eight or ten buzz bombs."

The *Treutlen* was towed back to Southampton and beached, where some of her cargo was salvaged. The ship itself was declared a constructive total loss. Both Gormley and Usselman survived their injuries and were assigned to other Armed Guard crews. *U-984* was sunk several months later during an attack by three British ships. There were no survivors.

The third Southeastern ship lost to enemy action was the *Jonas Lie,* the sixty-sixth ship launched at that yard. Her fate was announced by the WSA: "A submarine's torpedo ended the war career of the Liberty ship *Jonas Lie* a few weeks ago. . . . Two merchant seamen were missing after the blast; three others were injured."[1] The *Lie* was attacked by *U-1055* on January 9, 1945, in the Bristol Channel en route to New York from Milford Haven, Wales. Struck in the No.

4 hold, the *Lie*'s engine room was destroyed, and the hold was flooded. While the *Liberty*'s captain, Carl L. von Schoen, was confident that the ship was not in danger of sinking, she was drifting dangerously near pinnacle rocks, so the order was given to abandon ship. The captain and four crew members stayed on board for a short period, but as the ship drifted nearer the rocks, they, too, had to be taken off.

The next day, as the *Lie* drifted into and out of a minefield, fourteen members of the deck crew reboarded to assist with the attempt to take the ship under tow. After two abortive attempts at towing, the crewmen were again taken off, and the *Lie* was left on her own until heavier towing equipment could be brought out. She was never seen again.

Two merchant seamen died in the engine room when the torpedo hit the *Lie*. Twenty-three-year-old Wallace Dean Colson from Brookston, Minnesota, and Spanish citizen Ricardo Marino Garcia had gone down to the engine room to relieve the men on duty there so that they could have their evening meal. Colson and Marino, too, were never seen again. All of the rest of the *Lie*'s Merchant Marine and Navy crew members were rescued, including the seven Navy men and three merchant seamen who were injured in the attack, and also including the two seamen from Savannah, Joseph William Gerard and Jack Redmond Jordan.

U-1055 was lost with all hands sometime after April 5, 1945. No cause for the disappearance of this U-boat has ever been established.

A fourth Southeastern Liberty, the *Reuben Dario*, was torpedoed, but was able to make port under her own steam. Having sailed from New York, the *Dario* was in the Irish Sea, heading for Liverpool. As dawn broke on January 27, 1945, the weather was clear with small swells on the sea and winds at force 3–4. Liverpool was just thirteen hours away, and the crew of the *Dario* expected that the rest of their voyage would be downhill all the way. There was an obstacle in that downhill path—two obstacles to be exact. *U-825* and *U-1051* had been stalking the *Dario* and her convoy.

At noon ship's time, the *Dario* was steaming at 9.5 knots, her crew visualizing the Liver birds atop the twin towers of the Royal Liver Building and thinking of shore leave, when the convoy commodore signaled that U-boats were in the area. Armed Guard Ens. Samuel Pritchard recalled that "all Navy hands were ordered to their battle stations and guns were readied. At 12:37 [PM] we were hit by a torpedo, between our number 1 and 2 hatches on the starboard side." Holds No. 1 and 2 flooded immediately, but after surveying the damage, Capt. E. Carlson decided that since both holds were filled with grain, the ship would not take on too much water and had a good chance to make it to Liverpool.[2]

According to Pritchard, "The senior escort provided us with a standby, and under his direction we were detached from the convoy and traveled under his orders until we reached the bar. . . . At the bar a salvage boat tied up along side us and work was started to enable us to reach the dock."

The *Dario* was able to dock the next day and would spend six months in Liverpool undergoing repairs. When she was finally able to sail, the war in Europe had been over for six weeks. She would make four more voyages before being assigned to the Reserve Fleet in 1948.

U-825, whose torpedo probably struck the *Dario*, was a new boat on her first patrol. She was damaged during the attack but managed to return to her base in Norway three weeks later. Shortly after *U-825* began her second patrol, orders

Photo 48. The SS *James Jackson* in convoy on February 22, 1944. *The National Archives*

were issued by Dönitz, who had become chancellor of Germany after Hitler's death, for all U-boats to surface and surrender to the Allies. On May 8, 1945, *U-825* did surface and, flying the prescribed black flag, proceeded to Portland Harbour on the English Channel coast near Weymouth to be interned.

U-1051 was sunk by escorts during the attack on the *Dario's* convoy.

The four Savannah-built Liberty ships sunk or damaged by German U-boats never saw their assailants and never had the opportunity to defend themselves. They may have been large, slow merchant ships, but they were armed, and their crews would have given anything for a chance to hit back. Not a single round was ever fired from any of these ships, except during testing and during training exercises. One Southeastern Liberty, the *James Jackson*, did get a chance to hit back, although not until after several false alarms.

The *Jackson* left Savannah on her maiden voyage to New York and then went on to Liverpool on March 27, 1943, just ten days after the *Oglethorpe* had been sunk. With a mixed cargo of steel, pig iron, lumber, paper, and cotton, the *Jackson* headed north up the East Coast on her own. Even though U-boats no longer posed a threat in this area, her crew was nervous. Two incidents made them even more nervous. A U.S. Navy blimp signaled, asking if the *Jackson* was the ship requesting assistance. It was not, but the message was disturbing.

Then, lookouts spotted a large gray box that was very similar to the life jacket box on the *Jackson*'s bridge floating in the water alongside several other boxes. Had a ship been sunk? Was there a U-boat in the area? With these thoughts in mind, on March 30, the Navy lookout and the ship's third mate saw a suspicious looking wake that appeared to the mate to be caused by a "slightly submerged submarine traveling in the opposite direction of the *Jackson*."

Savannahian Clifford Thomas was that mate. "I was on watch, and this big black object showed up," he said. "Without having my mind in gear or anything else, I thought it was a submarine, so I jumped in a 20-milimeter gun tub and started firing. . . . A 20-milimeter couldn't have done anything. I turned in the alarm also, and by that time the captain and everybody else showed up."

The captain, Robert Lee Chaplin of Bluffton, South Carolina—just twenty miles from Savannah—who had seen action on Libertys in the Murmansk convoys, changed course hard to port, and the Navy Armed Guard crew began firing the 5-inch, .38-caliber aft gun. After three rounds the gun crew realized that they were firing at submerged wreckage, not a U-boat. Thomas was in for some ribbing. The chief mate presented him with a shell casing from one of the 20-milimeter rounds he had fired and a certificate that read, complete with blanks, "Shell of the first shot fired by the guns of the SS *James Jackson* in the fight against the Axis Submarine Blockade against Allied Shipping, fired by Third Officer Clifford C. Thomas, Latitude_____, Longitude_____, March 30, 1943." Fifty years later, Thomas still had the certificate, and there would be no teasing when he next spotted something suspicious in the Atlantic.

The *Jackson* left New York on April 5, 1943, as one of fifty-seven ships in Convoy HX.233. Her escort would be Capt. Paul R. Heineman's Group A3, an experienced team that had earned the nickname "Heineman's Harriers." Six other escorts would join later. The convoy was spotted by a U-boat on April 15, and after radioing the convoy's position, that U-boat continued on to complete a special mission.

Four other German submarines were ordered to attack the convoy. Several attacks were attempted during the next two days, but the escort group was successful in driving the U-boats off. That would change early in the morning of the 17th, when *U-628* evaded the escorts and torpedoed the British merchant ship *Fort Rampart*. The *Jackson*'s Armed Guard officer, Ens. Ray Dyke, said, "The lead ship in the first column [the *Jackson* was the last ship in that column] was torpedoed twice. The ship dropped out of the convoy in an orderly manner and fell astern on the port side of the convoy. An escort closely followed the vessel. It remained afloat until it was no longer visible."[3] The *Fort Rampart* sank four hours later after being hit by two more torpedoes.

It was now *U-175*'s turn to attack. A Type IX boat, *U-175*, under the command of Kapitänleutnant Henrich Bruns, was on her third patrol. She had sunk eight ships totaling 28,352 tons on her first patrol, but she had come up empty after a second patrol of eighty-six days. Her captain and crew were optimistic that this patrol would be very successful. *U-175* was ahead of Convoy HX.233, and there was, surprisingly, no escort in the area. The U-boat's crew thought that they were the beneficiaries of a major stroke of luck in finding such a wide gap in a screen composed of so many escorts.

The cutter USCG *Spencer*, however, was racing up through the convoy and almost immediately gained contact with the sub. It was 10:50 AM convoy time on the morning of April 17. The cutter dropped two patterns of eleven depth charges each, and the badly shaken U-boat went to 225 feet under the convoy to escape. The cutter followed *U-175* through the columns of merchant ships all the while, keeping the cutter USCG *Duane* abreast of her progress in order to bring that ship into the attack. Another depth charge attack resulted in an oil slick on the surface, but no U-boat. *U-175* had, in fact, been badly damaged.

One of the U-boat's officers later described the attack: "It is not easy down there, the bombs were bad. Inside it was all bad. Everything shaking, things fall down, it smelled and it hurt my eyes. . . . We don't like bombs. It was very weird when they shake the boat. We went down and the bombs started going off, things stopped and would not work, a lot of things broke."[4] The crew of *U-175* had lost control of their boat. Her hull was leaking, the shaft was broken, and with her planes jammed, she had to blow all tanks to surface.

The *Jackson* was in the convoy's coffin corner, and Thomas was on the ship's bridge. As he recalled, "I was on the 8 to 12 watch in the morning, and I was walking back and fourth on the bridge. There was one gunner in the 5-inch tub aft. I looked aft and kept on walking. I had to take a second look. Look here, I don't believe it. A black object surfaced about a thousand yards astern. It was definitely a sub, no problem about that. In fact, you could see men on the sub."

After his first experience in spotting a "sub," one might have expected Thomas to hesitate a bit before turning in the alarm. He did not. "I turned in the alarm, ran up the ladder, and got the signalman to run up the black flag, and then I blew the whistle for 'sub sighted,'" Thomas explained. "The gun crew got there in an instant. Everybody was always ready. There had been an awful lot of depth charges, and we had already lost one ship."

The *Jackson* was named for someone who always ready. The original James

Jackson was one of the "Liberty Boys," a group formed in Savannah to oppose the acts of King George III. During the Revolutionary War, Jackson rose to the rank of brigade major in the Georgia militia, and when the royal governor fled Savannah in July 1781, Jackson was given the honor of leading the militia into the city and receiving the keys to the city "in consideration of his severe and fatiguing service." He was elected governor of the state in 1799 and would later go to Washington as a U.S. senator for Georgia. Jackson's reputation as a fighter was earned not only because of his soldiering, but also because he fought in a number of duels—reputedly twenty-three—earning for himself the nickname "The Brawling Pygmy," and also earning an early death at the age of forty-nine owing to the cumulative effect of his many wounds.[5]

The *Jackson* found herself in a duel, albeit a one-sided one. At 11:35 AM the merchant ship's gunners opened fire at a range of five thousand yards, the noise and concussion from the old 5-inch, .51-caliber gun shaking the stern of the *Jackson*. According to Ensign Dyke, his ship was the first to open fire on the U-boat, and two rounds had been fired by his crew before the escorts changed course and headed for the surfaced submarine. Both cutters, the *Duane* and the *Spencer*, closed on *U-175*, firing as they approached. Ed Halon of Lebanon, Indiana, was a Coast Guardsman aboard the *Duane*. "This was my first trip out," Halon said. "I had just gotten out of boot camp and joined the *Duane* in Baltimore. We had depth charged the sub during the night, then when it surfaced, we hit the conning tower with a 5-inch shell."

Meanwhile, the *Jackson*'s gun crew had continued to fire at the sub as well. Dyke recalled, "Eight rounds were fired—the first seven short, and the eighth one hit on the base of the conning tower. From this observer's position, this appeared to be the second hit on the sub." Thomas swore that between twenty and thirty shells were fired by Dyke's crew before the hit was observed, but he did see the hit.

Navy gunners on the other merchant ships at the rear of the convoy were also firing by this time, and on board *U-175*, her crew knew that she had no chance of surviving. Most jumped into the sea to avoid the shelling, but one submariner, refusing to give up manning the 20-milimeter gun in the U-boat's "wintergarten"—or rear antiaircraft platform—began to fire at the *Spencer*. It was a futile gesture that cost the life of one man on the cutter and the lives of several Germans, including that of the gunner on the U-boat.

The *Spencer* moved into the area between the sub and the merchant ships, which were still firing. Dyke ordered his crew to cease fire, but a shell from one of the merchant ships struck the *Spencer* on her starboard side, sending a shower of shrapnel and splinters along her deck. The cutter suffered the only Allied casualties of the battle, with one dead and twenty-six injured—some by shrapnel, and others burned and deafened by the muzzle blasts from the ship's guns.

An attempt was made to board *U-175* and retrieve code books and other

Photo 49. One crewman still aboard the sinking *U-175* after it was hit by the USCG *Spencer* and the *Jackson*. *The National Archives*

sensitive material, but the boarding party had to abandon the sub quickly as she began to sink. Generally, Type IX U-boats carried a crew of forty-nine, and forty-one German submariners were picked up by the *Duane* and the *Spencer*. Kapitänleutnant Bruns was not among the survivors.

Two more unsuccessful attacks were made against Convoy HX.233, but on April 20, 1943, the convoy was turned over to a local escort off the southern coast of Ireland. Early in the morning of the next day, fifty-six of the fifty-seven ships that left New York arrived safely at Merseyside.

Dyke, in his recommendations for commendations and medals for his crew, did not mention the role played by Clifford Thomas or any of the merchant crew. No medals were approved, but Dyke was promoted to lieutenant, junior grade. When descriptions of the battle with *U-175* were written into the histories of the U.S. Navy and the U.S. Coast Guard after the war, the *Jackson*'s role was totally ignored. Samuel Eliot Morison, in his *History of the United States Naval Operations in World War II*, does mention that the Armed Guard crews on the merchant ships did open fire but does not record the *Jackson*'s hit on *U-175*.[6] In one of the two major histories of the U.S. Coast Guard during that period, Malcolm Willoughby, in *The U.S. Coast Guard in War II*, wrote only that "the Naval armed guards on the Merchantmen and the crews on both cutters opened a lot of fire."[7] Robert Erwin Johnson, in *Guardians of the Sea*, makes no mention at all of any merchant ships being involved.[8]

Capt. John Waters, a retired Coast Guard officer, acknowledged in his *Bloody Winter* that the merchant ships opened fire, but wrote, "The accuracy of the Armed Guard crews left much to be desired."[9] In a letter to the author, W. A. Haskell, author of the book *Shadows on the Horizon*, stated that "there is no evidence to support the claim by *James Jackson*. . . . I was indeed an eyewitness to the whole affair as I was then serving on the big Esso tanker *G. Harrison Smith* and from my position on the flying bridge watched the whole affair from the first to the last in an elevated position."[10]

For some members of the crew of the *Jackson* on their maiden voyage, it would be enough to know that they had been involved, that they had had an opportunity to hit back at the enemy, and that they had done so successfully. Exactly one month from the day that her sister ship the *Oglethorpe* had been torpedoed, the *Jackson*, also with many crewmen from Savannah, had exacted some revenge. This was not enough for one of the *Jackson*'s crew. Fifty years later Thomas, who would go on to become master of seven Liberty ships after the war, was still angry at the failure to give any credit to the crew of the *Jackson*. "The *Jackson* has never claimed that we sunk the sub, only claiming after the sub surfaced—almost surely as a result of depth charges—we scored a direct hit. I saw it," Thomas said.

A number of Savannah Libertys had close calls. Many were in convoys that lost a number of merchant ships and escorts to U-boat attacks. Several underwent heavy air attacks in harbors in Sicily and Naples. Eight Southeastern ships made numerous trips to the invasion beaches at Normandy. The *Thomas Wolf* at Utah Beach was missed by a bomb by just one hundred yards. Off Juno Beach the SS *Casimir Pulaski* had an even narrower escape, as two torpedoes sped by her stern, missing the ship by just fifteen feet. The German pilot who dropped the second torpedo was not so lucky.

Seaman First Class Mike Hrvol, a 20-milimeter gunner on the *Pulaski*'s starboard side, located the plane in the dark and opened fire. His shells ripped into the plane's belly as it swept over the ship from stern to bow. Badly hit, the aircraft crashed into the sea in the area just forward of the *Pulaski*, watched all the way by the gunners and several of the merchant seamen. A few seconds later several distress flares were fired from the direction of the crash, and the ship's crew heard voices in the water calling for help. In spite of the fact that the flares were illuminating the *Pulaski* while an air attack was still under way, the ship's crew tossed life rafts over the side. No survivors were picked up.[11]

The crews of the eight Savannah Libertys that took part in the Normandy invasion had front row seats at the beginning of a new era in warfare. At 4:13 AM on Tuesday, June 13, 1944, just one week after the first Allied troops went ashore in France, the first V-1 exploded harmlessly on open farmland near

Swanscombe in Kent. Seven minutes later a second came down at Cricksfield in Sussex again causing no damage. A third hit Bethnal Green in London's East End, killing six people and damaging several houses. The second Battle of Britain had begun, and by the end of June, 1,600 people had been killed, 4,800 had been seriously injured, and some 200,000 houses had been destroyed or damaged.

For the men on the merchant ships crisscrossing the English Channel, the V-1s were a novelty, something to marvel at and something for the gunners to fire at. The *John E. Ward* was making a return voyage after delivering a British regiment to the beaches of Normandy when her crew saw their first buzz bombs. "What was believed to be a rocket plane with a wingspan of about twenty-five feet and a fuselage much longer, with square wings and tail with an extension well behind the tail went directly over the convoy at 1,500 feet," recalled the *Ward*'s Armed Guard officer Ens. Leonard D. Hawley. "Four Spitfires gave chase and fired a few rounds, but were no match for its speed."[12]

A second V-1 flew over the *Ward*, watched by a fascinated crew. Hawley had his gunners ready for the third missile. "After the first two passed over I ordered the men to fire when in range. We opened up on the third with the 5-inch and the 20-milimeters. The LST on our stern brought this one down," he said.

After the first few days of buzz bomb attacks, the gun crews on the merchant ships received orders not to fire on the V-1s for fear of hitting other ships, but the crews saw quite a few shot down by Allied aircraft and coastal antiaircraft guns, some crashing into the sea near the ships. Several months after D-day, a V-1 did crash just one hundred yards away from the *Juliette Low* in the River Scheldt near Antwerp. The only real dangers posed by the new weapons to the ships crossing the English Channel or at the beachhead were from the possibility of a damaged one falling on or near a ship, from shrapnel from the shells fired at them falling on deck, or from friendly fire directed at the buzz bombs hitting them by mistake. This was a segment of the war that the crews of the merchant ships could observe with a great deal of interest and relative safety.

Contrary to the exciting and very dangerous German attacks suffered by some ships, most of the Libertys built at Southeastern completed a number of voyages across the North Atlantic at the end of which the ship's Armed Guard commander could complete his report with the sentence, "No enemy contact." For merchant and naval crewmen alike, time on these trips was taken up with station-keeping, chipping and painting—the Navy, particularly, was positively generous with the amount of paint provided to gun crews—safety drills, and gunnery practice. Off-duty hours were spent playing cards, reading, and sleeping. As the *Ward*'s master, Capt. Richard Braithwaite, noted, "Most of war is boring. That's the thing you remember most of all, and even when you are at sea, most of the time it is boring."

Unusually, after three North Atlantic voyages, Braithwaite's ship, the *Ward* finished the war sailing in the Pacific. Because of the distance and the resulting costs in time and money, most Libertys built at Southeastern and other shipyards on the East Coast never sailed to Pacific war zones. A few did. "If you saw another ship, it was the enemy," was how Merchant Seaman August Lewis later characterized sailing on a Liberty in the Pacific. Sailing independently was the rule in that theater of operations. Only when supporting landings or sailing close to islands still occupied by the Japanese did merchant ships sail in convoys protected by warships. Lewis had signed on as third mate on the *Robert Toombs* for her maiden voyage to Karachi, which was part of India at that time. That particular voyage would eventually last for six months, total 37,000 miles, and exemplify the differences in sailing across the Pacific rather than the Atlantic. Pacific voyages were long, both in distance and time, generally routine, and often, as Captain Braithwaite put it, boring.

Chapter Seventeen

A Mixed Blessing

The year 1945 brought the promise of victory to the Allies. The so-called turning point battles at Midway, El Alemein, and Stalingrad, had been fought and won. The Battle of the Atlantic, the invasion of North Africa, the fight for Rome, and the Normandy Invasion—all difficult and hard-fought struggles—had also ended with crushing Axis defeats. By New Year's Day 1945, the skies had cleared over the Ardennes, allowing Allied airpower to strike again at German troops and armor and the outcome of Hitler's last major offensive in Europe, the Battle of the Bulge, had been decided.

In the Pacific theater the successful island hopping campaigns for the Solomon, Gilbert, and Marshall Islands and the costly victories in New Guinea, at Guadalcanal, and at Tarawa had begun to close the ring on Imperial Japan. The "Great Marianas Turkey Shoot" and the Battle of Leyte Gulf had all but destroyed Japanese air and naval strength, and Gen. Douglas MacArthur had led Allied forces in the return to the Philippines.

Still ahead would be the battles for northern Italy and Germany, as well as the final defeat of the U-boats in the European theater. In the Pacific theater, Iwo Jima, Okinawa, Burma, and a possible invasion of the Japanese home islands were still to come, and those major battles would doubtless—and did—result in horrific casualties. Nevertheless, the Allies held the upper hand, and it was no longer a question of if, but when, the war would be won.

Certainly, one of the reasons for the Allied successes to this point had to be the tremendous industrial strength of the United States. Unprepared at the beginning of the war, the American defense industries had geared up quickly and were, by the beginning of 1945, turning out vast quantities of guns, tanks, planes, and ships for both the U.S. military and for the Allies. U.S. shipyards had already played a major part in winning the Battle of the Atlantic by launching ships in far greater numbers than Dönitz could ever have imagined, far exceeding those he had used in his calculations for planning the ultimate U-boat victory.

Liberty ships had been a major factor in the Battle of the Atlantic. But as early as the spring of 1943, a bigger and faster successor was being planned. The development of a design for a new turbine engine and the ability of American industry to produce that engine in large numbers made it possible for the Maritime Commission to award contracts for the construction of Victory ships. Only slightly larger than the Liberty, the Victory was some five to six knots faster, which meant that cargoes could be delivered faster and with less danger from U-boats. Another factor in opting for a bigger and faster ship design was that Maritime Commission officials were, even as early as 1943, concerned about America's ability to compete in the postwar maritime market.

In early May 1943 officials at Southeastern, where Libertys were being built under an original thirty-six ship contract, were informed by the Maritime Commission that the yard had been awarded a new contract to build twenty-two of the new Victory ships and sixteen more Libertys. The May 8, 1943, edition of the *Savannah Morning News* reported that Southeastern President William Smith "looked upon this new contract as a forecast of Savannah's permanency in the shipbuilding program of the Nation after hostilities have ended and the war emergency is over."[1]

This contract was to be as diaphanous as some of those announced in 1941 by the Savannah Shipyards Company, but this time it was the government and not the yard that was at fault. Because of a dispute between the Maritime Commission and the War Production Board, the start of construction of Victory ships was seriously delayed, and the number to be built was drastically reduced. A new contract was announced for Southeastern to build fifty-two more Libertys, but no Victory ships. It was a bigger contract, but did the elimination of the Victorys portend something less than postwar permanency for this shipyard?

Any fears in this area were soon allayed when the commission announced in January 1944 that "there are a large number of ships still to be built at Southeastern and the Commission looks forward to the awarding of additional work for Southeastern in the form of new contracts for either new ships or for conversions."[2] The contracts would be for new ships. In May 1944 two contracts were awarded—one for twenty AV-1 cargo ships, and the second for fourteen ships of the same type. The AV-1s, designed for island-hopping in the Pacific, were smaller than Libertys at 5,000 deadweight tons and 338 feet 6 inches in length, with a draft of only 23 feet 5 inches. Officials and workers at Southeastern were elated and felt some sense of security.

Events in the war were escalating. The Allies were advancing on Berlin from both the west and the east, and also moving, island by island, closer to Japan in the Pacific. On April 12, 1945, President Roosevelt died at Warm Springs, Georgia. Work at Southeastern stopped briefly, but there was still a war to be won, and construction of the AV-1s had to continue. Crews aboard the Liberty ships raised and then lowered ships' colors, but sailed on. By the end of April, both Hitler and the Italian dictator Benito Mussolini were dead. In Germany Dönitz became chancellor, and, at 2:41 AM on May 7, General Alfred Jodl acting on behalf of the "Last Fuhrer," signed the act of unconditional surrender.

VE Day brought a tremendous feeling of euphoria to the workers at Southeastern. The announcement of Allied victory in Europe was celebrated with a prayer, but also with a lot of noise. The air was filled with the sound of whistles blowing and of men and women cheering and banging on anything that would add to the overall cacophony of victory. Fifty years later, welder Joseph Williams still maintained that he would never forget the pandemonium in the yard on VE Day. People in the city were a bit more reserved. Sirens wailed, church bells rang, and there were thanksgiving services at various churches, but schools and businesses remained open and there were no public demonstrations.

Work continued on the AV-1s on the ways and at the wet dock at the yard, but Southeastern officials were concerned that workers would consider that the war was basically over and begin to slack off a bit. Workers, on the other hand, were afraid that the impending end of the war meant the end of their jobs. As part of the effort to keep workers focused on the continuing need to meet production quotas, the yard's new managing director, J. F. McInnis, sent the following message to all employees:

> The signing of peace terms in Germany is a great relief to the peoples of many countries, but this is only the end of the first half. You may all be proud of the part you have played in furnishing your share of the Liberty ships which have played such an important part of the success of our Armed Forces. We have an equally important part of the war yet to be won in the Pacific as the vessels presently under construction are one of the most important factors necessary to carry to completion the tremendous problem of supply in the Far East. In order that we may complete our contract on time we must all pull together. I want to assure you of my full cooperation and I know that together we can win.[3]

While construction continued at Southeastern, Allied forces were battling closer to the Japanese home islands. Iwo Jima was secured on March 10, 1945, after weeks of difficult fighting and at a tremendous cost of dead and wounded on both sides. Burma fell to British, Indian, and Gurkha troops under the command of Lieutenant General William Slim on May 4. Okinawa was finally captured on June 21, making round-the-clock bombing of Japan possible, and Trinidad, the last major objective in the Philippines fell on the 27th. The day before, the Potsdam Declaration was issued, demanding the unconditional surrender of all Japanese military forces but allowing the emperor and the

Imperial government to remain in place. It was hoped that this face-saving gesture would generate a positive response, but none was forthcoming.

Faced with the prospect of an invasion of Japan and the ensuing huge number of casualties on all sides, the United States decided to use atomic weapons. On August 6, 1945, the first bomb was dropped on the city of Hiroshima. When there was still no response from the Japanese, a second bomb leveled Nagasaki three days later. "Atom Bomb (2000 Times More Powerful as Any Ever Made Before) Dropped on Japs" exclaimed the headlines of the August 6 edition of the *New York Post*. With more insight than even they knew at the time, the British newspaper the *Daily Express* described it as "The Bomb That Changed the World." Everyone everywhere was talking about the new secret weapon and also, as it was secret, speculating.

Welder Red Pitts arrived at work at Southeastern as usual that day. "I come in and everybody was talking about it," he said. "They had dropped something on Japan . . . the first atomic bomb. We didn't know how big it was . . . might not be any bigger than a golf ball. All around people were trying to guess what it was."

After a tradition-breaking intervention by the emperor, the Japanese government agreed to the terms of the Potsdam Declaration, and, at 7:00 PM on August 15, President Harry Truman announced by radio to the nation, "I have just received a note from the Japanese government in reply to the message forwarded to that government by the secretary of state on August 11. . . . I deem that reply a full acceptance of the Potsdam Declaration which specifies the unconditional surrender of Japan."[4]

Lt. Jack Sparks, who was serving on the *Casimir Pulaski*, which was docked at Manila on the day Allied victory over Japan was declared, probably spoke for most of the world when he wrote in his log, "August 15, 0808—Japan's surrender announced. Hooray!"[5]

For Southeastern crane operator Wallace Beasley, VJ Day would always be a special memory. As he told the story decades later,

> When the war ended, I remember that day. . . . The announcement was given to us in the morning before noon. They had all the employees of the shipyard, about six thousand. . . . They announced . . . for everybody to meet together at noon. They selected one man who happened to be a friend of mine to give a prayer of thanksgiving. This was Evan D. Grant, a real nice guy. I remember they had a PA system hooked up where [you] could hear all over the yard, and they asked everyone to remove their hats. . . . They did, just as reverently as you would expect, and they offered a beautiful prayer of thanksgiving for the ending of the war. That was a historical thing in my memory.

If Savannahians were somewhat subdued when they received the news of victory in Europe, they more than made up for it on VJ Day. At the end of President Truman's announcement, thousands of people swarmed into downtown streets. Automobile horns, sirens, church bells, and people shouting and screaming combined to create a terrific din. Broughton Street, the city's main shopping area, filled rapidly and police had to stop all east-west traffic. British merchant seamen in the crowd were overheard to say, "If only we were in London," but everyone else was happy to be right where they were.

As in larger cities around the country, every young man, in or out of uniform, wanted to kiss every young woman. Few were turned down. Bars closed, but churches opened for services. Rival bonfires were lit in the middle of downtown squares, with that in Washington Square adjudged to be the largest.

The African-American celebration on West Broad Street was not as big as the one on Broughton, but it was just as enthusiastic. Smaller communities had their own celebrations. On Tybee Island, with its normal population swollen by summer residents even during wartime, the noise and enthusiasm rivaled those on Broughton Street. Every family automobile was jammed with people inside, with more sitting on the fenders and hanging on to running boards, all screaming, waving flags, and blowing whistles and horns. The ensuing parade up and down Butler Avenue was as long as the island itself. Hastily built bonfires appeared on every street, and even more hastily drawn pictures of Tojo, Hirohito, and Japanese Rising Sun flags all done in red crayon on pieces of bed sheets were ceremoniously burned.

The thoughts of the adults involved were undoubtedly on the end of the killing and the return of loved ones. For the then-eight-year-old author, fortunate that no family member or close relative had been lost during the conflict, thoughts revolved around the hope that Fleer's Dubble Bubble bubble gum would appear again quickly on store shelves.

By midnight the streets in Savannah and the other areas of celebration were quiet again. The next day government offices and most stores and businesses were closed. Southeastern, however, behind on its contracts because of the recent machinist strike, remained open.

August 15, 1945, brought a sense of elation, of thanksgiving, and of concern to the shipyard's employees. The killing had ended; the war that had taken family members, friends, and fellow workers was over. But Southeastern employees could also not help but wonder how long would they have jobs. There had already been layoffs and a reduction from three shifts to two as the war wound down and contracts were modified. Would the country still need the ships they were building? Would there be new contracts for new ships for use in America's peacetime merchant fleet? These workers had been told over and over to work hard, that only through their hard work would there be a chance for new contracts after the war. They would hear that mantra again, and they would not have to wait long to find out what lay ahead.

Beasley described what happened: "The next day they started laying off and cutting down. I don't remember them laying off everybody. What they did was, as they completed the ship that was under construction, they laid off that crew. Then they laid off everybody except essential people that were needed to dispose of surplus materials and supplies. Just overnight they had a big lay off. I guess everybody looked at it as a mixed blessing . . . all happy the war was over, but their jobs were going to end."

It was actually two days after VJ Day. On the 17th, McInnis issued a statement to all employees in which he told them that the AV-1s begun at Southeastern and which the Maritime Commission had earlier ordered to be sent to Tampa for completion would be completed and delivered by the Savannah yard, but hulls 19 through 28 under the present contract had been cancelled. To that point three AV-1s had been delivered, thirteen were being outfitted at the wet dock, and two were still under construction on the ways. Those eighteen ships would be the last under the existing contract.

Once again workers were exhorted to do their best. "The excellence of your work in completing these fifteen vessels will have a direct bearing on whether or not management is able to secure any additional contracts, which may enable this yard to remain open in the future." Then came the news that all the shipyard workers expecting but did not want to hear: "It is necessary, however, that management reduce employment at the yard to approximately 4,500 persons, including employees of sub-contractors. This effects a reduction of approximately 2,500 from the present force."[6]

The statement went on to say that officials at Southeastern hoped to make an announcement within a few weeks about the future of the shipyard. They were doing everything possible to keep the yard operating beyond the end of 1945 and, thereby, provide employment for a substantial number of *men*. On September 14, the eighteenth and last AV-1 was launched, and everyone knew by then that there would be no more contracts for ships at Southeastern. The *Savannah Morning News* knew:

Savannah's big Southeastern Shipyard which put 106 telling blows into Uncle Sam's Battle of Ships sent its last vessel down the ways yesterday afternoon while hundreds of employees and civic leaders, all a bit tearful, looked on. . . .

In the main, it was the usual type of launching ceremony so familiar to Savannahians. Gay bunting floated on the breeze, the band played martial airs and there was the customary bashing of a good bottle of champagne across the bow. But there was a difference—it was the final launching, the end of a job well done. You could see the tinge of sadness in the faces of the workmen who flocked around.[7]

Those who spoke at the ceremony knew. The Right Rev. Middleton Barnwell, the Episcopal bishop of the Diocese of Georgia, and the yard's executive vice president, Charles Atwell, were both confident that new industrial doors would open for the workers and the site. Henry Dunn, the yard's local attorney and a member of the company's board of directors, knew and expressed the hope that "the men behind the shipyard would find some peacetime industry which could be established at the shipyard site."[8]

First-class welder Shorty Beasley knew seven months earlier, explaining later, "They had cut down the shifts from three to two. That's when I left. I was real young, but I guess I was smart enough to figure the war must be coming to an end. Nobody mentioned it, but that is what I was thinking. I wanted to get me a steady job, because when the war ended, they weren't going to need all those ships." Beasley went to Sears Roebuck, which was then located downtown on Broughton Street, and filled out an application. As he recalled,

> The man said, "I don't think you want this job. We can't afford to pay you the kind of money you've been making at Southeastern."
>
> "Well," I said, "What I want is a regular job. I'm thinking Southeastern is going to close pretty soon, and then I won't have a job."
>
> That was the first day of March 1945 that I went to work at Sears. After the war ended everybody had to leave Savannah because there weren't any other jobs. People told me that I was smart at that young age to think ahead like that.

Beasley retired from Sears Roebuck as manager of their shipping department many years later.

Welder Joseph Williams, who was laid off just before the last ship was launched, tried to stay in Savannah. According to Williams,

> We were just terminated. I can remember it like yesterday. In other words, the old pink slip. I had a service station briefly at Price and Gwinnett, but even back then people broke into it and gave me a hard time. I said to myself, "I'll go home and do something even if it is wrong."
>
> I had this relative, William J. Meskar, who owned this property, and he and I went into business together. Built a store in 1947. My mother was afraid we'd starve to death. We started up with hardware and dry

goods. She said, "You can't make it. You have to have a well-rounded store." So we added groceries. Stayed there for forty-one years.

Welding quarterman Red Pitts left the yard before the last days, too. "They asked me to stay and help," Pitts said. "But by that time they were building a different kind of boat. They had to finish them up, but I decided I better get me a job while the getting was good. Right then I could get a job with Steel Products, so I haven't been out of work but three days since 1933."

Welding leaderman Myrtice Hammock was also asked to stay on, but thought better of it. He explained, "They started laying off people toward the end. They laid them off when they launched a boat. After that last boat went down . . . they asked me to move over to the wet dock. The best welders went to the wet dock, but the war was over so I didn't go. I left there and went to work in a service station, $28 a week, on Bay Street. Been in that business ever since."

Bob Fennel, the outside machinist leaderman, went to work at Southern Oil after the war. Gantry Operator Robert Smith moved out west, worked in California and Texas for twenty-seven years, then returned to the Coastal Empire to retire. Sue Donahue resigned her job as a clerk-typist to attend Draughons Business College and then took a job as secretary making half of what she was paid at Southeastern. Henry C. Beatty, the shipyard's electrical superintendent, joined Rollason Engineering in 1947, and he was appointed city engineer for the City of Savannah in 1967. Sheet metal apprentice Jeff Dukes never did become a fighter pilot. He did learn to fly, however, and after a number of years in the U.S. Army, he retired as a lieutenant colonel.

As for M. C. Nettles, the welder who was given the war bond for his good idea that later proved costly, well, "I quit the day Germany surrendered and went to work the next day. I went out and got me a job with an electrical contractor. He was in electrical and air conditioning. I was the air conditioning part. I finally bought the business from him."

The Southeastern workers who remained on the job at the yard after VJ Day had less time than they originally thought. On September 29 word came from the Maritime Commission that eight of the remaining ships at the wet dock would not be completed at Southeastern or any other shipyard. The reason given was that the commission already had a sufficient number of that type of vessel.

On November 8 shipyard officials announced that Southeastern would cease operation in the near future and that after the last AV-1 was delivered, only a skeleton force would remain at the site to facilitate the closing down. Wallace Beasley was included in that skeleton force. "They shut the shipyard down," he recalled. "And then the Maritime Commission took over, and they laid off everybody except essential employees. . . the security men, a couple of electricians, a couple of plumbers, and two crane operators. Enough to keep going because they were responsible for all those surplus materials. After a couple of months the War Assets Administration [WAA] took over and raised my salary to $1.60 an hour. There was one other crane operator, who was president of the union, and myself."

The *Sou'Easter* published its final issue on November 9, 1945. The tone of that swan song was proud but sad, proceeding from a review of the history of the yard and its accomplishments to a listing of the important employees and production statistics. Editor C. Winn Upchurch also briefly outlined the history of the publication and then concluded with this paragraph, "Newspapermen at the end of their copy put the mark '30' which means the end, no more to come. So it is with reluctance that the final indentation of our typewriter is this—'30!'"[9] It would not be long before "30" would be placed after the name Southeastern Shipbuilding Corporation.

Southeastern went out of business on Saturday, April 20, 1946, when the Maritime Commission took over the site.[a] W. W. Cantrell, plant engineer for the commission, announced that about 175 employees, including Beasley, would be retained for possibly several more months until all surplus material was shipped. The real estate was declared surplus, and shortly thereafter, the War Assets Administration put the property up for sale.

Officials of the City of Savannah, anxious to bring in private industry to replace the shipyard, decided to try and purchase the site, and in a council meeting on May 29, 1946, an appropriation on $10,000 was approved for use by the Ports Authority as a binder deposit in negotiations with the WAA for the purchase. In June 1946 a delegation of Georgia's congressional leaders contacted the WAA to voice support for the city's attempt to purchase the Southeastern site, and it was announced that several large industries had sent representatives to inspect the buildings and facilities with a view toward starting operations.

In September the federal government announced that former Maritime Commission shipyard sites, including Southeastern, would be converted to scrap as part of a campaign to provide enough raw materials to keep American steel mills operating at close to 90 percent capacity. The official notice of this new policy in the *Savannah Morning News* read, in part, "Movable equipment and other material of a non metal type, it is expected will be offered for sale by the W.A.A. in the usual manner. The rest of the yard . . . will await the pleasure of the junk dealers."[10]

In November the city submitted a bid of $100,000 to the government. The City of Savannah was the sole bidder for the Southeastern site, but the bid was rejected and a counteroffer of $524,350 was made by the WAA. The city's

---

[a] Actually, the company was dissolved three and a half years later. On Friday, November 25, 1949, a petition for the dissolution of the company's charter was filed in superior court by the legal firm of Anderson, Connerat, Dunn and Hunter. Judge David Atkinson granted the petition, formally winding up the affairs of the largest industry ever located in Savannah, before or since.

rejection of this higher WAA price led to protracted negotiations that continued through 1946 and into 1947. The city made a "final offer" of $357,000 and set a deadline of October 15, 1947, for the WAA to accept or the city would abandon its efforts to acquire the site. Two days before the deadline the government agreed to the sale.

The Savannah City Council acted quickly. Council members met on October 15 to approve the purchase at a final price of $345,000 and then approve the sale of movable property and the large fabrication building to Chatham Iron and Metal Company for $253,000.85. This sale, and the sale of $17,000 worth of personal property, brought the city's net expenditure down to just $75,000.[11]

The city had originally sold the land, mostly marsh and mud, to the federal government in 1941 for $40,000. Five years later and at a premium of $35,000, the city resumed ownership, but of property that had been vastly improved, having clean running water and electrical systems, railroad tracks, roads, and ready-to-occupy buildings. Members of the City Council and the Port Authority were justly proud of themselves, and Mayor John G. Kennedy congratulated all concerned.

"It was hard work, but I know that all of us feel relieved that it is now behind us and that the Southeastern Shipyard property is now ours," Kennedy told the *Savannah Morning News* on October 16. "I know for a fact that that a number of industries have had their eyes on this location and I feel that the City and the Port Authority have made a definite step forward. We have bought this property reasonably. I expect it will be the means of bringing to Savannah new industry, greater employment and a larger payroll."[12]

Finally, it was time for Beasley to leave the yard. As Beasley remembered, "I was the next to the last one that left the yard. I could operate any of the cranes they had, so I guess that was the reason they retained me. They sold all the equipment, even sold the cranes and everything else." He went straight to a job at Union Bag, now the Union Camp Corporation. "I didn't have to go looking for a job; they had one waiting for me," he said. Beasley retired after a thirty-year career with that company.

Chapter Eighteen

Then, as Camelot, It Disappeared

The Southeastern Shipbuilding Corporation may have gone out of existence in 1946, but most of the Liberty ships built there sailed on. At the end of the war, eighty-five of the eighty-eight Savannah-built ships entered "duration-plus" service, and there was still work for some of them. Some were sold to private owners and would continue to sail for decades, helping to create fortunes for men such as Aristotle Onassis. Fifty-five of the Savannah-built Libertys went into the National Defense Reserve Fleet.

After the war, even with all of the cargoes that had to be moved across oceans in one direction or another, there was a surplus of merchant ships, especially Liberty ships. There was, however, still the desire among politicians and the leaders of the various maritime industries that America should never again have to face an emergency with a paucity of ships as it did in 1941 and never again have a need for an emergency shipbuilding

Photo 50. The SS *John E. Ward* in the Hudson River Reserve Fleet, July 16, 1970. *Photo courtesy of Bill Hultgren*

Photo 51. The SS *William W. Seaton* sailed on after the war as the *Menites*.
Photo courtesy of Bill Hultgren

program. To that end, Congress created the Reserve Fleet in 1946 and established eight sites around the country where surplus ships could be preserved and held ready for future use.

As time passed, and the need for eleven-knot ships passed as well, the Reserve Fleet Libertys that were in the poorest condition were sold to ship breakers. A few others were briefly brought out of mothballs and leased for short periods to shipping companies. In the 1950s when American farmers produced more wheat than could be stored normally, a new use was found for the ships in the Reserve Fleet. Three hundred and thirty Libertys were filled with 225,000 bushel each, enough wheat to bake 15 million loaves of bread.[1]

One Southeastern Liberty even went to war again. Or at least it was modified to go to war. In 1966 during the Vietnam War, the *Harry L. Glucksman* was selected by the Navy for conversion into a special purpose minesweeper. Her superstructure was stripped down; her decks, engines, boilers, and all interior and exterior fittings were removed; and all of her hold openings were plated over. A ballast of urethane foam was sprayed into every crevice of her hull, a bridge was mounted on shock absorbers, and five deck-mounted diesels were installed. All of this work was completed in August 1969, and she was reclassified as the USS *Harry L. Glucksman* (MSS-1).

The outboard engines gave the ship a speed of ten knots and the ability to maneuver sideways up and down rivers clearing mines in a path the width of the ship. With the modification and the foam in her hull, she would be able to explode mines without damaging herself. The author has found no evidence that the *Glucksman* ever made it to Vietnam. She was stricken from the Navy register in 1974 and broken up in 1976.[2]

At the end of 1972 just four ships built at Southeastern still remained in the Reserve Fleet. Three would be withdrawn for a special purpose, so the last to be scrapped was the *James Jackson*. Perhaps it was fitting that she should be the last to go. During the war she fought off air attacks, landed French troops during D-day, and was the only Liberty built in Savannah to fire shots that helped to sink a U-boat. In June 1973, forty years after she was launched at Southeastern, the *Jackson* was broken up in Mobile, Alabama.[3]

The other three ships withdrawn from the Reserve Fleet are still serving today—after a fashion. All three were scuttled to become fish reefs. The SS *Richard Upjohn* was sunk in the fall of 1975 off Horn Island, Mississippi,[4] and the SS *Joseph E. Brown* was sunk off Panama City, Florida, in 1977.[5] The third, the SS *Addie Bagley Daniels*, came home. Withdrawn from the Reserve Fleet on March 21, 1975, the *Daniels* was towed to Newport News, Virginia, for preparation for scuttling off the coast of Savannah. In Virginia,

Photo 52. The SS *Addie Bagley Daniels* ready for scuttling to become a fish reef off the coast of Georgia. *Photo by Nancy Heffernan*

the ship's superstructure, deck equipment, all machinery, movable objects, and nonferrous metal were removed, and she was thoroughly cleaned. The *Daniels*' hull was then cut down to twenty-seven feet to allow clearance for boats above once she was sunk and in place. Openings were cut in her deck to provide entrance for water, to allow for the penetration of some light, and to facilitate the movement of marine life. Looking at the ship just before she was scuttled, it would have been difficult to realize what she had been, where she

Photo 53. (left) Explosions rip through the hull of the *Daniels*. **Photo 54.** (Right) The *Daniels* going down off the Georgia coast to become a fish reef. *Photos by Nancy Heffernan*

had been, the cargoes she had carried, or the role she had played in helping to defeat the Axis powers.

Betty Mansfield wrote this description of the *Daniels* in the *Savannah Morning News* on July 10, 1975: "She was not very beautiful as ships go, and shorn of her superstructure she looked barge-like and defenseless."[6]

The *Daniels* was towed out and anchored in place sixteen miles off St. Catherine's Sound on July 9, 1975, and a U.S. Marine Corps demolition team was transferred aboard to place the ninety-two charges that would send the ship to the bottom. Venetia Butler and her husband, Rusty, had been asked to use their shrimp boat to assist with setting the Liberty ship in the proper position. They would have front row seats. "All of a sudden we heard a couple of gun shots," Venetia said. "That was the signal for everybody to get off the ship. You could see people running all over the deck . . . climbing down ropes and jumping into the water . . . actually jumping off the ship into the water to swim to their boats. . . . And then we all moved away from it, maybe half mile to a mile away."

A small charge went off to alert the observers that the main explosions would take place in one minute. Then, according to Venetia, "A flash, almost simultaneous billows of smoke, and a thunderous report . . . and moments later the stern began to lead the decent to the ocean floor. It took the *Daniels* just over six minutes to go under. It went down just like they show in the movies, where one end of it would kind of start going and it would just slide under."

Several days later, like the *Upjohn* and the *Brown*, few would know who or where the *Daniels* was. There was a veil of anonymity in her demise that characterized her career and that of all Liberty ships.

The *Brown*, scuttled in September 1977, was the last of the Liberty ships built at the Southeastern Shipbuilding Corporation to be decommissioned.

When the Southeastern Shipbuilding Corporation closed down and its site was purchased by the City of Savannah, there was tremendous optimism for the shipyard's potential use by private industry. The forecast of "new industry, greater employment and larger payroll" by Mayor John G. Kennedy in 1947 was as ethereal as some of those announced earlier by the two shipyards.[7] Private industry did not beat down the city's door to locate on the site.

In December 1954 part of the area was leased to the Kraft Equipment Co., which manufactured specialized equipment for pulp and paper mills. Three years later Sea Trains, Inc., signed a fifty-year lease for twenty-eight acres of the property. Neither company was doing business there forty years later. Walking around the area some fifty years after the shipyard closed, one would never imagine that a giant industry once operated there, one whose total payroll poured $112 million into the economy of the city, and one where 46,766 people came together for just longer than forty-nine months to build large cargo ships that helped bring about victory in World War II.

While the former Southeastern site did not develop into the industrial park envisioned by Savannah's city fathers, the shipyard's impact on those who worked there during world War II and on the community was enormous. Men and women came to work at the yard from a variety of backgrounds. The yard and its work drew farmers whose families had tilled their lands for generations and had little or no experience of city life, musicians, teachers, salesmen, and professional athletes. People from all walks of life learned new skills and became welders, pipefitters, carpenters, electricians, riveters, and shipwrights.

In the fall of 1945, some of these people went back to their former jobs, but, for many, their new skills provided access to new opportunities. Some had saved enough money to start their own businesses, buy houses, and begin very different lives.

For women, even though most went back to traditional jobs or family life, the experiences at the shipyard not only gave them new skills, but a new confidence that they could perform jobs that had been male-only and could deal with situations and problems in their personal lives that had been previously left to men.

African Americans did not come out of their years at Southeastern with the same positive experiences as women. For them, their immediate postwar experience was more of the same, but the dissatisfaction of Sam Williams and

Photo 55. Remnants of the ways at the site of the Southeastern Shipbuilding Corporation in May 1992. *Photo by the author*

others with their lack of opportunity and general treatment did not disappear when the shipyard did. And while it would generally be the next generation that would successfully demand and fight for change, perhaps it was what that generation saw and heard from their parents who worked at Southeastern and defense plants across America along with those who served in the armed forces that created the impetus for the civil rights movement. The first *V* in the Double V was won in 1945. The fight for the second, while won in large part over the next several decades, is still being fought.

After the war many defense plant workers left Savannah to start new lives elsewhere, but many stayed. With the thousands of service men and women returning, housing could have been a major problem. The housing projects built to house shipyard workers also did not disappear when the shipyard did, and, like the Liberty Ships originally built only for the duration, the housing developments provided affordable places for families to live in Savannah for decades after the end of the war. The last were finally torn in the early 2000s.

Not many Savannahians who are still alive remember that there was a huge shipyard just downriver from the city during World War II. Those who worked there, however, remember. They remember the din of construction and the heat and the cold. The former Southeastern employees remember the sometimes monotonous, often dangerous, work. They remember the experience of working so closely together with so many, and they remember the excitement of a launching and the pride they felt as a loaded Liberty ship sailed past the yard on her way to war. Some who were never allowed to learn craft skills or to use those they already possessed remember the frustration and the anger.

Still, those former welders, burners, riggers, shipwrights, cooks, and drivers remember. Those who worked as laborers, painters, office staff, machinists, and crane operators all remember what happened there. For most, men and women who had survived the Depression, it was the best time of their lives. They had money in their pockets, and they were doing something important. As former rivet catcher Jimmy Hodges said, "Those were times that kinda stuck with you."

In the last issue of the *Sou'Easter*, editor C. Winn Upchurch finished his brief history of the shipyard by writing, "It was a hard fight for our boys on the battle fronts. And it was a tough job for our men and women in shipyards and factories of America. But it was a perfectly geared teamwork that brought us the victory of which we never had any doubts of winning. The men and women of Southeastern are proud of the part they took in the war effort." Six decades later, they still were.

Knowing what went on there, a tour of the Southeastern site in the early 1990s was depressing. The buildings were gone, the scaffolding on the ways— once six stories tall—had crumbled and disappeared, and no docks or railroad tracks remained. Just a few concrete slabs baked by the sun and cracked by weeds still bore witness to buildings once filled with the activity of heavy construction. At low tide the only hint of what once went on there, the six ways where eighty-eight Liberty ships and eighteen AV-1s were launched, could still be seen—the pilings rotted down to the level of the mud, and the concrete twisted and broken.

Perhaps the former sheet metal apprentice and would-be fighter pilot Jeff Dukes best described what happened on the stretch of the Savannah River: "To me the grand thing about this is, something was created that drew all of these people, thousands of people, and for a thousand days they worked in concert. Then, as Camelot, it disappeared."

The ships built at Southeastern, like all Libertys, had their detractors. As the *Sou'Easter* reported, the ships were "much maligned and slandered more than once." But from March 1943 the ships built in Savannah were involved in the Battle of the Atlantic, the invasion of Normandy, the invasion of southern France, the fight for North Africa and Italy, and in the island-hopping battles of the Pacific. They carried guns, planes, tanks, gliders, tugboats, locomotives, landing craft, medicine, food, post exchange supplies, and raw materials to American and Allied troops and embattled civilian populations around the world. Perhaps the Libertys were not as fast as some would have liked. A few did develop cracks. But they faced the dangers of the U-boats, bombers and torpedo planes, mines, shore batteries, kamikazes, collisions, and storms, and they did get into port.

Built for the duration and considered a success if they completed a single voyage, the Libertys did their job better and certainly longer than anyone ever planned or hoped. In 1941 when he first saw the plans for the Liberty ship, President Roosevelt remarked, "I think this ship will do us very well."[9] It did indeed!

Those eighty-eight ships built in Savannah and the shipyard that built them are gone now. So, too, are most of the people who built them and sailed them. The shipyard workers, the merchant seamen, and the Navy gunners have also been cloaked in that veil of anonymity that descends with the passage of time. Those too young to have been part of those times have worked next to them, met them, sat behind them in churches and synagogues, been taught by them, and cheered them at ball games, but the youngsters never knew what those of the older generation had done or the role that they played in what will hopefully be the last world war. The workers and veterans, both Navy and merchant seamen, have not talked much about those days, either because nobody has asked them or because they thought that young people were not interested or were too busy to listen. A few reunions are still held where they can talk to each other, but when they bring those times up at home, they are greeted with, "Aw Dad!" or "Aw Mom, that's ancient history."

Today, there is no monument to the people of Southeastern or to the ships built at the site of the shipyard. Not many would see it if there were. There is no monument commemorating the merchant seamen from Savannah who died on the Liberty ships during World War II or on merchant vessels in any other war. Many local men did go to sea during the war years, and the number of Savannahians who were killed in the Merchant Marine was the highest of any seaport in the United States in proportion to population.[10] There was a monument once, in Emmett Park on the bluff above the Savannah River, but it was removed to provide space for a monument to the dead of another war. The bronze plaques from the first memorial have been stored with the hope that someday money will be found to create another.

There are small displays devoted to Southeastern and Liberty ships in Savannah at the Ships of the Sea Maritime Museum, the Savannah History Museum, the Juliette Gordon Low Birthplace, and the Coastal Heritage Society's Fort Jackson, but the shipyard, the ships, and the people are, for the most part, forgotten now. The Southeastern Shipbuilding Corporation rose out of the mud and the marsh, drew people from everywhere, became a city in itself, and built ships that crossed every ocean. Then, when no longer needed, it vanished, leaving traces only in the memories of those who were part of it all. For them, perhaps, it was Camelot.

Appendix A

"Song for the Victory Fleet"

We'll build 'em and sail 'em

We'll never fail 'em

The Victory Fleet will be complete we know

On every ocean, we'll be in motion

The Victory Fleet will soon defeat the foe.

We'll have a bridge of ships beyond compare

We'll soon be able to walk from here to over there

The world is cheering

The skies are clearing

With the Victory Fleet—let's go.

In the factories hear the hammers night and day

In the shipyards everyone is on his way

On the ocean every seaman joins the fray

We heard the buglers blow

We answered our country's call we're ready one and all.

Appendix B

Shipbuilding in the Savannah Area

Colonial Period
The Colonial Shipyard on Shipyard Creek built and overhauled shallow-draft, square-rigged men-of-war for use in protecting the Georgia colony against the Spanish.

Civil War Period
The ironclad CSS *Atlanta*, formerly the blockade runner *Fingal*, was reconstructed in Savannah.

Willink's Shipyard on Hutchinson Island constructed the ironclad CSS *Savannah*, a casement-type armored ship, and was in the process of building the ironclad CSS *Milledgeville* when the city was evacuated.

The CSS *Georgia*, once described as a "marine abortion," was also constructed in Savannah.

World War I Period
In 1909 the Forrest City Foundry constructed a yacht that was used as an auxiliary patrol vessel during World War I. The yard was purchased in 1912 by Walter Lee Mingledorff and renamed the Savannah Machine and Foundry Company.

At its site on the Brampton tract, four and a half miles from the city, the Savannah yard of the Foundation Company constructed twenty-eight minesweepers for the French government.

The Terry Shipbuilding Company built several composite cargo ships of 3,600 tons, the second of which was named the *James Oglethorpe*. This Terry yard also built the 5,186-ton tankers *Darden*, *Danford*, *Gladysbe*, *Lilmar*, and *Pearldon*.

World War II Period
The Savannah Machine and Foundry Company constructed twenty-five steel-hulled minesweepers and four submarine rescue and salvage vessels for the U.S. Navy. The yard also converted Liberty ships to limited-capacity troop ships.

The MacEvoy Shipbuilding Corporation built seven 6,000-ton concrete oil barges.

The Southeastern Shipbuilding Corporation built eighty-eight Liberty ships and eighteen AV-1 cargo vessels.

In Brunswick, Georgia, the J. A. Jones Construction Company built eighty-five Liberty ships and fourteen AV-1s.

Postwar Period

The Savannah Machine and Foundry Company operated a ship repair facility and built barges for several major oil companies.

In 1968 Savannah Machine and Foundry was sold to the Aegis Corporation, which had a contract to convert bulk carriers into container ships and Victory ships into missile carriers. Saylor Marine purchased the yard in 1984, and it became a repair facility for U.S. Coast Guard and commercial vessels.

The Diamond Manufacturing Company constructed barges and towboats ranging in size from 26 feet to the largest ocean-going towboats in the world, the 167-foot-long *Port Everglades* and the *Tampa*.

Thunderbolt Marine Industries, located on the Wilmington River, built small towboats and barges for a number of years.

The Lockheed Shipbuilding Company purchased the site of Thunderbolt Marine Industries and constructed two landing craft utility 2000s for the U.S. Army. Trinity Marine bought out this operation and moved production to its Gulf Coast yard.

The Thunderbolt site was then leased to Palmer Johnson, Savannah, which opened a repair and remodeling facility for large yachts to complement its yacht construction business in Wisconsin.

In 2003 Palmer Johnson purchased the Intermarine facility on the Savannah River and moved its operations to that site. Palmer Johnson, in turn, closed its Savannah operations in 2004 and sold the yard to Global Ship Systems, which continued in the yacht repair business and had a contract with the U.S. Coast Guard for the repair work. Global closed in June 2007.

Today, Thunderbolt Marine operates a repair and conversion facility for large yachts at the former Palmer Johnson site on the Wilmington River.

Appendix C

Basic Design Schematic for the Standard Liberty Ship

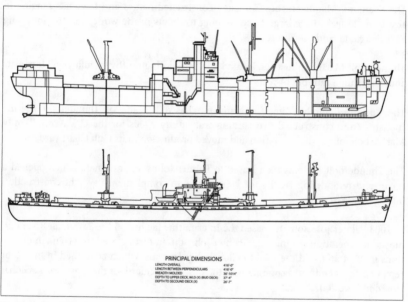

PRINCIPAL DIMENSIONS

LENGTH OVERALL	416'-0"
LENGTH BETWEEN PERPENDICULARS	416'-0"
BREADTH-MOLDED	36'-101⁄4"
DEPTH TO UPPER DECK, WLD (X) (BUD DECK)	37'-4"
DEPTH TO SECOUND DECK (X)	28'-7"

This was the typical interior and exterior design of the standard dry cargo Liberty ship as constructed in eighteen shipyards throughout the United States during World War II. Some Libertys, purpose-built to be tankers or colliers, varied from this standard design.

Appendix D

Ships Built by the Southeastern Shipbuilding Corporation in Savannah

Table 1. Liberty Ships

Yard Hull No.	Name	Launch Date
1	James Oglethorpe	November 20, 1942
2	George Handley	December 7, 1942
3	James Jackson	December 27, 1942
4	George Walton	January 21, 1943
5	Lyman Hall	February 6, 1943
6	John Milledge	February 21, 1943
7	Robert Toombs	March 19, 1943
8	Robert M. T. Hunter	March 28, 1943
9	Crawford W. Long	April 10, 1043
10	John C. Breckenridge	April 22, 1943
11	Button Gwinnett	May 2, 1943
12	Felix Grundy	May 15, 1943
13	Langdon Cheves	May 22, 1943
14	Nicholas Herkimer	June 8, 1943
15	Casimir Pulaski	June 25, 1943
16	Hamlin Garland	July 6, 1943
17	Andrew Pickens	July 20, 1943
18	William L. Yancey	July 25, 1943
19	George Whitfield	August 6, 1943
20	Joseph E. Brown	August 19, 1943
21	Dudley M. Hughes	August 27, 1943
22	Jerome K. Jones	September 6, 1943
23	Hoke Smith	September 16, 1943
24	William Black Yates	September 27, 1943
25	James H. Couper	October 1, 1943
26	Joseph Habersham	October 9, 1943
27	Joseph H. Martin	October 18, 1943
28	Robert Fechner	October 28, 1943
29	Charles C. Jones	November 5, 1943
30	Florence Martus	November 11, 1943
31	Charles H. Herty	November 17, 1943
32	John E. Ward	November 25, 1943
33	Edwin L. Godkin	November 30, 1943

Table 1. continued

Yard Hull No.	Name	Launch Date
34	A. Frank Lever	December 6, 1943
35	Thomas Wolfe	December 15, 1943
36	Louis M. Godey (Samvannah)	December 20, 1943
37	Ben Robertson	January 4, 1944
38	Samuel T. Darling	January 8, 1944
39	Isaac S. Hopkins	January 26, 1944
40	Samhorn	February 5, 1944
41	A. Mitchell Palmer	February 12, 1944
42	Samdart	February 23, 1944
43	John E. Sweet	March 3, 1944[a]
44	Clark Howell	March 14, 1944
45	Earl Layman	March 17, 1944
46	John A. Treutlen	April 10, 1944
47	Ben A. Ruffin	April 11, 1944
48	William D. Hoxie	April 14, 1944
49	Samcebu	April 23, 1944
50	Harry L. Glucksman	April 29, 1944
51	Juliette Low	May 12, 1944
52	Francis S. Bartow (Themistocles)	May 22, 1944
53	Jacob Sloat Fassett	May 31, 1944
54	Richard Upjohn	June 8, 1944
55	William G. Lee	June 15, 1944
56	Ruben Dario	June 22, 1944
57	Benjamin Brown French	June 29, 1944
58	Stephen Leacock	July 11, 1944
59	Charles A. Keffer	July 15, 1944
60	Risden Tyler Bennett	July 22, 1944
61	Alexander R. Shepherd	August 3, 1944
62	James Swan	August 12, 1944
63	Martha Berry	August 19, 1944
64	Frank P. Walsh	August 28, 1944
65	Floyd Gibbons	August 31, 1944
66	Jonas Lie	September 7, 1944
67	John P. Harris	September 13, 1944
68	Richard Coulter	September 22, 1944
69	Addie Bagley Daniels	September 28, 1944
70	William H. Edwards	October 5, 1944
71	Joseph Murgas	October 12, 1944
72	Milton J. Foreman	October 21, 1944
73	Joseph S. McDonagh	October 27, 1944
74	Josiah Tattnall	November 3, 1944
75	Moina Michael	November 9, 1944
76	Robert Parrot	November 16, 1944
77	Josiah Cohen	November 23, 1944
78	Rudolph Kauffman	November 29, 1944

Table 1. continued

Yard Hull No.	Name	Launch Date
79	James H. Price	December 9, 1944
80	William L. McLean	December 13, 1944
81	Edwin J. Berwind	December 16, 1944
82	William W. Seaton	December 22, 1944
83	Mack Bruton Bryan	December 30, 1944
84	William Terry Howell	January 6, 1945
85	William Leroy Gamble	January 13, 1945
86	Harry Kirby	January 20, 1945
87	Arlie Clark	January 27, 1945
88	Thomas W. Murray	January 31, 1945

Table 2. Coastal Cargo Vessels (C1-M-AV1)

Yard Hull No.	Name	Launch Date
1	Check Knot	January 1945[a]
2	Becket Bend	January 26, 1945
3	Flemish Knot	February 9, 1945
4	Snakehead	February 24, 1945
5	Linksplice	March 17, 1945
6	Diamond Hitch	March 1945[a]
7	Persian Knot	April 5, 1945
8	Marline Bend	April 13, 1945
9	Ring Hitch	April 23, 1945
10	Grass Knot	April 30, 1945
11	Sailmaker's Splice	May 14, 1945
12	Long Eye	June 6, 1945
13	Crossing Knot	June 19, 1945
14	Solid Sinnet	June 30, 1945
15	Flat Knot	July 11, 1945
16	Horseshoe Splice	July 14, 1945
17	Double Loop	September 6, 1945
18	Half Knot	September 14, 1945

[a]The exact launch dates for these ships were not recorded.

APPENDIX E

Monthly Wages for Merchant Seamen Sailing on the SS *James Oglethorpe*

Rate	Wage (U.S Dollars)	Rate	Wage (U.S Dollars)
Master	Not specified in shipping articles	Third Assistant Engineer	187.50
		Engine Cadets (2)	81.25
Chief Mate	250.00	Deck Engineer	117.50
Second Mate	212.50	Oilers (3)	110.00
Third Mate	187.50	Firemen/Watertenders (3)	110.00
Deck Cadets (2)	81.25	Wipers (2)	87.50
Radio Operator	137.50	Steward	157.50
Boatswain	122.50	Clerk	137.50
Able-Bodied Maintenance	110.00	Chief Cook	137.50
Able-Bodied Quartermaster (6)	110.00	Second Cook	122.00
Ordinary Seaman (3)	87.50	Assistant Cook	112.00
Chief Engineer	375.00	Messmen (3)	87.50
First Asst. Engineer	250.00	Utility (3)	87.50
Second Assistant Engineer	212.50		

APPENDIX F

Sponsors and Maids or Matrons of Honor for Liberty Ships Launched at the Southeastern Shipbuilding Corporation

Yard Hull No. 1
Ship: James Oglethorpe
Sponsor: Mrs. Walter F. George, wife of Georgia's U.S. senator
Maid or Matron of Honor: Mrs. Archibald B. Lovett,[a] wife of a U.S. district court judge

Yard Hull No. 2
Ship: George Handley
Sponsor: Mrs. Robert W. Groves, wife of the president of the Savannah Port Authority
Maid or Matron of Honor: Mrs. Sam L. Varnadoe, assistant to the coordinator of the Savannah-Chatham Defense Council

Yard Hull No. 3
Ship: James Jackson
Sponsor: Mrs. Charles S. Atwell, wife of the vice president of the Southeastern Shipbuilding Corporation
Maid or Matron of Honor: Mrs. J. R. Waiseman, wife of the assistant to the president of Southeastern

Yard Hull No. 4
Ship: George Walton
Sponsor: Mrs. Henry M. Dunn, wife of the director and local attorney for Southeastern
Maid or Matron of Honor: Mrs. Samuel A. Cann, sister of Mrs. Dunn

Yard Hull No. 5
Ship: Lyman Hall
Sponsor: Mrs. George A. Rentschler, wife of the chairman of the board of Southeastern
Maid or Matron of Honor: Unknown

Yard Hull No. 6
Ship: John Milledge
Sponsor: Mrs. L. R. Portney, wife of the assistant treasurer of Southeastern
Maid or Matron of Honor: Mrs. A. H. Vanderhoof, wife of the U.S. Navy hydrographic officer in Savannah

Yard Hull No. 7
Ship: Robert Toombs
Sponsor: Miss Natalie Todd Smith, daughter of the president of Southeastern
Maid or Matron of Honor: Miss Julia Butler, daughter of Col. and Mrs. E. George Butler

Yard Hull No. 8
Ship: Robert M. T. Hunter
Sponsor: Mrs. John I. Weeks, "wife of East Coast shipbuilder"
Maid or Matron of Honor: Mrs. Harry J. Fair, wife of the purchasing agent at Southeastern

Yard Hull No. 9
Ship: Crawford W. Long
Sponsor: Miss Merilyn Milton, daughter of the Southeastern director
Maid or Matron of Honor: Miss Audrey Dunn, daughter of the Southeastern director

Yard Hull No. 10
Ship: John C. Breckenridge
Sponsor: Mrs. Arnold A. Wilcox, descendent of John C. Breckenridge
Maid or Matron of Honor: Mrs. Charles S. Atwell, wife of the vice president of Southeastern

Yard Hull No. 11
Ship: Button Gwinnett
Sponsor: Mrs. P. L. Goldsboro, sister-in-law
of the treasurer and director of Southeastern
Maid or Matron of Honor: Miss Nancy
Goldsboro, daughter of the sponsor

Yard Hull No. 12
Ship: Felix Grundy
Sponsor: Mrs. J. F. McInnis, wife of the
director of construction, East Coast, U.S.
Maritime Commission
Maid or Matron of Honor: Miss Mary
Evdemon, secretary to the comptroller at
Southeastern

Yard Hull No. 13
Ship: Langdon Cheves
Sponsor: Mrs. Patience Peterson, wife of
the U.S. congressman for Georgia's First
District Rep. Hugh Peterson and sister of
U.S. Senator Richard B. Russell
Maid or Matron of Honor: Mrs. A. S. Reid
"of Washington D.C."

Yard Hull No. 14
Ship: Nicholas Herkimer
Sponsor: Mrs. J. J. Stevenson, daughter of
the former Ohio congressman and South-
eastern legal adviser
Maid or Matron of Honor: Mrs. George
Hollister, wife of a Southeastern public
relations official

Yard Hull No. 15
Ship: Casimir Pulaski
Sponsor: Mrs. Remer Y. Lane "of Savannah"
Maid or Matron of Honor: Mrs. Jack E.
Cay Jr., "of Savannah"

Yard Hull No. 16
Ship: Hamlin Garland
Sponsor: Mrs. T. W. Langford, wife of
a Southeastern employee
Maid or Matron of Honor: Mrs. W. S.
Fulghum, sister of a Southeastern employee

Yard Hull No. 17
Ship: Andrew Pickens
Sponsor: Mrs. C. H. Crabtree, direct
descendant of Andrew Pickens
Maid or Matron of Honor: None[b]

Yard Hull No. 18
Ship: William L. Yancey
Sponsor: Mrs. William Burns, wife of
a Maritime Commission attorney
Maid or Matron of Honor: Mrs. M. T.
Osborne, secretary to a labor relations
official at Southeastern

Yard Hull No. 19
Ship: George Whitfield
Sponsor: Miss Dorothy Leach, daughter of
an assistant foreman of the welding depart-
ment at Southeastern
Maid or Matron of Honor: Mrs. J. R.
Cowart, wife of an assistant foreman of the
welding department at Southeastern

Yard Hull No. 20
Ship: Joseph E. Brown
Sponsor: Mrs. Thomas H. Fowler, daughter
of the president of Southeastern
Maid or Matron of Honor: Mrs. Edgar
Hart, a burner at Southeastern

Yard Hull No. 21
Ship: Dudley M. Hughes
Sponsor: Mrs. Denise Schley, wife of Maj.
Gen. Julian Larcombe Schley
Maid or Matron of Honor: Mrs. R. L.
Schley, sister-in-law of sponsor's husband

Yard Hull No. 22
Ship: Jerome K. Jones
Sponsor: Miss Joan Jones, granddaughter
of Jerome K. Jones
Maid or Matron of Honor: Mrs. W. J.
Cooney, wife of the vice president of the
Georgia Federation of Labor

Yard Hull No. 23
Ship: Hoke Smith
Sponsor: Miss Sallie Cook, president of the
Georgia 4H Council
Maid or Matron of Honor: Miss Lottie
Gay, vice president of the Georgia 4H
Council

Yard Hull No. 24
Ship: William Black Yates
Sponsor: Miss Grace Tully, private
secretary to President Franklin D. Roosevelt
Maid or Matron of Honor: Miss Audrey
Turner, White House staff member

Yard Hull No. 25
Ship: James H. Couper
Sponsor: Mrs. Myrtle L. Cowart, a layout
pusher in the Southeastern fabrication shop
Maid or Matron of Honor: Mrs. E. J.
Hughes, a shipfitter at Southeastern

Yard Hull No. 26
Ship: Joseph Habersham
Sponsor: Mrs. W. Spencer Connerat, a
direct descendent of Joseph Habersham
Maid or Matron of Honor: Miss Mary
Crisfield, sister of the sponsor

Yard Hull No. 27
Ship: Joseph H. Martin
Sponsor: Mrs. William Perrott, wife of
the Southeastern vice president
Maid or Matron of Honor: Mrs. J. R.
Wakeman, wife of the assistant to the
president of Southeastern

Yard Hull No. 28
Ship: Robert Fechner
Sponsor: Mrs. Robert Fechner, wife of
Robert Fechner
Maid or Matron of Honor: Mrs. Clarence
E. Weaver, sister of the sponsor

Yard Hull No. 29
Ship: Charles C. Jones
Sponsor: Mrs. Hilmer Lundbeck, wife of
the Southeastern director
Maid or Matron of Honor: Unknown

Yard Hull No. 30
Ship: Florence Martus
Sponsor: Mrs. J. Rogers Cohan, wife of the
local manager of maintenance and repair
for the War Shipping Administration
Maid or Matron of Honor: Mrs. Roy J.
Baugh, daughter of the sponsor

Yard Hull No. 31
Ship: Charles H. Herty
Sponsor: Mrs. Sidney D. Walton, sister of
the Southeastern chairman of the board
Maid or Matron of Honor: Mrs. Joseph
Page, "of Detroit"

Yard Hull No. 32
Ship: John E. Ward
Sponsor: Mrs. Ethelbert Wakefield, wife of
the New York attorney for Southeastern
Maid or Matron of Honor: Unknown

Yard Hull No. 33
Ship: Edwin L. Godkin
Sponsor: Ens. Josephine Butler, WAVE
Maid or Matron of Honor: Ens. Julia Butler,
WAVE and sister of the sponsor

Yard Hull No. 34
Ship: A. Frank Lever
Sponsor: Mrs. A. Frank Lever, widow of
A. Frank Lever
Maid or Matron of Honor: Unknown

Yard Hull No. 35
Ship: Thomas Wolfe
Sponsor: Mrs. Nonnie Skinner, senior
keypunch operator in the tabulating depart-
ment at Southeastern
Maid or Matron of Honor: Miss Rosemary
Walsh, senior clerk in the payroll depart-
ment at Southeastern

Yard Hull No. 36
Ship: Louis A. Godey (Samvannah)
Sponsor: Mrs. J. R. Wakeman, wife of an
assistant to the president of Southeastern
Maid or Matron of Honor: Unknown

Yard Hull No. 37
Ship: Ben Robertson
Sponsor: Mrs. Julian Longley, sister of Ben
Robertson
Maid or Matron of Honor: Mrs. Snyder
Atwell, wife of the director of personnel at
Southeastern

Yard Hull No. 38
Ship: Samuel T. Darling
Sponsor: Mrs. Ernest Dupont Jr., daughter of Samuel T. Darling
Maid or Matron of Honor: Mrs. J. W. Middleton, wife of the president of Smith and Kenny Steamship Lines

Yard Hull No. 39
Ship: Isaac S. Hopkins
Sponsor: Miss Ruth Hopkins, daughter of Isaac S. Hopkins
Maid or Matron of Honor: Mrs. M. L. Brittain, wife of the president of the Georgia Institute of Technology

Yard Hull No. 40
Ship: Samhorn
Sponsor: Mrs. Joseph F. Johnson, wife of the principal hull inspector for the U.S. Maritime Commission at Southeastern
Maid or Matron of Honor: Miss Mary E. Jones, secretary to the hull inspector

Yard Hull No. 41
Ship: A. Mitchell Palmer
Sponsor: Mrs. A. Mitchell Palmer, widow of A. Mitchell Palmer
Maid or Matron of Honor: Mrs. George Crawford, "of New York"

Yard Hull No. 42
Ship: Samdart
Sponsor: Mrs. Albert E. Thiele, "of Scarsdale, N.Y."
Maid or Matron of Honor: Mrs. R. P. Darsey Jr., chief telephone operator at Southeastern

Yard Hull No. 43
Ship: John E. Sweet
Sponsor: Mrs. Homer J. Lohse, wife of the principal machinery inspector at Southeastern
Maid or Matron of Honor: Mrs. D. O. McIntyre, secretary to the machinery inspector

Yard Hull No. 44
Ship: Clark Howell
Sponsor: Mrs. Clark Howell Jr., daughter-in-law of Clark Howell
Maid or Matron of Honor: Mrs. Albert Howell, sister-in-law of the sponsor

Yard Hull No. 45
Ship: Earl Layman
Sponsor: Mrs. C. D. Layman, mother of Earl Layman
Maid or Matron of Honor: Miss Josephine Munsona, fitter in the fabricating shop at Southeastern

Yard Hull No. 46
Ship: John A. Treutlen
Sponsor: Mrs. G. Philip Morgan, wife of Philip Morgan, who sold pilings for yard foundations
Maid or Matron of Honor: Unknown

Yard Hull No. 47
Ship: Ben A. Ruffin
Sponsor: Mrs. Ben A. Ruffin, widow of Ben A. Ruffin
Maid or Matron of Honor: Mrs. T. Martin Holloway, daughter of the sponsor

Yard Hull No. 48
Ship: William D. Hoxie
Sponsor: Mrs. William D. Hoxie, widow of William D. Hoxie
Maid or Matron of Honor: Miss Janey Louise Middleton, granddaughter of the sponsor

Yard Hull No. 49
Ship: Samcebu
Sponsor: Mrs. A. Burton Closson, "of Cincinnati"
Maid or Matron of Honor: Miss Emma Grace Snead, secretary in the purchasing department at Southeastern

Yard Hull No. 50
Ship: Harry L. Glucksman
Sponsor: Mrs. Celia W. Glucksman, widow of Harry L. Glucksman
Maid or Matron of Honor: Miss Evelyn Kaminsky, secretary to the head of the rigging and erections department at Southeastern

Yard Hull No. 51

Ship: Juliette Low

Sponsor: Mrs. Samuel C. Lawrence, niece of Juliette Gordon Low and the first registered Girl Scout in America

Maid or Matron of Honor: Mrs. Thomas M. Johnson, president of the Girl Scout Association of Savannah

Yard Hull No. 52

Ship: Francis S. Bartow (Themistocles)

Sponsor: Miss Virginia Walton Purse, employee at Southeastern and past president of the Winnie Davis Chapter of the Children of the Confederacy

Maid or Matron of Honor: Mrs. Leon W. Johnson, wife of the Brig. Gen. Leon W. Johnson, who had been awarded the Medal of Honor

Yard Hull No. 53

Ship: Jacob Sloat Fassett

Sponsor: Mrs. Jennie Fassett Nevin, daughter of Jacob Sloat Fassett

Maid or Matron of Honor: Miss Melba Markham, women's counselor at Southeastern

Yard Hull No. 54

Ship: Richard Upjohn

Sponsor: Mrs. Philip Naylor Israel, "of Washington D.C."

Maid or Matron of Honor: Mrs. Henry Kavenel, "of Chevy Chase, Md."

Yard Hull No. 55

Ship: William G. Lee

Sponsor: Mrs. Helen Baker Beckman, great niece of William G. Lee

Maid or Matron of Honor: Mrs. E. Kenneth Baker, mother of the sponsor and a niece of William G. Lee

Yard Hull No. 56

Ship: Ruben Dario

Sponsor: Sra. Lillian Somoza de Seville-Sacasa, daughter of the president of Nicaragua and wife of Nicaragua's ambassador to the United States

Maid or Matron of Honor: Mrs. Charles Ellis Jr., "of Savannah"

Yard Hull No. 57

Ship: Benjamin Brown French

Sponsor: Mrs. Carl H. Claudy, wife of the past grandmaster of the Masonic Grand Lodge of Washington, D.C.

Maid or Matron of Honor: Mrs. Arthur W. Harrington, secretary to the general manager of Southeastern

Yard Hull No. 58

Ship: Stephen Leacock

Sponsor: Mrs. John E. Bulloch, wife of a member of the firm serving as chief council for Southeastern

Maid or Matron of Honor: Miss Eugenia Elaine Willis, clerk in the International Business Machines department at Southeastern

Yard Hull No. 59

Ship: Charles A. Keffer

Sponsor: Miss Inez Mikel, a 4H member from Tennessee

Maid or Matron of Honor: Mrs. Corine L. Cobb, secretary to the welding foreman at Southeastern

Yard Hull No. 60

Ship: Risden Tyler Bennett

Sponsor: Mrs. Mary Bennett Little, daughter of Risden Tyler Bennett

Maid or Matron of Honor: Mrs. Kenneth Weeks, niece of the sponsor, and Miss Sarah Dabney Little, granddaughter of the sponsor

Yard Hull No. 61

Ship: Alexander R. Shepherd

Sponsor: Mrs. Arthur S. Chadwick, sister of the secretary of the Maritime Commission

Maid or Matron of Honor: Mrs. A. J. Williams, wife of the secretary of the Maritime Commission

Yard Hull No. 62

Ship: James Swan

Sponsor: Mrs. H. Harvey, wife of superintendent of the burning department at Southeastern

Maid or Matron of Honor: Mrs. Edra Bruton, secretary to the superintendent of the burning department

Yard Hull No. 63
Ship: Martha Berry
Sponsor: Mrs. Virginia Campbell, niece of Martha Berry
Maid or Matron of Honor: Mrs. William Henry, former secretary to Martha Berry

Yard Hull No. 64
Ship: Frank P. Walsh
Sponsor: Miss Ruth Harrison, clerk in the timekeeping department at Southeastern
Maid or Matron of Honor: Miss Leila R. Trowell, secretary to the superintendent of the tool room at Southeastern

Yard Hull No. 65
Ship: Floyd Gibbons
Sponsor: Mrs. Zelda Gibbons Mayer, sister of Floyd Gibbons
Maid or Matron of Honor: Mrs. Donald Gibbons, sister-in-law of Floyd Gibbons

Yard Hull No. 66
Ship: Jonas Lie
Sponsor: Mrs. S. R. Sharpton, sister of Senator Richard B. Russell
Maid or Matron of Honor: Mrs. W. E. Penney, niece of the sponsor

Yard Hull No. 67
Ship: John P. Harris
Sponsor: Mrs. Eleanor H. Harris, widow of John P. Harris
Maid or Matron of Honor: Mrs. Edwin Zurhorst, daughter of John P. Harris

Yard Hull No. 68
Ship: Richard Coulter
Sponsor: Miss Emma Coulter, granddaughter of Richard Coulter and a WASP service pilot
Maid or Matron of Honor: Mrs. Richard Coulter, mother of the sponsor

Yard Hull No. 69
Ship: Addie Bagley Daniels
Sponsor: Miss Elizabeth B. Daniels, granddaughter of Addie Bagley Daniels
Maid or Matron of Honor: Miss Patricia B. Daniels, granddaughter of Addie Bagley Daniels

Yard Hull No. 70
Ship: William H. Edwards
Sponsor: Mrs. Herbert K. Twitchell, sister of William H. Edwards
Maid or Matron of Honor: Unknown

Yard Hull No. 71
Ship: Joseph Murgas
Sponsor: Mrs. Bayard Kilgore, "of Cincinnati"
Maid or Matron of Honor: Mrs. Louise Swann, "of New York"

Yard Hull No. 72
Ship: Milton J. Foreman
Sponsor: Mrs. Harry J. Fair, wife of a Southeastern purchasing agent
Maid or Matron of Honor: Miss Lillian M. Meitzler, senior tabulator in the International Business Machines department at Southeastern

Yard Hull No. 73
Ship: Joseph S. McDonagh
Sponsor: Miss Mary A. McDonagh, sister of Joseph S. McDonagh
Maid or Matron of Honor: Mrs. Alice E. Britt, "of Brooklyn"

Yard Hull No. 74
Ship: Josiah Tattnall
Sponsor: Miss Abby Milton, daughter of the Southeastern director
Maid or Matron of Honor: Miss Ruth Harrison, college roommate of the sponsor

Yard Hull No. 75
Ship: Moina Michael
Sponsor: Miss Mary Florence Michael, great-niece of Moina Michael
Maid or Matron of Honor: Mrs. Schley Howard Jr., niece of Moina Michael

Yard Hull No. 76
Ship: Robert Parrot
Sponsor: Mrs. Burnham Carter, wife of "advertising firm partner" at Southeastern
Maid or Matron of Honor: Mrs. W. A. McCoy, wife of plant engineer at Southeastern

Yard Hull No. 77
Ship: Josiah Cohen
Sponsor: Mrs. Marion A. O'Connor, wife of the labor relations director at Southeastern
Maid or Matron of Honor: Mrs. Paul T. Blanton, wife of the assistant to the chief planner at Southeastern

Yard Hull No. 78
Ship: Rudolph Kauffman
Sponsor: Mrs. Rudolph Max Kauffman, daughter-in-law of Rudolph Kauffman
Maid or Matron of Honor: Mrs. Godfrey W. Kauffman, wife of a grandson of Rudolph Kauffman

Yard Hull No. 79
Ship: James H. Price
Sponsor: Mrs. Louise Ware, "of Winnetka, Ill."
Maid or Matron of Honor: Mrs. Thomas Ware, daughter-in-law of the sponsor

Yard Hull No. 80
Ship: William L. McLean
Sponsor: Mrs. Harold Palmer, mother of the news carrier who won a war stamp sales contest in order to have the ship named after him
Maid or Matron of Honor: Mrs. J. Raymond Sherlock, wife of the personnel director at Southeastern

Yard Hull No. 81
Ship: Edwin J. Berwind
Sponsor: Mrs. Henry J. Ross, wife of the general hull superintendent at Southeastern
Maid or Matron of Honor: Mrs. M. J. Brennan, wife of the assistant general hull superintendent at Southeastern

Yard Hull No. 82
Ship: William W. Seaton
Sponsor: Mrs. H. C. Smith, wife of a shipwright foreman at Southeastern
Maid or Matron of Honor: Mrs. George M. Brannon, wife of an assistant shipwright foreman at Southeastern

Yard Hull No. 83
Ship: Mack Bruton Bryan
Sponsor: Miss Mary Jane Lundbeck, daughter of "Southeastern sponsor"
Maid or Matron of Honor: Miss Clare Lundbeck, sister of the sponsor

Yard Hull No. 84
Ship: William Terry Howell
Sponsor: Mrs. Claire Louise Howell, widow of William Terry Howell
Maid or Matron of Honor: Miss Carolyn Frances Hall, a shipfitter at Southeastern

Yard Hull No. 85
Ship: William Leroy Gamble
Sponsor: Mrs. Florence M. Gamble, widow of William Leroy Gamble
Maid or Matron of Honor: Mrs. L. S. Mason, a pipefitter at Southeastern

Yard Hull No. 86
Ship: Harry Kirby
Sponsor: Mrs. Frank Fordham, wife of a member of the timekeeping department at Southeastern
Maid or Matron of Honor: Mrs. C. R. Winge, wife of the shipfitter inspector at Southeastern

Yard Hull No. 87
Ship: Arlie Clark
Sponsor: Mrs. Robert E. Banks, wife of the industrial relations council at Southeastern
Maid or Matron of Honor: Mrs. J. Milledge Cummings, secretary to the Industrial Relations Council

Yard Hull No. 88
Ship Thomas W. Murray
Sponsor: Mrs. Dorothy Murray, widow of Thomas W. Murray
Maid or Matron of Honor: Sgt. Cecile Bordelon, WAC, voted "G.I. Jane" of Hunter Army Airfield

---

[a]Following the convention of the time, newspaper and newsletter accounts of ships' launchings generally identified married women only by their husband's names.

[b] The sponsor's daughters, Olga and Emily Crabtree, and the sponsor's nephew, Stephane Turner, were named as "attendants."

APPENDIX G

Steamship Company Assignments for Liberty Ships Built by the Southeastern Shipbuilding Corporation

South Atlantic Steamship Company

Yard Hull No.	Ship
1	James Oglethorpe
3	James Jackson
5	Lyman Hall
6	John Milledge
7	Robert Toombs
8	Robert M. T. Hunter
11	Button Gwinnett
12	Felix Grundy
17	Andrew Pickens
22	Jerome K. Jones
28	Robert Fechner
32	John E. Ward
35	Thomas Wolfe
46	John A. Treutlen
51	Juliette Low
55	William G. Lee
58	Stephen Leacock
59	Charles A. Keffer
62	James Swan
65	Floyd Gibbons

International Freighting Company

Yard Hull No.	Ship
9	Crawford W. Long
25	James H. Couper
56	Ruben Dario
72	Milton J. Foreman
84	William Terry Howell

J. H. Winchester & Co.

Yard Hull No.	Ship
10	John C. Breckenridge
18	William L. Yancey
29	Charles C. Jones
71	Joseph Murgas

Stockard Steamship Company

Yard Hull No.	Ship
48	William D. Hoxie
53	Jacob Sloat Fassett
75	Moina Michael

T. J. Stevenson & Co.

Yard Hull No.	Ship
24	William Black Yates
54	Richard Upjohn
78	Rudolph Kauffman
82	William W. Seaton

Overlakes Freight Company

Yard Hull No.	Ship
68	Richard Coulter
73	Joseph S. McDonagh
77	Josiah Cohen

British Ministry of War Transport

Yard Hull No.	Ship
36	Louis A. Godey (Samvannah)
40	Samhorn
42	Samdart
49	Samcebu

Dickman Wright & Pugh

Yard Hull No.	Ship
76	Robert Parrot
79	James H. Price
87	Arlie Clark

A. H. Bull Steamship Company

Yard Hull No.	Ship
19	George Whitfield
37	Ben Robertson
70	William H. Edwards

Black Diamond Steamship Company

Yard Hull No.	Ship
43	John E. Sweet
63	Martha Berry
67	John P. Harris

Agwilines Inc.

Yard Hull No.	Ship
13	Langdon Cheves
14	Nicholas Herkimer
66	Jonas Lie

Wessall Duvall & Company

Yard Hull No.	Ship
27	Joseph H. Martin
74	Josiah Tattnall

Polarus Steamship Company

Yard Hull No.	Ship
30	Florence Martus
45	Earl Layman

Merchants and Miners Transportation Co.

Yard Hull No.	Ship
4	George Walton
50	Harry L. Glucksman
83	Mack Bruton Bryan

Luckenbach Steamship Company

Yard Hull No.	Ship
33	Edwin L. Godkin
57	Benjamin Brown French

States Marine Lines

Yard Hull No.	Ship
34	A. Frank Lever
69	Addie Bagley Daniels

Greek Government in Exile

Yard Hull No.	Ship
52	Francis S. Bartow (Themistocles)

Isbrandsten Steamship Co.

Yard Hull No.	Ship
39	Isaac S. Hopkins
41	A. Mitchell Palmer

American Export Lines

Yard Hull No.	Ship
23	Hoke Smith

Marine Transport Lines

Yard Hull No.	Ship
2	George Handley
47	Ben A. Ruffin

North American and Gulf Steamship Co.

Yard Hull No.	Ship
16	Hamlin Garland

United Fruit Company

Yard Hull No.	Ship
15	Casimir Pulaski

Grace Lines

Yard Hull No.	Ship
21	Dudley M. Hughes
38	Samuel T. Darling

Isthmian Steamship Company

Yard Hull No.	Ship
26	Joseph Habersham

Cosmopolitan Steamship Co.

Yard Hull No.	Ship
20	Joseph E. Brown
88	Thomas W. Murray

Union Sulfur Company

Yard Hull No.	Ship
85	William Leroy Gamble

American West African Line

Yard Hull No.	Ship
60	Risden Tyler Bennett

Blidberg Rothchild

Yard Hull No.	Ship
86	Harry Kirby

A. I. Burbank & Co.

Yard Hull No.	Ship
61	Alexander R. Shepherd

Wilmore Steamship Co.

Yard Hull No.	Ship
81	Edwin J. Berwind

Parry Navigation Company

Yard Hull No.	Ship
44	Clark Howell

U.S. Navigation Co.

Yard Hull No.	Ship
31	Charles H. Herty

R. A. Nichol Company

Yard Hull No.	Ship
64	Frank P. Walsh

William J. Roundtree Co.

Yard Hull No.	Ship
80	William L. McLean

NOTES

CHAPTER 1. THE "JIM"

1. Thomas Causton to his wife, March 12, 1733, in *General Oglethorpe's Georgia: Colonial Letters, 1733–1743*, vol. 1, ed. Mills Lane (Savannah, Ga.: Beehive Press, 1975), 9.

2. Anna C. Hunter, "Liberty Ship Is Launched," *Savannah Evening Press*, November 20, 1942.

3. Ibid.

4. Ibid.

5. Ibid.

6. Sarah Wilkerson, "New Vessel Joins Bridge of Ships," *Savannah Morning News*, November 21, 1942, 12.

CHAPTER 2. NEW YORK, NEW YORK

1. Sloan Taylor, "The Sea Baptizes a Liberty Ship," *New York Sunday News*, March 28, 1943, 6.

2. Ibid.

3. Ibid.

4. Ibid.

5. Ibid.

6. Ibid.

7. Martin Middlebrook, *Convoy: The Battles for SC.122 and HX.229* (London: Penguin Books, 1978), 87.

8. Ibid.

9. Ibid.

CHAPTER 3. THIS SHIP WILL DO US VERY WELL

1. Peter Elphick, *Liberty: The Ships That Won the War* (Annapolis, Md.: Naval Institute Press, 2001), 65.

2. John Gorley Bunker, *Liberty Ships: The Ugly Ducklings of World War II*, reprint (Salem, N.H.: Ayer Co., 1991), 6.

3. *Savannah Morning News*, April 5, 1941.

4. "Ships Built Here Be for Britain," *Savannah Morning News*, April 4, 1941.

5. "Crowley Finishes Giving Testimony," *Savannah Morning News*, July 15, 1942, 12.

CHAPTER 4. IF YOU BUILD IT, THEY WILL COME . . . AND BUILD SHIPS

1. Margaret Curtis, "War Work Done in Savannah," *Savannah Morning News*, May 8, 1945, 3.

2. "Shipyard Buys Hundred Acre Tract," *Savannah Morning News*, May 7, 1941, 14.

3. Bill Fielder, "Trees and Grass to Aid Protection of New Project," *Savannah Morning News*, September 14, 1942.

4.   *Savannah Morning News*, March 10, 1942.
5.   Ibid.
6.   Want Ads, *Sou'Easter*, June 1, 1945.
7.   Want Ads, *Sou'Easter*, May, 15, 1945.
8.   W. L. Marshall, principal construction auditor, letter to J. A. Hosnick, Construction Audit Section, U.S. Maritime Commission, December 24, 1941.
9.   Want Ads, *Sou'Easter*, December 1, 1943.
10. "Police Busy Rounding Up Speeders," *Sou'Easter*, August 15, 1943.

CHAPTER 5. WENDY THE WELDER AT SOUTHEASTERN
1.   "Expert Welders," *Sou'Easter*, February 15, 1944, 15.
2.   Quoted in Paul D. Casdorph, *Let the Good Times Roll: Life at Home in America during World War II* (New York: Paragon House, 1991), 85.
3.   Bob Bach and Ginger Mercer, eds., *Johnny Mercer: The Life, Times and Song Lyrics of Our Huckleberry Friend* (Secaucus, N.J.: Lyle Stuart, Inc., 1982), 114.
4.   Charles Wollenberg, *Marinship at War: Shipbuilding and Social Change in Wartime Sausalito* (Berkley, Calif.: Western Heritage Press, 1990), 62–63.
5.   Ibid., 63.
6.   *Savannah Morning News* (supplied by Bob Fennel).
7.   *Wollenberg, Marinship at War*, 65.
8.   *Sou'Easter*, July 1, 1943.
9.   Joseph C. Goulden, *The Best Years, 1945–1950* (New York: Atheneum, 1976), 42.

CHAPTER 6. YOU WERE A LABORER NO MATTER WHAT SKILLS YOU HAD
1.   Frederic C. Lane, *Ships for Victory: A History of Shipbuilding under the U.S. Maritime Commission in World War II* (Baltimore: Johns Hopkins Press, 1951), 252.
2.   Ibid.
3.   *Sou'Easter*, November 1, 1943.
4.   *Sou'Easter*, February 15, 1944, 5.
5.   "Sober Threesome," *Sou'Easter*, June 15, 1945, 10.
6.   "Spearmen," *Sou'Easter*, August 1, 1944.
7.   *Sou'Easter*, May 1, 1943.
8.   *Sou'Easter*, August 1, 1943.

CHAPTER 7. IF YOU DON'T JOIN, YOU DON'T WORK
1.   "Southeastern May Close Today," *Savannah Morning News*, July 24, 1945.
2.   Ibid.
3.   "Hope to Avert Closing of Yard," *Savannah Evening Press*, July 24, 1945.
4.   "Shipyard Outlook Seen as Improving," *Savannah Morning News*, July 27, 1945.
5.   "S.E. Shipyards Operating Again," *Savannah Morning News*, July 28, 1945.

CHAPTER 8. DOING THE SAME THING OVER AND OVER
1.   Lane, *Ships for Victory*, 454.
2.   Ibid., 299.
3.   "A Brief History," *Sou'Easter*, November 9, 1945.

4.   *Savannah Morning News*, May 23, 1942, 12.

5.   *Sou'Easter*, April 1, 1945, 6.

6.   *Savannah Morning News*, May 23, 1944.

7.   *Sou'Easter*, January 15, 1944.

8.   *Sou'Easter*, August 1, 1943.

9.   "Horseplay in Defense Work Scoured by FBI," *Savannah Morning News*, October 3, 1943.

10. Lane, *Ships for Victory*, 299.

11. Wollenberg, *Marinship at War*, 1990, 49.

CHAPTER 9. YOU CAN'T SPELL VICTORY WITH AN ABSENT *T*

1.   "Progress Noted in Shipbuilding," *Savannah Morning News*, January 26, 1943, 12.

2.   *Sou'Easter*, November 15, 1944.

3.   "To the 1,288 Men Who Are Absent Every Day," *Sou'Easter*, August 15, 1943.

4.   "Draft Board Seeks Absentees," *Sou'Easter*, May 1, 1943.

5.   "Do You Believe It," *Sou'Easter*, August 15, 1943, 12.

6.   Lane, *Ships for Victory*, 449.

7.   Ibid.

8.   "Riggers Shaded by Death When Cable Breaks," *Sou'Easter*, May 15, 1945, 3.

9.   *Sou'Easter*, April 15, 1944, 10.

10. "Riding Gantry Fall Found Dull," *Sou'Easter*, May 1, 1943, 11.

11. "Big Crane Fall at Southeastern," *Savannah Morning News*, April 11, 1943, 36.

12. Winn C. Upchurch, "Around the Yard," *Sou'Easter*, October 15, 1945, 8.

CHAPTER 10. WHO ARE ALL THESE CHAPS?

1.   William G. Schofield, *Eastward the Convoys* (Chicago: Rand McNally & Co., 1965), 54.

2.   Bunker, *Liberty Ships*.

3.   Felix Riesenberg Jr., *Sea War: The Story of the U. S. Merchant Marine in World War II* (New York: Rinehart & Co., 1956), 84.

4.   Ibid., 91.

5.   "Ogelthorpe to Be Ship's Name," *Savannah Morning News*, April 20, 1942, 12.

6.   *Sou'Easter*, April 20, 1942, 12.

7.   Peter Wyatt, Dartmouth, England, letter to the author, March 1, 1992.

CHAPTER 11. FIFTEEN MINUTES OF FAME

1.   Agnes E. Meyer, *Journey Through Chaos* (New York: Harcourt Brace & Company, 1943), 98.

2.   Elphick, *Liberty*, 274–75.

3.   "Shipwright Saves the Day," *Sou'Easter*, July 1, 1944, 3.

4.   Sou'Easter, July 15, 1943, 3.

5.   "He Wouldn't Trade His Job," *Sou'Easter*, December 1, 1943.

6.   "Vessel Honors Southern Leader," *Savannah Evening Press*, July 22, 1944.

7.   Lane, *Ships for Victory*, 69.

8.   Lane, *Ships for Victory*, 70.

9.   Harry G. Proctor, "The Wm. L. McLean Is Launched," *Philadelphia Evening*

Bulletin, December 13, 1944, 3.

10. "S. S. Addie Bagley Daniels Slides Down the Ways," *Savannah Morning News*, September 29, 1944, 14.

11. William F. O'Toole, letter to Mrs. Samuel Lawrence, January 23, 1945.

12. Proctor, "The Wm. L. McLean," 4.

13. Ibid.

14. "S. S. Button Gwinnett Slides Gracefully Down to the Savannah Sunday," *Savannah Morning News*, May 3, 1943, 10.

15. "Vessel Launched by Southeastern," *Savannah Morning News*, August 28, 1943.

16. Sarah W. Wilkenson, "Records Fall as Ship Is Launched," *Savannah Morning News*, November 26, 1943, 10.

17. "Launching Is a Colorful Affair," *Savannah Evening Press*, February 2, 1944.

18. *Savannah Evening Press*, February 2, 1944.

CHAPTER 12. GETTING READY FOR WAR

1. *Sou'Easter*, May 5, 1943.

2. U.S. Navy, Armed Guard Report, SS *James Jackson*, Voyage No. 1, beginning March 26, 1943, by Ens. Ray Dyke (Washington, D.C.: National Archives).

3. Norman Howe Jr., letter to Mr. and Mrs. Norman Howe Sr., September 26, 1943.

4. Ibid.

5. Ibid.

6. The letters Capt. Norman Howe Jr. wrote home to his parents during June 1943 are in the author's collection.

7. Walter W. Jaffe, *The Last Liberty: The Biography of the SS Jeremiah O'Brien* (Palo Alto, Calif.: Glencannon Press, 1993), 236.

8. Bunker, *Liberty Ships*, 7.

9. U.S. Maritime Commission, Memorandum for File to Port Director, Port of Savannah, March 30, 1943.

CHAPTER 13. NEW YORK TO GREAT BRITAIN

1. Ash Gerecht, "Sinking of the S. S. Oglethorpe Is Recalled on Anniversary," *Savannah Morning News*, March 17, 1948.

2. Middlebrook, *Convoy*, 137.

3. Ibid., 150.

4. "Survivor Sinking James Oglethorpe at Southeastern," *Savannah Morning News*, January 1, 1944, 1.

CHAPTER 14. IT SOUNDED JUST LIKE A TWO-INCH FIRECRACKER

1. Jurgen Rohwer, *Axis Submarine Successes, 1939–1945* (Annapolis, Md.: Naval Institute Press, 1983), 152.

2. L. A. Sawyer and H. M. Mitchell, *The Liberty Ships: The History of the "Emergency" Type Cargo Ships Constructed in the United States during the Second World War*, 2nd ed. (Colchester, UK: Lloyds of London Press Ltd., 1985), 103; Arthur R. Moore, *A Careless Word . . . A Needless Sinking: A History of the Staggering Losses Suffered by the U.S. Merchant Marine, Both in Ships and Personnel, during World War Two* (Kings Point, N.Y.: American Merchant Marine Museum, 1990), 420.

3. Middlebrook, *Convoy*, 153.

4. Like so many fateful encounters in history, this was a chance meeting in every sense. Suppose Lieutenant Commander Luther had not taken it upon himself to order the course change the day before. Suppose that change had been made fifteen minutes before or after it was. Suppose U-boat headquarters had not relieved the five boats from the Raubgraf group when it did. And suppose the sailor on the deck of that ship had obeyed regulations and not lit his cigarette. Would the lookouts on the bridge of *U-653* have seen the convoy?

    Suppose, then, that the three convoys had been sent out at regular intervals, or that the British codes had been changed a month earlier. What would have been the outcome?

    War and history are full of such chance occurrences that determine when lives are spared or lost.

5. Jurgen Rohwer, *The Critical Convoy Battles of March 1943* (London: Ian Allen Ltd., 1977), 119.

6. Middlebrook, *Convoy*, 173.

7. Ibid., 170.

8. Ibid., 176.

9. Gerecht, "Sinking."

10. Ibid.

11. Sworn statement of William Ford, deck cadet, SS *James Oglethorpe*, April 20, 1943, 1.

12. Ibid.

13. Gerecht, "Sinking."

14. Sworn statement of William Ford, 1.

15. Ibid.

16. "Survivor Sinking," *Savannah Morning News*.

17. Gerecht, "Sinking."

18. Ibid.

19. Sworn statement of William Ford, 3.

20. Ibid.

21. Middlebrook, *Convoy*, 177.

22. Ibid.

23. Gerecht, "Sinking."

24. Sworn statement of William Ford, 2.

25. "Survivor Sinking," *Savannah Morning News*.

CHAPTER 15. ST. PATRICK'S DAY, 1943

1. It is difficult to determine how many and which crewmen were still on board the *Oglethorpe* at this point. British historian Martin Middlebrook wrote in *Convoy* that Captain Long, Second Mate Joseph Duke, and thirty-one other men were still on board. Engine Cadet Fajans, however, testified later that he saw Duke in the water and was sure that Duke had drowned.

    In *The Critical Convoy Battles of March 1943*, German historian Jurgen Rohwer indicated that the *Oglethorpe's* captain and "some 30" men remained on boarOut of a regular crew of seventy-two plus two U.S. Navy enlisted passengers, thirty were picked up by the *Beverly* and the *Pennywort*. Fajans identified nine men in the water who were never picked up, and William Brantley saw another jump for boat No. 6, miss, fall into the ocean, and disappear. That would make forty men accounted for, plus the others Fajans saw in the water but whose names he could not recall. It would also leave fewer than thirty-four men on board the ship. But because neither the numbers nor the identity of the men seen by Fajans, other than Captain Long, who spoke by hailer to the captain of one of the escorts, are known, it is impossible to tell which crewmen were still on board the ship.

2.   Sworn statement of William Ford, 2.

3.   Middlebrook, *Convoy*, 182.

4.   This view of the final moments of the *Oglethorpe* comes from German records re-searched by Jurgen Rohwer, the long time director of the Bibliothek fur Zeitgeschicte in Stuttgart. The account here draws from Rohwer's *The Critical Convoy Battles of March 1943*, which was published in 1977, and his *Axis Submarine Successes, 1939–1945*, which was first published in 1967 and then updated and translated into English in 1984.

      Martin Middlebrook, whose 1976 *Convoy: The Battle for SC.122 and HX.299* provides another well-researched and detailed account of the battle, states that the *Oglethorpe* was not torpedoed again. She was too far west to have been the victim of *U-91*, the boat that claimed to have sunk her, Middlebrook argued, and there were no other U-boat claims of sinkings for a ship in the area. According to Middlebrook, the *Oglethorpe* may have been more seriously damaged than first thought, or she may have foundered in a storm that passed through the area the next day, March 18. For whatever reason, the *Oglethorpe* never reached St. John's.

      No American records that might shed some light on this situation have been found. The principal witnesses to the *Oglethorpe's* sinking were on the ship herself, and none survived. While Rohwer's research indicates that the *Oglethorpe*—in catch ing up to the previously torpedoed *Eustis*—was sailing east instead of west as Captain Long had voiced the intention of doing, the German U-boat commander's description of the event was very clear and detailed. He was specific in stating that there were two ships. If that was the case, one of those ships would have to have been the *Oglethorpe*. No other ship from the convoy could have been at that location. They were all ac counted for as being elsewhere.

5.   *Savannah Morning News*, March 18, 1943.

6.   *Sou'Easter*, March 18, 1943, 11.

7.   The other merchant crewmen who were probably on board during the second attack on the *Oglethorpe* were Deck Cadet John Robert Laubert of Del Rio, Texas; Able-Bodied Seaman Charles Frank Puckett of Tarvorn, North Carolina; Able-Bodied Seaman Samuel Instant Bullard Jr., who was born in Savannah but lived in Alamo, Georgia; Able- Bodied Seaman Harold Samuel Smithson of Rutherford, New Jersey; Able-Bodied Seaman Floyd James Williams of Bellaire, Ohio; First Assistant Engineer Gilbert B. Parks, who was born in Savannah but lived in Beaumont, Texas; Wiper John J. Thomas of Melbourne, Florida; Stewart Carl Frederick Salzman of Norfolk, Virginia; Chief Cook Thomas Jefferson Thomas of Griffin, Georgia; Messman J. D. Carter of Lamont, Florida; Utilityman Charles Thomas White of Jacksonville, Florida; and Capt. Albert W. Long of Miami, Florida.

      The U.S. Navy Armed Guardsmen who were probably on the ship included Lt.(jg) James F. Bayne of Michigan, SM3 Russell Clyton Parrish of Virginia, SN1 Francis Aloysius Weed of Pennsylvania, SN2 Harold Franklin Daggs of Indiana, SN2 Kenneth Paul Dryer of Indiana, SN2 John DeFrancisco of Illinois, SN2 Maurice Joseph Demers of Massachusetts, SN2 Clyde William Pelton of Washington, SN2 William James Smith of Massachusetts, SN2 William Poe Sheaks of Washington, D.C., and SN3 Frank Loran Roales of Indiana.

    Also lost were two U.S. Navy enlisted men sailing on the *Oglethorpe* as passengers. The author has not been able to determine the identity of those two men.

8.   Middlebrook, *Convoy*, 96–97.

9.   Dan van der Vat, *The Atlantic Campaign: World War II's Greatest Struggle at Sea* (New York: Harper and Row, 1988), 322.

10.   Middlebrook, *Convoy*, 314.

11.   Ibid., 251.

12.   Ibid., 287.

13.   Sworn statement of William Ford, 2.

14.   Gerecht, "Sinking."

15.   J. C. Outler, director of the Division of Security and Communication, Navy Department, letter to Mr. Raymond Sullivan, South Atlantic Steamship Company, March 22, 1943.

16.   Commander, Naval Forces Europe, Daily Serial No. 25, March 16, 1943.

17.   Western Union telegram from Vice Adm. R. R. Waesche, commandant, U.S. Coast Guard, to Mrs. Bertie Von Dolteren, April 19, 1943, 6:34 PM.

18.   Mrs. Jernigan's request regarding the Gold Star insignia was forwarded to the War Shipping Administration, and while no record of a reply from that office has been found, she was probably given the information that a special flag had been approved for display by members of the immediate family of merchant mariners serving in the war. The flag displayed a white silhouette of a merchant ship at the top and a white star for each family member in the Merchant Marine. If the family member was killed or died while in the service, a small gold star was superimposed so that the white star would form a border. The flags were not issued by the WSA, but they could be purchased from companies manufacturing them according to the approved design.

19.   Lt. Cdr. R. H. Farinholt, U.S. Coast Guard, letter to Beatrice F. Parks, August 12, 1944.

20.   Ibid.

21.   Lt. Cdr. R. H. Farinholt, U.S. Coast Guard, letter to Miss Beatrice F. Parks, October 4, 1945.

22.   Cdr. P. G. Prins, chief, Merchant Vessel Personnel Records and Welfare Section, U.S. Coast Guard, letter to Miss Ava Mary Stevens, n.d.

23.   "More Seamen Are Reported Missing," *Savannah Morning News*, April 22, 1943, 14.

24.   "Splicer on Wet Dock Survived Sinking of 'James Oglethorpe,'" *Sou'Easter*, January 1, 1944, 1.

25.   Gerecht, "Sinking."

26.   Richard Hough, *The Longest Battle: The War at Sea, 1939–45* (London: Weidenfeld and Nicolson, 1986), 60.

CHAPTER 16. A SUBMARINE'S TORPEDO ENDED THE CAREER OF . . .

1.   War Shipping Administration, Advanced Release: Sunday Papers, February 25, 1945.

2.   U.S. Navy, Armed Guard Report, SS *Ruben Dario*, Voyage No. 3, beginning January

13,   1945, by Ens. Samuel N. Pritchard (Washington, D.C.: National Archives).

3.   U.S. Navy, Armed Guard Report, SS *James Jackson*.

4.   John M. Waters Jr., *Bloody Winter* (Annapolis, Md.: Naval Institute Press, 1994), 228.

5.   Preston Russell and Barbara Hines, *Savannah: A History of Her People Since 1733* (Savannah, Ga.: Frederick C. Bell, 1992), 72, 94.

6. Samuel Eliot Morison, *The Battle of the Atlantic*, vol. 1, *History of United States Naval Operations in World War II* (Boston: Little, Brown and Company, 1984), 345.

7. Malcolm F. Willoughby, *The U. S. Coast Guard in World War II* (Annapolis, Md.: Naval Institute Press, 1957), 201.

8. Robert Erwin Johnson, *Guardians of the Sea: History of the United States Coast Guard, 1915 to the Present* (Annapolis, Md.: Naval Institute Press, 1987).

9. Waters, *Bloody Winter*, 226.

10. W. A. Haskell, letter to the author, 1999.

11. U.S. Navy, Armed Guard Report, SS *Casimir Pulaski*, Voyage London to Normandy Beachhead, June 11, 1944, by Lt. (jg) Herbert K. Hurst (Washington, DC: National Archives).

12. U.S. Navy, Armed Guard Report, SS John E. Ward, Voyage No. 2, beginning June 7, 1944, by Ens. Leonard D. Hawley (Washington, D.C.: National Archives).

CHAPTER 17. A MIXED BLESSING

1. "New Victory Ships to Be Built in Savannah," *Savannah Morning News*, May 8, 1943, 12.

2. "Southeastern to Get Added Work," *Savannah Morning News*, January 18, 1944, 12.

3. Ibid.

4. Library of Congress, "War's End: VJ Day," *Experiencing War: Stories from the Veterans History Project*, May 10, 2005, http://www.loc.gov/vets/stories/vj-day. html.

5. U.S. Navy, Armed Guard Report, SS *Casimir Pulaski*, Voyage No. 8, beginning May 5, 1945, by Lt. Jack Sparks (Washington, D.C.: National Archives).

6. *Savannah Evening Press*, August 17, 1945, 18.

7. "Last S.E. Ship Goes Down the Ways," *Savannah Morning News*, September 15, 1945, 10.

8. Ibid.

9. "A Brief History," *Sou'Easter*, November 9, 1945, 2.

10. "U.S. Will Scrap S.E. Shipyards," *Savannah Morning News*, September 17, 1946, 16.

11. "City Buys Yard," *Savannah Morning News*, October 16, 1947, 18.

12. Ibid.

CHAPTER 18. THEN, AS CAMELOT, IT DISAPPEARED

1. Bunker, *Liberty Ships*, 200.

2. Sawyer and Mitchell, *Liberty Ships*, 165–66.

3. Ibid., 164.

4. Ibid., 165.

5. Ibid., 166.

6. *Savannah Morning News*, July 10, 1975.

7. "City Buys Yard," *Savannah Morning News*.

8. "'30' for the Sou'Easter," *Sou'Easter*, November 9, 1945, 18.

9. Bunker, *Liberty Ships*, 204.

10. The International Seafarer's Union, quoted in the *Savannah Morning News*, April 6, 1946.

SOURCES

A Note on Archival Sources

A number of archival collections were consulted during the writing of this book. The existing records of the Southeastern Shipbuilding Corporation, kept by the Georgia Historical Society (GHS) in Savannah, proved invaluable. Various U.S. Maritime Commission Production Division records regarding the operation of Southeastern were also consulted (http://www.archives.gov/research/guide-fed-records/groups/178.html#178.8).

General and specific information about the design and building of Liberty ships was culled from resources at Project Liberty Ship (http://www.liberty-ship.com), and Savannah's Ships of the Sea Maritime Museum (http://shipsofthesea.org). Additionally, the records of the Maritime War Emergency Board are maintained by the National Archives (http://www.archives.gov/research/guide-fed-records/groups/248.html#248.5).

Copies of the *Sou'Easter*, the in-house publication at Southeastern, were obtained from the Coastal Heritage Society in Savannah, Georgia, and microfiche copies of Georgia newspapers were reviewed at the Savannah Public Library. Photographs and information about Savannah during World War II were obtained from the GHS. Information regarding the purchase of the land on which Southeastern was built was drawn from files kept by Chatham County and the City of Savannah. Records relating to the condemnation proceedings against Savannah Shipyards, Inc., were obtained from the U.S. District Court for the Southern District of Georgia. Photographs and information regarding the construction of the housing projects built for Southeastern workers were taken from the Housing Authority of Savannah.

Correspondence among representatives of American Export Lines, South Atlantic Steamship Lines, and Southeastern provided information on the assignment of Savannah-built Liberty ships to shipping companies. Similarly, letters to and from Capt. William F. O'Toole of the SS *Juliette Low* and various girl scouts archived at the Juliette Gordon Low Birthplace in Savannah were reviewed.

Finally, information about and contact information for merchant seamen and Navy Armed Guardsmen was collected from the U.S. Merchant Marine Veterans of World War II (http://www.usmm.org/usmmv.html) and the U.S. Navy Armed Guard Center in Brooklyn, New York (http://www.armed-guard.com/about-ag.html).

INTERVIEWS AND PERSONAL CORRESPONDENCE

SHIPYARD WORKERS
Dewey "Shorty" Beasley
Wallace Beasley
Albert E. Blackburn Sr.
Jack W. Brady
Robert F. Brannen
Bertha W. Brown
Robert Cannon
Ed Carson
Edward Cetti
Ruby Clifton
N. H. "Nick" Creasy
Sue Donahue
Amelia Dreese
Jeff Dukes
Bob Fennel
Joe Gerbasi
Myrtice Hammock
W. A. Haskell
Nanthalee Hiott
Jimmy Hodges
Thelma Hodges
Leon W. Judy
Clinton E. Lance
Ida Royal McCullogh
Harold Miller
Thomas E. Nease
M. C. Nettles
Nathan H. Page
Red Pitts
H. O. "Buck" Rahn
Tracey Rainey
Walter Simmons
Robert "Buddy" Smith
Carolyn Strong
Peggy Strong, mother worked at
   South eastern Shipbuilding Corporation
Joe Switz
Carl Thompson
Joseph Williams
Sam Williams
Woodrow Williams

MERCHANT SEAMEN
United States
Gordon Bell

Richard W. Braithwaite
W. Burroughs
Edward Cetti
N. H. "Nick" Creasy
Robert Dickey
Paul J. Doyle
Adele Fleetwood, wife of Purser
   William Fleetwood
Terry Goodwin
Joe Harwell

Great Britain
Billy Joe Head
William Russell Hiers
Barbara Howe, wife of Capt. Norman Howe Jr.
Norman Howe Jr., letters to his parents,
   June 1943
Richard Philip Homm
Tom Houston
Charles D. Kromer
Peter Lange
August Lewis
Walter W. Luikart
Earl E. Martin
Ben MClendon
Neil J. Osburn
Alec G. Parker
Joe Ramsey
George Harrison Reid
Bill Schwartzhoff
Harold Scott
Kenneth Strickland
Stuart Swords
W. Clifford Thomas Jr.
Howard Vier Sr.
Al Williams
Dave Williams
Dorothy Wise, daughter of Anthony "Andy"
   Von Dolteren
Lawrence Wurtz
James Blears
A. M. Forbes
Ian Gorrie

U.S. COAST GUARD
Ed Halon

U.S. NAVY ARMED GUARD

Frank S. Baczuk
Henry A. "Hank" Burttschell Jr.
William Bushen
Dean E. Cain
Ken Caplan
Frank Capobianco
E. D. Denbinski
William G. Frick
Marilyn Fry, wife of Darwin Fry
Fred W. Goddard
Gerald C. Gormley
Frederic C. Lane
Thomas Mischler
John Pettry
Donald D. Royer
Clarence Scott
Ivan E. Shenberger
Raymond Stanley
John B. Taylor
Leo Usselman

ROYAL NAVY

Captain Peter Wyatt

SHIP SPONSORS AND MAIDS AND MATRONS OF HONOR

Josephine Connerat
Mary Crisfield
Evalynn Finnegan, daughter of Nonnie Skinner
Mary Lane

DOCK WORKERS

Charlie Gross
Dave Williams

OTHERS

Venetia Butler, participant in the scuttling of the SS *Addie Bagley Daniels*

Nancy Heffernan, photographer and participant in the scuttling of the SS *Addie Bagley Daniels*

Bill Hultgren, photographer participant in the scuttling of the SS *Addie Bagley Daniels*

Ed Morgan, helped cut and haul trees used as pilings at Southeastern Shipbuilding Corporation

OFFICIAL CORRESPONDENCE

U.S. Coast Guard, letters to and from the relatives of seamen lost at sea
U.S. Coast Guard, Merchant Marine Personnel Records and Welfare Section
U.S. Consulate General, Belfast, Northern Ireland, letters to and from the author
  regarding the port of Belfast during World War II
U.S. Department of Commerce, Bureau of Marine Inspection and Navigation
U.S. Department of the Navy, letters to and from the relatives of seamen lost

GOVERNMENT DOCUMENTS

United States

Administrative History: Arming of Merchant Ships and Naval Armed Guard Service in World War II. U. S. Naval Administration in World War II OPNAV-P421-514. Washington, D.C.: Office of Naval Operations, 1946. http://www.ibiblio.org/hyperwar/USN/Admin-Hist/172-ArmedGuards/index.html (accessed April 3, 2009).

Final Report of a Board of Inquiry Convened by Order of the Secretary of the Navy: The Design and Methods of Construction of Welded Steel Merchant Vessels. Washington, D.C.: Government Printing Office, 1946.

Fischer, Gerald J. *Statistical Summary of Shipbuilding under the U.S. Maritime Commission during World War II.* Historical Reports of the War Administration. Washington, D.C.: Government Printing Office, 1949.

Land, Emory Scott. *U.S. Merchant Marine at War.* Washington, D.C.: War Shipping Administration, 1946. http://ibiblio.net/hyperwar/ATO/Admin/WSAMMatWar-44/index.html.

Library of Congress. "War's End: VJ Day." *Experiencing War: Stories from the veterans History Project*, May 10, 2005. http://www.loc.gov/vets/stories/vj-day.html.

Operation and Maintenance of Main Boilers: U. S. Maritime Commission Vessels Design EC2-S-C1. New York: Combustion Engineering Co., Inc., n.d.

U.S. Congress. Senate. Special Committee Investigating the National Defense Program. *Additional Report of the Special Committee Investigating the National Defense Program Pursuant to S.Res. 71,* 77th Cong., 2d sess., January 15, 1942. Washington, D.C.: Government Printing Office, 1942.

U.S. Maritime Commission Supplement No. 12 to Administrative Order No. 33.

U.S. Maritime Commission Training Manual. Published for the Maritime Service. Cambridge, Md.: Cornell Maritime Press, 1943.

U.S. Maritime Commission, War Shipping Administration. *United States Merchant Marine Insignia and Honors Awards.* Washington, D.C.: Government Printing Office,1944.

U.S. Maritime Service. *Officers' Handbook.* Washington, D.C.: War Shipping Administration, 1944.

U.S. Merchant Ship Losses. Washington, D.C.: U.S. Coast Guard, n.d.

U.S. Navy. Armed Guard Report, SS *Casimir Pulaski*, Voyage London to Normandy Beachhead, June 11, 1944, by Lt. (jg) Herbert K. Hurst. Washington, D.C.: National Archives.

——. Armed Guard Report, SS *Casimir Pulaski*, Voyage No. 8, beginning May 5, 1945, by Lt. Jack Sparks. Washington, D.C.: National Archives.

——. Armed Guard Report, SS *John E. Ward*, Voyage No. 2, beginning June 7, 1944, by Ens. Leonard D. Hawley. Washington, D.C.: National Archives.

——. Armed Guard Report, SS *Ruben Dario*, Voyage No. 3, beginning January 13, 1945, by Ens. Samuel N. Pritchard. Washington, D.C.: National Archives.

——. Armed Guard Report, SS *James Jackson*, Voyage No. 1, beginning March 26, 1943, by Ens. Ray Dyke. Washington, D.C.: National Archives.

War Shipping Administration. *Merchant Marine Training, Federal Register* 8, January 9, 1943.

Warner, John C., and John H. Leeper. *Shipbuilding Research and Development.* Washington, D.C.: Maritime Transportation Research Board. National Research Council, 1973.

World War II Commemoration Committee. *World War II.* Fact Sheet. Washington, D.C.: Headquarters Department of the Army, 2005.

Great Britain

British Central Office of Information. *The Battle of the Atlantic.* London: His Majesty's Stationery Office, 1946.

British Merchant Vessels Lost or Damaged by Enemy Action during the Second World War. London: His Majesty's Stationary Office, 1947.

Director of Merchant Shipbuilding. *Notes on Merchant Ship Production in the United States of America: Report to the Admiralty.* London: Admiralty, November 3, 1942.

SECONDARY SOURCES

Books

Bach, Bob, and Ginger Mercer, eds. *Johnny Mercer: The Life, Times and Song Lyrics of Our Huckleberry Friend.* Secaucus, N.J.: Lyle Stewart Inc., 1982.

Bunker, John Gorley. *Liberty Ships: The Ugly Ducklings of World War II.* Reprint. Salem, N.H.: Ayer Co., 1991.

Carse, Robert. *The Long Haul: The United States Merchant Marine in World War II.* New York: W. W. Norton & Co., 1965.

Casdorph, Paul D. *Let the Good Times Roll: Life at Home in America during World War II.* New York: Paragon House, 1991.

Causton, Thomas. Thomas Causton to his wife, March 12, 1733. *In General Oglethorpe's Georgia: Colonial Letters, 1733–1743,* vol. 1, ed. Mills Lane. Savannah, Ga.: Beehive Press, 1975.

Edwards, Bernard. *The Merchant Navy Goes to War.* London: Robert Hale, 1990.

Elphick, Peter. *Liberty: The Ships That Won the War.* Annapolis, Md.: Naval Institute Press, 2001.

Gleichauf, Justin F. *Unsung Sailors: The Naval Armed Guard in World War II.* Annapolis, Md.: Naval Institute Press, Annapolis, 1990.

Goulden, Joseph C. *The Best Years, 1945–1950.* New York: Atheneum, 1976.

Hoehling, A. A. *The Fighting Liberty Ships; A Memoir.* Kent, Ohio: Kent State University Press, 1990.

Hough, Richard. *The Longest Battle: The War at Sea, 1939–45.* London: Wiedenfield and Nicholson, 1986.

Jaffe, Walter W. *The Last Liberty: The Biography of the SS* Jeremiah O'Brien. Palo Alto, Calif.: Glencannon Press, 1993.

Johnson, Robert Erwin. *Guardians of the Sea: History of the United States Coast Guard, 1915 to the Present.* Annapolis, Md.: Naval Institute Press, 1987.

Land, Emory S. *Winning the War with Ships: Land, Sea and Air—Mostly Land.* New York: Robert M. McBride & Co., 1958.

Lane, Frederic C. *Ships for Victory: A History of Shipbuilding under the U.S. Maritime Commission in World War II.* Baltimore: Johns Hopkins Press, 1951.

Meyer, Agnes E. *Journey Through Chaos.* New York: Harcourt Brace & Company, 1943.

Middlebrook, Martin. *Convoy: The Battles for SC.122 and HX.229.* London: Penguin Books, 1978.

Moore, Arthur B. *A Careless Word . . . A Needless Sinking: A History of the Staggering Losses Suffered by the U.S. Merchant Marine, Both in Ships* and *Personnel, During World War Two.* Kings Point, N.Y.: American Merchant Marine Museum, 1990.

Morison, Samuel Eliot. *The Battle of the Atlantic.* Vol. 1, *History of United States Naval Operations in World War II.* Boston: Little, Brown and Company, 1984.

Riesenberg, Felix Jr. *Sea War: The Story of the U.S. Merchant Marine in World War II.* New York: Rinehart & Co., 1956.

Rohwer, Jurgen. *Axis Submarine Successes, 1939–1945.* Annapolis, Md.: Naval Institute Press, 1983.

——. *The Critical Convoy Battles of March 1943.* London: Ian Allan Ltd., 1977.

Russell, Preston, and Barbara Hines. *Savannah: A History of Her People since 1733* Savannah, Ga.: Frederick C. Bell, 1992.

Sawyer, L. A., and W. H. Mitchell. *The Liberty Ships: The History of the "Emergency" Type Cargo Ships Constructed in the United States during the Second World War.* 2nd ed. Colchester, UK: Lloyds of London Press Ltd., 1985.

Schofield, William G. *Eastward the Convoys.* Chicago: Rand McNally & Co., 1965.

Van der Vat, Dan. *The Atlantic Campaigns: World War II's Greatest Struggle at Sea.* New York: Harper and Row, 1988.

Waters, John M. Jr. *Bloody Winter.* Annapolis, Md.: Naval Institute Press, 1994.

Willoughby, Malcolm F. *The Coast Guard in World War II.* Annapolis, MD: Naval Institute Press, 1957.

Wollenberg, Charles. *Marinship at War: Shipbuilding and Social Change in Wartime Sausalito*. Berkley, Calif.: Western Heritage Press, 1990.

PERIODICALS

Bennett, Stanley. "The Liberty Ships: Part One." *Sea Breezes* 36 (1963), 373–87.

——. "The Liberty Ships: Part Two." *Sea Breezes* 36 (1963), 455–78.

Britton, Beverly L. "Navy Stepchildren: The Armed Guard." *Proceedings* 73 (1947).

Curtis, Margaret. "War Work Done in Savannah." *Savannah Morning News*, May 8, 1945, 3.

Dorn, David R. "Ships for Victory." *Proceedings* 71 (1945).

Fielder, Bill. "Trees and Grass to Aid Protection of New Project." *Savannah Morning News*, September 14, 1942.

Gerecht, Ash. "Sinking of the S. S. *Oglethorpe* Is Recalled on Anniversary." *Savannah Morning News*, March 17, 1948.

Hunter, Anna C. "Liberty Ship Is Launched." *Savannah Evening Press*, November 20, 1942.

Proctor, Harry G. "The Wm. L. McLean Is Launched." *Philadelphia Evening Bulletin*, December 13, 1944, 3.

Ruark, Robert C. "They Called 'Em Fishfood." *Saturday Evening Post*, May 6, 1944.

Savannah Evening Press. "Hope to Avert Closing of Yard." July 24, 1945.

——. "Launching Is a Colorful Affair." February 2, 1944.

——. "Vessel Honors Southern Leader." July 22, 1944.

——. February 2, 1944.

——. August 17, 1945, 18.

Savannah Morning News. "Big Crane Fall at Southeastern." April 11, 1943, 36.

——. "City Buys Yard." October 16, 1947, 18.

——. "Crowley Finishes Giving Testimony." July 15, 1942,

——. "Horseplay in Defense Work Scoured by FBI." October 3, 1943.

——. "Last S.E. Ship Goes Down the Ways." September 15, 1945, 10.

——. "More Seamen Are Reported Missing." April 22, 1943, 14.

——. "New Victory Ships to Be Built in Savannah." May 8, 1943, 12.

——. "Oglethorpe to Be Ship's Name." April 20, 1942, 12.

——. "Progress Noted in Shipbuilding." January 26, 1943, 12.

——. "S.E. Shipyards Operating Again." July 28, 1945.

——. "Ships Built Here Be for Britain." April 4, 1941.

——. "Shipyard Buys Hundred Acre Tract." May 7, 1941, 14.

——. "Shipyard Outlook Seen as Improving." July 27, 1945.

——. "Southeastern to Get Added Work." January 18, 1944, 12.

——. "S.S. *Addie Bagley Daniels* Slides Down the Ways." September 29, 1944, 14.

——. "S.S. *Button Gwinnett* Slides Gracefully Down to the Savannah Sunday." May 3, 1943, 10.

——. "Survivor Sinking *James Oglethorpe* at Southeastern." January 1, 1944, 1.

——. "U.S. Will Scrap S.E. Shipyards." September 17, 1946, 16.

——. "Vessel Launched by Southeastern." August 28, 1943.

——. April 5, 1941.

——. March 10, 1942.

——. May 23, 1942, 12.

——. March 18, 1943.

——. May 23, 1944.

——. April 6, 1946, 10.

——. July 10, 1975.

Sou'Easter. "'30' for the Sou'Easter." November 9, 1945, 18.

——. "A Brief History." November 9, 1945.

——. "Do You Believe It." August 15, 1943, 12.

——. "Draft Board Seeks Absentees." May 1, 1943.

——. "Expert Welders." February 15, 1944, 15.

——. "He Wouldn't Trade His Job." December 1, 1943.

——. "Police Busy Rounding Up Speeders." August 15, 1943.

——. "Riding Gantry Fall Found Dull." May 1, 1943, 11.

——. "Riggers Shaded by Death When Cable Breaks." May 15, 1945, 3.

——. "Shipwright Saves the Day." July 1, 1944, 3.

——. "Sober Threesome." June 15, 1945, 10.

——. "Spearmen." August 1, 1944.

——. "Splicer on Wet Dock Survived Sinking of 'James Oglethorpe.'" January 1, 1944, 1.

——. "To the 1,288 Men Who Are Absent Every Day." August 15, 1943.

——. Want Ads. December 1, 1943.

——. Want Ads. May, 15, 1945.

——. Want Ads. June 1, 1945.

——. April 20, 1942, 12.

——. March 18, 1943, 11.

——. May 1, 1943.

——. May 5, 1943.

——. July 1, 1943.

——. July 15, 1943, 3.

——. August 1, 1943.

——. January 15, 1944.

——. February 15, 1944, 5.

——. November 15, 1944.

——. April 1, 1945, 6.

Taylor, Sloan. "The Sea Baptizes a Liberty Ship." *New York Sunday News*, March 28, 1943, 6.

Upchurch, Winn C. "Around the Yard." *Sou'Easter*, October 15, 1945, 8.

Wilkerson, Sarah. "New Vessel Joins Bridge of Ships." *Savannah Morning News*, November 21, 1942, 12.

——. "Records Fall as Ship Is Launched." *Savannah Morning News*, November 26, 1943, 10.

UNPUBLISHED MANUSCRIPTS

Frick, William. "Voyage No. 1." San Francisco, Calif., April 1945.

Howe, Norman. Personal Diary, 1943.

Martin, Leon W. "A Brief Look at the Most Ambitious Shipbuilding Activity in U.S. History, 1941–1946." Savannah, Ga., n.d.

——. "A Brief Study of Shipbuilding Activity in the Savannah Area, 1900–1987." Savannah, Ga., n.d.

Index

Page numbers followed by an *n* or *f* indicate notes and figures. All ships are American flagged unless otherwise indicated.

About the Author

Tony Cope is a native of Savannah, Georgia, who retired after thirty years in public education, serving as a teacher, head baseball coach, administrator, and creator and longtime director of the award-winning environmental education facility, the Oatland Island Education Centre. He was a member of a long list of state and local boards, served three terms as president of the Savannah Symphony, and was featured in the book *Movers and Shakers of Georgia*. Since moving to Ireland he has received a Rotary Club award for his leadership with Toward a Better Understanding, an exchange program involving students from Cork City and Belfast. Tony now lives with his wife, Ellen, and five cats near Kinsale in County Cork, dividing his time between writing, playing golf (badly), and building dry stone walls.